THE DYNAMICS OF MODERNIZATION

THE DYNAMICS

HARPER TORCHBOOKS

OF MODERNIZATION

A Study in Comparative History

C. E. BLACK

Harper & Row, Publishers
New York, Evanston, and London

To Corinne, Jim, and Christina

A publication of the Center of International Studies, Princeton University.

First HARPER TORCHBOOK edition published 1967 by
Harper & Row, Publishers, Incorporated,
New York, N.Y. 10016.

Library of Congress Catalog Card Number: 66-20757.

Contents

Preface

I have written this book to explain things to myself. I hope that others find it interesting.

The first version of this study, in a very different form, was prepared for the James W. Richard Lectures in Comparative History at the University of Virginia in November 1960. If it had not been for this challenging invitation, this book might not have been written.

An early brief statement of a few of the themes was formulated in "Political Modernization in Historical Perspective," a paper prepared for the Conference on Political Modernization organized by the Social Science Research Council in 1959. Certain aspects of these materials were also presented in the Witherspoon Lectures, sponsored by the Undergraduate Council of Princeton University, in the spring of 1964. The first section of Chapter 2 was read at the meeting of the Modern European History Section of the American Historical Association in Washington, D.C., in December 1964.

The work on this book has been generously supported over a period of several years by Princeton University through the Department of History, the Council of the Humanities, and the Center of International Studies. It is being published as one of the studies sponsored by the Center.

A year at the Center for Advanced Study in the Behavioral Sciences, at Stanford, with the assistance of a grant from the Rockefeller Foundation, provided an opportunity to explore the relationship between history and the social sciences in an atmosphere unexcelled for relaxed contemplation.

I have also benefited from the advice and assistance of friends and associates too numerous to name. Particularly valuable have been the stimulation and criticism received from colleagues and students at Princeton University in formal seminars and in informal discussions over a number of years, and also at Stanford University and Hokkaido University in the summers of 1964 and 1965.

Princeton University   C. E. BLACK
May 1966

1. Modernization

Prologue: The Challenge of a Revolutionary Age

We are experiencing one of the great revolutionary transformations of mankind. Throughout the world in widely differing societies man is seeking to apply the findings of a rapidly developing science and technology to the age-old problems of life. The resulting patterns of change offer unprecedented prospects for the betterment of the human condition, but at the same time threaten mankind with possibilities of destruction never before imagined. The search for an understanding of these forces of change is compelling, for failure may lead to catastrophe. The mastery of this revolutionary process has become the central issue of world politics—the ultimate stake for which peoples struggle in peace and risk annihilation in war. The initiative in guiding this transformation in a manner beneficial to human welfare belongs to those who understand most clearly the ways in which different societies around the world are affected, what must unavoidably be changed, and what must at all costs be preserved.

The change in human affairs now taking place is of a scope and intensity that mankind has experienced on only two previous occasions, and its significance cannot be appreciated except in the context of the entire course of world history. The first revolutionary trans-

1

formation was the emergence of human beings, about a million years ago, after many thousands of years of evolution from primate life. It has been estimated through analysis of radioactive material that the universe, as it can be perceived today, has been in existence for ten to twenty billion years and that our solar system was formed about four and a half billion years ago. Another two and a half billion years passed before elementary forms of life appeared, and not until a billion years ago did the antecedents of man emerge.

This infinitely slow process may be termed a revolution by virtue of the significance of the differences that separate prehuman from human life, and when one examines these differences, the term does not seem extravagant. Today anthropologists study baboon troops and other primate societies as a means of understanding prehuman life, and their findings serve to dramatize the contrast between these two levels of existence. Although the primates are not entirely lacking in social graces or in organizing ability, the capabilities of even the most primitive humans were of an entirely different character. Primitive man could make tools, weapons, shelter, and means of transportation; he could communicate by means of speech and written signs and markings; he could organize large groups for security and mutual assistance; and he could exercise some control over his fate by raising, preserving, and storing food and by taming nature to his purposes in a wide variety of other ways. In the course of this transformation the volume of the human brain grew to about three times its original size, and the rate of growth accelerated after man began to use tools.

The second great revolutionary transformation in human affairs was that from primitive to civilized societies, culminating seven thousand years ago in three locations, the valleys of the Tigris and Euphrates (Mesopotamia), the valley of the Nile, and the valley of the Indus. Revolutions of similar import occurred subsequently, and in all likelihood independently, on the island of Crete, in the valley of the Yellow River, in Middle America, and in several Andean river valleys. The Cretan and Chinese civilized societies emerged five thousand years ago and the Middle American and Andean about four thousand. In these seven regions the transformation from simple tilling of the soil to organized agriculture, from villages and tribes to cities and states, took a definite form. The civilized societies, much larger and more complex than the primitive ones, possessed written systems of communication, although the Middle American and Andean were still quite primitive.

Most important of all, the civilized societies had sophisticated conceptions, expressed in religious beliefs, of the identity of man, of his relationship to his environment, and of those profound truths that experience had taught them were beyond full human comprehension. These early religions had a common concern for water, earth, and fertility, and employed symbols of varying abstraction to express their perception of the eternal truths inherent in the world as it was known. This level of understanding reflected an attitude of mind in which significant extensions of knowledge no longer took hundreds of thousand of years, as was the case with primitive man, but developed with sufficient dynamism to give human affairs a capacity for change and even an instability that they had never known before. Within a few centuries civilized societies altered their character and developed rapidly, sometimes failing to solve the problems confronting them.

Two of the seven primary civilized societies, the Indian and the Chinese, have had a continuing existence to the present time despite many changes in fortune and have found expression in the Hindu, Buddhist, and Confucian religions. The Middle American and the Andean disintegrated, and were absorbed without leaving significant traces. The remaining three—the Mesopotamian, the Egyptian, and the Cretan—have transmitted their knowledge and institutions to later societies that have intermingled and interacted over the centuries without losing their essential distinctiveness. This distinctiveness, in its broadest sense representing different conceptions of the fundamental nature of man and his environment, is reflected at its most abstract level in the great religions: Hebrew, Greco-Roman, Iranian, Christian, in its Eastern and Western forms, and Islamic. These societies may also be perceived in various configurations as civilizations, as cultures, as linguistic groups, or as political or economic systems, depending on the interest or angle of vision of the observer.

These successors to the primary civilized societies did not all face the same problems, nor did they experience equal success in meeting the problems that they faced. It is still a matter of speculation why some failed and others succeeded, although at the most fundamental level it must have been the leaders' inability to keep the delicate balance required for survival between the maintenance of the traditional pattern of values that serves as the basis of social cohesion and the adaptation to new knowledge that requires a revision of the traditional value system. What distinguished these societies from one another was the particular adaptation of traditional institutions, expressed in religion, language, literature, art, and music. What they had in common was a general understanding of their environment that kept them all at similar levels of technology and an attitude toward knowledge that relied heavily on truths received from the past and very little on objective experimentation. These traditional societies coexisted and influenced one another, but none had a sufficient edge in knowledge or power to dominate the others.

The process of change in the modern era is of the same order of magnitude as that from prehuman to human life and from primitive to civilized societies; it is the most dynamic of the great revolutionary transformations in the conduct of human affairs. What is distinctive about the modern era is the phenomenal growth of knowledge since the scientific revolution and the unprecedented effort at adaptation to this knowledge that has come to be demanded of the whole of mankind. Man perceives opportunities and dangers that for the first time in human existence are global in character, and the need to comprehend the opportunities and master the dangers is the greatest challenge that he has faced.

This study is concerned with this process of change in the modern era, one of the great revolutionary transformations of human affairs. The present chapter defines the characteristics of modernity that may be assumed to be of universal validity and explores in general terms the problems confronting societies in the process of adapting traditional institutions to modern functions. The second is concerned with the comparative method in formulating generalizations about the totality of the human experience in modern times, and with related problems. The third chapter examines the course of modernization from a chronological point of view, setting forth certain main phases of change that appear to be common to all societies. The fourth considers on a comparative basis, in terms of seven main patterns, the experience of the more than 170 contemporary societies in facing the political problems characteristic of modernization. The fifth and sixth chapters study the impact of this process on international relations and its implications for policy in the foreseeable future. The seventh, finally, explores the problems that historians and social scientists have faced in seeking to understand the development of man in the modern era and examines the present state of the study of modernization.

Modernization

"Modernization" as a general term describing the process of rapid change in human affairs since the scientific revolution is of comparatively recent origin, but "modern" as a term denoting the quality of a contemporary era can be traced to late Latin usage of the sixth century. First in Latin and later in English and other languages the word was used to distinguish between contemporary and "ancient" writers and themes, and by the seventeenth century "modernity," "modernizers," and "modernization" were employed in a variety of more or less limited and technical contexts. "Modern" in earlier times frequently had the pejorative meaning of commonplace and trite, and Shakespeare invariably used the term in this sense. When English writers referred to the French revolutionary leaders as "modernizers," they were doubtless using the word disparagingly. It was also used in a more objective sense, however, and in the seventeenth and eighteenth centuries historians in Europe gradually abandoned the accepted periodization based on the Christian era and began to refer to ancient, medieval, and modern periods. Modern history was at first thought of as starting rather abruptly with the fall of Constantinople or the discovery of America—at sunrise on May 29, 1453, or at 2:00 A.M. on October 12, 1492, if one wishes to be literal—but it is now more commonly regarded as beginning "about 1500."

Within the past generation "modernity" has come to be rather widely employed to describe the characteristics common to countries that are most advanced in technological, political, economic, and social development, and "modernization" to describe the process by which they acquired these characteristics. "Modernization" may at first strike one as a tautology—making things more modern, or like that which follows what precedes it—but it is no more a tautology than the use of "Christianization" or "industrialization" to denote the introduction of Christianity or of industry. The difference is that there is general agreement as to what Christianity and industry mean, whereas "modernity" does not convey a meaning that is as yet widely understood or accepted. It is the purpose of this chapter to clarify the term.

"Modernization" is not the only word used to describe the process. "Europeanization" and "Westernization" are employed in this general sense, particularly to describe the impact in recent times of the more advanced countries on the less advanced. Yet this is only a part of the process, although a very important one, and it fails to take into account not only the initial transformation of the advanced countries themselves but also the impact of the less advanced countries on the still less advanced. One would not, then, refer to the "Westernization" of England and France in the seventeenth and eighteenth centuries or to the "Europeanization" of Manchuria by Japan in the twentieth century. In a different sense, "industrialization," "industrial revolution," and "the revolution of rising expectations" are also too narrow. They stress the economic aspect alone, the immediate consequences of the technological revolution, and do not convey the complexity and all-pervading character of the process. "Innovation," on the other hand, is a much broader term, insofar as it is used to describe the entire sweep of change that has occurred since the beginning of recorded history. At the same time, it can also be employed with specialized reference to technical improvements.

"Modernization" as it is used here refers to the dynamic form that the age-old process of innovation has assumed as a result of the explosive proliferation of knowledge in recent centuries. It owes its special significance both to its dynamic character and to the universality of its impact on human affairs. It stems initially from an attitude, a belief that society can and should be transformed, that change is desirable. If a definition is necessary, "modernization" may be defined as the process by which historically evolved institutions are adapted to the rapidly changing functions that reflect the unprecedented increase in man's knowledge, permitting control over his environment, that accompanied the scientific revolution. This process of adaptation had its origins and initial influence in the societies of Western Europe, but in the nineteenth and twentieth centuries these changes have been extended to all other societies and have resulted in a worldwide transformation affecting all human relationships. Political scientists frequently limit the term "modernization" to the political and social changes accompanying industrialization, but a holistic definition is better suited to the complexity and interrelatedness of all aspects of the process.

The culture-bound or deterministic character of most of the widely accepted explanations has obstructed efforts to understand this process. It seems clear that the liberal view of "progress" was a projection for the whole world of a conception of change that was believed, erroneously, to be true of the societies of Western Europe and of the English-speaking world. Other widely held views have more often than not been characterized by a narrow-minded determinism that has sought to explain all change in terms of some simple original cause or motivating factor. A characteristic reflection of a lack of appreciation on the part of these theories of the ultimate complexity and unpredictability of the social process is the assurance they offer that a resolution of fundamental problems lies just ahead, perhaps even within one's own lifetime, if only the program implied by the theory is generally accepted. The advantage of a term such as "modernization" is not only that it has a broader scope than "Westernization," "Europeanization," "industrialization," or even "progress," but also that it is less encumbered with accretions of meaning.

What would an educated man from fifteenth-century England find familiar and what would he find strange in contemporary Britain? The written language he might be able to understand in some measure, some aspects of religious services might be familiar, a few of the great architectural monuments of his day would still be standing, and in the countryside there might be features of rural life that at least at first glance would not appear to have changed a great deal. Yet how much more striking has been the transformation, and how completely new and incomprehensible would be most of what he saw and read.

The process by which this transformation has taken place may be discussed in terms of the adaptation of a given set of institutions to changing functions. In historical perspective, the institutions undergoing this process may be defined as the traditional institutions of the societies of the world. "Traditional" and "modern" are, then, relative terms, but they are used here in a specific sense. For the societies of Western Europe, the traditional institutions are those of the Middle Ages, and the challenge of modernity to the traditional system occurred between the twelfth and eighteenth centuries. Comparable traditional periods before the challenge of modernity may be discerned in all other societies. In the least developed societies, the traditional period has lasted until well into the twentieth century. Since the challenge of modernity in the societies that modernized earliest was primarily internal, the process of transformation took place gradually over several centuries. In the later-modernizing societies this challenge has been increasingly external, hence more rapid and even abrupt. These traditional eras were, of course, diverse, highly sophisticated in some cases and no more than tribal in others, but the common factor is that in each case they formed the setting for the particular pattern of historically evolved institutions that is adapted to the functions of modernity and that gives each modernized society its distinctive character.

The modern does not share the diversity of the traditional, insofar as the particular functions characteristic of modernity tend to be common to all mankind, but the identification of these common characteristics is fraught with problems. The principal of these is that most societies, embracing the great majority of human beings, have not advanced to the point where these characteristics can be fully discerned. Even the most advanced countries are still modernizing, and it is only by an effort of the imagination that one can conjecture which of their features are likely to be characteristic of all modern societies and which are simply culture-oriented idiosyncrasies of individual societies.

Tradition and Modernity

All aspects of human activity have been undergoing transformation at the same time, and the process of modernization is too complex to be reduced to simple terms without the danger of grave distortion. Assume for the purposes of this study, however, that all of human activity can be discussed in terms of five aspects: intellectual, political, economic, social, and psychological. It is clear that these are essentially arbitrary categories adopted for the sake of convenience, familiar terms that it would probably be a mistake to try to define too closely. It should also be apparent that the various aspects of human activity, however categorized and defined, are continually interacting and can be discussed in discrete compartments only by a deliberate act of gross oversimplification.

Intellectual. It is appropriate to start with the intellectual realm, since the growth of man's understanding and control over his environment in all of its complexity plays such a vital role in the process of change in modern times. Indeed, it is clear that in a sense little has changed except man's knowledge, for the diversity of the physical environment was present before man began to understand its potentialities, and evolutionary changes in man and his environment have not been significant in historical times. Historians trace the immediate origins of modern knowledge in Western Europe to the renaissance of the twelfth century, when the writings of Greek and Arabic scholars became available and creative work of a lasting order was initiated in many fields. The basis of this renaissance was the recognition that it was possible to seek a rational explanation of physical and social phenomena. In the natural sciences, which have stamped such a forceful impression on the modern era, the level of achievement of the Greeks and Arabs was reached in Western Europe in the thirteenth and fourteenth centuries. By the sixteenth century the revolutionary growth in the understanding of nature, which has placed in man's hands instruments of great power and peril, was under way.

The revolution in science has no doubt fostered the most dramatic change in man's understanding of his environment, but it was in fact only one part of a much more comprehensive re-evaluation of accepted ways of doing things. Indeed, all of man's conceptions were subjected to scrutiny, and all fields of intellectual activity underwent a rapid transformation. Each generation toppled the idols of the last, in one respect or another, and the view came to be generally accepted that change was the normal state of all knowledge.

It would be gratifying if one could trace in the realm of ideas a neat pattern of growth and of interaction between empirical experimentation, political thought, art and literature, and speculations regarding the nature of man, of God, and of the universe. Interaction was continual, and before the accumulation of knowledge reached its present state of complexity, it was possible for individual great minds to work creatively at the frontiers of many fields of learning. Rather than seek a simple pattern, one must think of many minds working in many directions with growing facilities for intercommunication and mutual stimulation, but also with increasing specialization to the point where eminent men in different fields today can scarcely understand the nature of one another's work.

Historians of Europe have found it convenient to describe the evolution of man's understanding in terms of a Renaissance, a Reformation and Counter Reformation, an Age of Enlightenment, and perhaps an Age of Materialism, and a traditional periodization such as this remains a useful frame of reference. What is particularly significant is that from the twelfth to the nineteenth century this

Scientific rev.

intellectual revolution was almost exclusively the product of Europe. The earlier debt to the Greeks, the Arabs, and the Hindu mathematicians and astronomers is well known, and there were significant parallel and contributing developments in China and Southeast Asia. [The great modern effort to understand the world of men and matter was nevertheless essentially a European achievement until the nineteenth century, when other societies attained the sophistication necessary to participate in this great adventure. Even today, when universities and research institutes encircle the globe, the original intellectual centers of Europe still possess the greatest accumulation of talent in many fields of endeavor, and are rivaled in some fields and surpassed in others chiefly by the English-speaking countries overseas and by the peoples of Russia who have been their pupils. It is in this sense that many think of modernization as being "Europeanization" or "Westernization." The accumulation of knowledge, and the methods of rational explanation by which it was achieved, is no doubt the most generally recognized aspect of modernization, and as an attitude of mind it lies at the center of this process.]

An important feature of the intellectual revolution was the application of science to the practical affairs of man in the form of technology. One of the most consistent themes of the modern era has been the opportunity offered by the new knowledge for the betterment of man's material life, and this is a sphere where great achievements have been registered. Whether in manufacturing, transportation, communications, agriculture, or medicine, the new technology has revolutionized the ways in which man conducts his affairs. For the first time in the history of mankind it is possible to anticipate that adequate food, shelter, education, and medical care can eventually be made available to everyone and that want can be abolished forever. Not only do goods and services multiply in ever-increasing quantities, but the amount of energy available per capita is continually growing. The further reduction through automation of the need for human exertion is advancing rapidly, and the possibility of significant man-made modifications in the climate can now be envisaged.

The scientific attitude has also influenced the values by which men live. Theological systems and religious beliefs based on earlier conceptions of the nature of the world have been confronted with the need for a reassessment of the distinction between those aspects of a faith that represent eternal verities and those that reflect the outlook of particular periods and cultures. Beliefs and values are always subject to change, but the modern age is one in which particular emphasis has been placed on a critical approach. In this reassessment of values it is natural that the welfare of man should have become a matter of primary concern. The potentialities of the modern age for the material betterment of the conditions of human existence are so great that this concern has taken precedence over others. History has become increasingly preoccupied with economic and social matters. In literature the novel has become a favorite form of expression, perhaps because it is particularly suited to the exploration of the infinitely complex problems characteristic of the modern age. The great works of modern literature have been deeply concerned with social change, the conflicts between traditional and modern values, and the fate of man in an era peculiarly lacking in stable norms of behavior. In all these respects, man—his nature, well-being, and prospects—has become the central concern of modern thought.

In contemplating the profound and infinitely varied consequences of the spirit and methods of inquiry that have evolved since the twelfth century, it is important to recognize that some of the most dramatic contributions have been made in our own time and that we live in an era of great intellectual productivity. It has been estimated that in the most advanced countries as much as a quarter of all human and material resources is devoted to the production and distribution of knowledge in all its forms, and that this one-quarter is about triple the proportion at the turn of the century. The number of currently published scientific periodicals in the world was about 100,000 in 1850 and will probably be 1 million by the year 2000. The number of books published has about doubled every twenty years since 1450, and some 30 million have by now been published; the projected figure is 60 million by 1980. The number of people employed in science in the advanced countries is increasing at an even more rapid rate. Certainly the rate of increase of the share of the production and dissemination of knowledge in the total expenditure of time and energy will have to abate, if only because at the present rate it will before long absorb all people and resources, but it is important to recognize how central this concern for knowledge is in a modern society.

B) Political. The political implications of modernization are most strikingly apparent in the consolidation of policy-making that has occurred in both the public and the private domains. This consolidation has doubtless been the result in part of technical developments in communications and transportation that permit the administration of increasingly larger enterprises and areas from a single base. It is due more, however, to the desire on the part of modernizing leaders in both government and private enterprise to mobilize and rationalize the resources of society with a view to achieving greater control, efficiency, and production.

In the public domain this has taken the form of the increasing centralization of the administrative organs of the state. Although traditional political forms have varied greatly around the world, the authority of the state has in the past not normally reached down to every citizen. It has tended to be limited to defense against foreign attacks, the preservation of law and order at home, the maintenance of essential public works, and the collection of sufficient taxes to perform these functions. Even in the case of such exceptionally authoritarian and centralized traditional states as China and Russia, the authority of the central government reached down to the individual peasant only indirectly and through a variety of intermediaries. Before modern times, political power was in most instances shared by numerous authorities, and only after a long struggle did kings and emperors succeed in subduing the various bodies that exercised power at the local level and in consolidating their power on a nationwide basis. Some of the most dramatic pages in the history of political modernization have been concerned with the civil wars in which the struggle between centralizing, regional, and local authorities was waged.

The modern state arose from this consolidation of local authorities and then proceeded to extend its power on a functional basis to many activities that had hitherto been in the private or local domain. Functions that the family, the village, the landlord, the church, and a variety of other agencies had originally performed all tended to be gathered into the hands of the state. In some societies practically all education, communications, transportation, and social security, as well as much manufacturing, are functions of the state, and most other activities come under state regulation in one form or another. Even in societies with a strong tradition of local rights, such as Switzerland and the United States, the trend over the years has been for the central authorities to increase their power at the expense of the local. Private enterprise in those societies where it is firmly rooted is not incompatible with a strong central government, and is generally the most efficient method of production. Where the state has traditionally played a large role, or where war and other catastrophes have undermined private enterprise, modernization is often accompanied by one form or another of statism. In either case, the state tends to absorb functions that other agencies are not able to perform effectively, and the relationship between public and private enterprise varies with the traditionally evolved capabilities of the particular society. Modern states today collect revenues in an amount equivalent to between one-quarter and one-half of the gross national product to reimburse the costs of general administration, public enterprises, and social security, whereas in traditional societies such revenues may be as low as 5 percent or less of the wealth produced.

The relatively centralized and rationalized functions of a modern state would not be possible without the rule of law maintained by a highly organized bureaucracy, and a close rapport between the state and every member of society. Indeed, the replacement of the arbitrary administration of individuals by a legal system is the hallmark of modernization in the political realm, for modern administration with its vast undertakings would not be able to operate effectively on any other basis. Arbitrary decisions are still necessary at a high level of policy, and even at lower levels a legal system does not rule out a wide variety of choices, but unless the range of choices is restricted by generally accepted norms, a modern state will not function well. Large bureaucracies arc called for, manned by persons who devote their lives to civil service. Principles of organization suitable for a wide variety of organizations have been evolved, and modern methods of administration and techniques of management permit the effective implementation of complex policies.

A closer rapport between the modern state and its citizens is necessitated by the fact that for the first time, the state has direct relations with every member of society. The state cannot fulfill its functions in regard to taxation, foreign policy, education, social security, and a myriad of other matters unless the citizenry understands and in considerable measure accepts its role. Public participation in politics may nevertheless take many forms. In societies with a deeply rooted tradition of individual rights, modern government has typically been democratic in the sense that all citizens participate to some degree in the choice of political leaders and policies, and that the right of individual choice is guaranteed by effective civil liberties. In other societies this rapport is maintained by various forms of popular enlightenment and propaganda, and the consensus is enforced by police methods when it cannot be won by other means. Even in the most tightly controlled police states, however, great reliance is placed on propaganda and economic incentives to gain the necessary degree of acceptance and participation on the part of the public. It is not possible to run a modern political system by sheer terror, and modern dictators depend on their ability to win public support through thought control, plebiscites, and nominally representative bodies.

[Modern societies rely to such a degree on the acceptance and participation in one form or another of its inhabitants that the structure of the state has been determined to a large extent by its ability to gain such acceptance.] Geography, economic viability, or security might dictate very different political units from those that have emerged. Indeed, some would argue that continentwide or worldwide political systems are the only ones that make sense today. In fact, however, a state can be no larger than the basis of its support, voluntary or enforced, and this basis has generally been the result of a variety of factors among which common historical experience is no doubt the most significant. In most cases a common language has been the principal feature of this experience, and nationalism has been a characteristic rallying point for modern states. It has proved to be the most effective means of consolidating loyalties that would otherwise be divided by attachments to many other associations. Yet linguistic nationalism is by no means the only, or even a necessary, prerequisite of nationhood; and there are numerous instances of states that are multinational or that are held together by religious or other beliefs. Indeed, state boundaries have rarely coincided precisely with those of linguistic or other forms of nationality, and efforts to bring the two into close rapport have led to endless strife. The location of groups of peoples with common linguistic traditions is often such as to make discrete political entities out of the question, and a variety of provisions for federalism and minorities rights have been evolved in an effort to bridge this gap.

The organization of peoples into the relatively watertight compartments of modern states has meant that problems of organization involving two or more states have had to be solved by other than conventional political methods. The main method has been the development since the seventeenth century of principles of international law and diplomacy that make it possible for modern states to handle certain types of problems without recourse to violence. A significant aspect of this development has been the establishment of international organizations for the purpose of handling specialized functions affecting many states—such as communications—and, more recently, worldwide organizations with a more general political function of preserving the peace.

These observations about the consolidation of policy-making under modern conditions apply to the private domain as well as to the public. Private enterprise, to consider one area, has also tended to become centralized and bureaucratized. There are legitimate differences of opinion as to the efficacy of sheer size, and the degree of centralization of an enterprise must of necessity depend to a considerable extent on the nature of its activity. It is sometimes maintained that publicly owned enterprises are inherently more modern than those that are privately owned, in that the state is better able to coordinate and integrate the complex elements of a society. Experience has not, however, shown this to be the case. The consideration essential to modernity is efficiency, and organizational forms that are efficient in one society are not necessarily efficient in another. Efficiency depends in part on the nature of the activity involved, for no modern society has found it possible to administer armed forces, universal elementary education, or major construction enterprises on a purely private basis. In regard to other types of activity, however, efficiency depends largely on the traditional culture of a society. Some societies have excelled for many centuries in the management of private enterprise, whereas others have over equally long periods relied primarily on public administration, and have not evolved the personnel or the value system for other forms of enterprise. The relationship of public to private enterprise in a society is, then, more a function of its cultural heritage than of its level of development.

Even in those societies where private enterprise is most strongly rooted, property devoted to production has been transferred largely from private to corporate ownership. In this corporate form persons who may not be owners manage such property, and its use is restricted by limitations the state imposes in the interest of public welfare. Nationalization of property devoted to production is a rather primitive form of control, and was characteristic in the Western European societies of the era when kings were seeking to strengthen the state by expropriating the estates of recalcitrant lords and ecclesiastical institutions. In advanced societies corporate property devoted to production is more rigorously controlled by the state—through taxation and other forms of regulation—than is publicly owned property in less advanced societies that are in principle statist or totalitarian. Property used for consumption, on the other hand, continues to be less rigorously controlled in free-enterprise societies than in statist societies. What is characteristic of modernity in this regard is the public regulation of productive property in the interest of the public welfare as interpreted by political leaders. Whether this public regulation is exercised through public ownership—as in statist, socialist, or communist societies—or by means of legal controls depends on the traditional culture of a society and on the contingencies of politics and leadership, rather than on the degree of modernity.

Economic. Economic development may be discussed in terms of the two essential and interrelated functions of saving and investment. Traditional economies tend to consume virtually all that is produced, leaving little for investment and growth. Even modest savings may be of no avail in an undeveloped economy if the population grows more rapidly than production. The saving of resources for investment presupposes a net surplus per capita, and it is the availability of this surplus that makes development possible. When rapid economic development was getting under way two or three centuries ago in the countries that are now advanced, it had the benefit of rather high levels of income and of agricultural land per capita. This was certainly one of the reasons that the countries of Western Europe got a head start. These levels were on the whole several times higher than those of undeveloped countries today, and the application of the new technology to this relatively prosperous economy resulted in very rapid growth. Accompanying this growth was a degree of specialization that permitted the production of a much greater surplus than before, hence greater savings.

Specialization was accompanied in turn by an expansion of domestic and foreign trade that made it possible to integrate a wide range of resources and peoples into a relatively well-knit economic system. A traditional rural community may be virtually self-sufficient, producing most of its food, clothing, and implements from resources available locally and only occasionally purchasing goods from itinerant merchants, whereas a modern community may devote all of its efforts to a few products and purchase the greater part of its needed supplies from outside. Savings may take the form of private profits or of public taxes, and in either case many problems of policy are raised concerning the means by which savings should be achieved.

Investment is the complementary function of allocating resources, and saving and investment are generally performed by the same institutions: governments, banks, business enterprises, and individuals. The policy of investment depends on the capabilities of an economy and on the purposes and sophistication of the investor. Generally speaking, a large investment in producer goods—transportation, the production of raw materials, factories, and heavy machinery—will result in more rapid economic development but will impose a heavier burden on the population. A large investment in consumer goods, on the other hand, will benefit the population but will reduce the productive capacity of the economy. Societies, moreover, do not always have a free choice in this matter, for emphasis on consumer goods is not possible until a society is relatively well developed. Yet at every stage there exists a choice between patterns of investment, and this choice is essentially a political one. Some political leaders are prepared to demand maximum sacrifices of the people in the interest of the rapid development of producer goods, whereas others will prefer to provide for annual increments in the standard of living even in the earlier stages of development.

The economic aspect of modernization has been so dramatic that many have regarded it as the central and determining force in this process. In fact, however, economic development depends to a great extent on the intellectual and political aspects of the process, the growth in knowledge and the ability of political leaders to mobilize resources. Yet economic growth has no doubt been compelling in its effect on individuals. It seems likely that in the more advanced societies real income per person may have increased ten to twenty times or more in the past two or three centuries. At the heart of this growth has been the scientific and technological revolution, which has made possible a phenomenal increase in production through the mechanization of labor. Here, as in other fields, innovation in its modern form can be traced back to the Middle Ages, but it was the rapid industrialization of the nineteenth and twentieth centuries that brought this process to its most dynamic phase.

As a result of increased specialization the area in which goods and services are exchanged has been expanded, and barriers to travel and trade within and between states have gradually been broken down. This has permitted the creation of mass markets, supplied by mass production, with a corresponding reduction of costs per unit and increase in real income per hour of work. This expansion has affected agriculture no less than industry and trade, and the machine has come to the aid of man in every sphere of his activity.

The difference between tradition and modernity in the economic sphere can be graphically illustrated by a variety of quantitative measures. In gross national product per capita, a widely employed indicator despite many shortcomings, the dozen or more most advanced societies range from $800 to $2,500, whereas the twenty-five least developed countries with about one-half of the world's population have a gross national product per capita of less than $100. In modern societies one-sixth to one-quarter of the gross national product may be reinvested each year, stimulating a continuing rapid growth over a period of many decades. In traditional societies, by contrast, only one-twentieth or less of the gross national product may be so invested, and in some cases the rate of economic growth is slower than the growth of population, so that the inhabitants become gradually poorer over the decades. This profound difference in economic levels and patterns of growth between the societies that make effective use of technology and those that do not may be seen in the contrast both between advanced and undeveloped societies of today and between these advanced societies and the same societies several centuries ago. Differences between societies as to resources and skills are such that one cannot assume that all societies are capable of the same rates and levels of development as those that are now the most advanced, and indeed it appears that during the first half of the twentieth century the gap between the advanced and the undeveloped has grown. In seeking an explanation for this diversity of growth trends one must look beyond economics to the political, social, and psychological factors.

Social. Profound social changes have accompanied and complemented the intellectual, political, and economic aspects of modernization. In the course of this process societies that for many generations were composed predominantly of peasants, with perhaps no more than 10 percent of the population engaged in administration, manufacturing, and trade, may within a few generations change to the extent that a relatively small minority remains rural. A phenomenal migration to the cities accompanies this change in occupations, and within a few generations three-quarters or more of the population may live in urban areas. This urbanization generally involves a significant transformation of the family from the larger kinship units normally associated with agrarian life to the much smaller nuclear family consisting only of parents and younger children. In advanced societies there is also much more geographical mobility, and as much as one-fifth of the population may move each year from one locality to another in response to occupational demands.

These trends have been associated with a considerable leveling in terms of income, education, and opportunities. This is not matched by a similar leveling of social or political roles, however, and one may in fact question whether such distinctions will ever disappear. Not only do the natural endowments of individuals vary considerably but also the functional requirements of a society call for a wide variety of roles, ranging from imaginative leadership at the highest level to the equally necessary but less dramatic tasks of tending cattle and cleaning streets. What is called for by the rationalizing tendencies of modernization is less a leveling than an equalization of opportunity, so that the members of a society will find the roles best suited to their abilities and predispositions. In any society the composition and training of the leaders—or the "elite," as it is sometimes called— is a matter of the highest importance.

Modernization is also accompanied by the extension of literacy from a small proportion of the population in traditional societies to a practically universal ability to read and write. The associated expansion of education, to the point where in some societies virtually the entire population completes secondary education and as much as one-third of the relevant age group receives formal education at a higher level, has resulted in a revolution in the acquisition and dissemination of information.

Relations between men and women also undergo a marked change, for until the modern era the status of women was based on the circumstance that the livelihood of most people depended on heavy physical labor, which men are best able to perform. The gradual replacement of physical with mechanized labor and with clerical and intellectual work, greatly reducing this age-old functional inequality, has challenged the pattern of relations that had been accepted for many centuries. This change in the relationship of men and women is fraught with problems, and appropriate institutional forms to meet them are only now being elaborated in the more advanced societies. Education has been the principal vehicle for the emancipation of women, making professional, managerial, and clerical occupations available to them. At the same time, the legal and social status of women has undergone a transformation designed to give them opportunities and responsibilities equal to those of men.

Through a wide variety of media, interested persons can keep in touch with developments in many fields. This growth of the communications network contributes greatly to the integration of society and permits the maintenance of a close rapport among its many divergent elements. Modern societies have annual newspaper circulations of 250 to 500 per 1,000 population, exchange each year 100 to 350 items of domestic mail per capita, own 250 to 950 radios and 50 to 300 television sets per 1,000 population, and have an annual cinema attendance of 10 to 25 per capita. Traditional societies had none of these means of communication a century or more ago, and even today possess them in a limited degree.

With the aid of mechanization, only a small proportion of the population is needed to raise food, whereas in earlier times agriculture occupied the bulk of the population. In advanced societies the differences in income and conditions of labor between the various occupations are greatly reduced. Indeed, the role of labor itself assumes much smaller proportions as machines increasingly take over work formerly done by muscles. In such societies more than one-half of the population is engaged in the professions, services, and clerical work, and the role of manual labor is correspondingly reduced.

Equally striking has been the improvement of health as a result of modern medicine. In traditional societies the rates of both birth and death are normally between 3 percent and 4 percent, and have tended to remain relatively stable over long periods of time. With the advent of modern medicine and sanitation the death rate has been rapidly reduced, but the birth rate has remained high for much longer. In the advanced countries, as a result both of external pressures and of changes in family practices, the birth rate has been significantly reduced and the rate of population growth has become more gradual. Earlier, however, the population of Europe had grown from 188 million in 1800 to 462 million by 1914. In the countries that developed later, the impact of modern medicine has been much more strongly felt, but the birth rate has continued to follow traditional patterns, so that their populations have grown at an unprecedented rate. Infant mortality is as low as 16 to 30 per 1,000 live births and life expectancy as high as 70 to 75 years in modern societies. In traditional societies the corresponding levels may be as high as 100 to 225 for infant mortality and as low as 25 to 50 for life expectancy. In modern societies there is a trained physician for every 500 to 1,000 inhabitants, in traditional societies one for every 10,000 to 100,000.

At the same time, modernization fosters a more equal distribution of income. This is the case not only because graduated income taxes and provisions for social security tend to reduce differences of income in the more advanced societies but also because mass production is inexorably dependent on mass consumption. As societies industrialize, all of their members tend in the long run to become better off, and those with modest incomes benefit relatively more than those with large ones. Indeed, a mass-production economy would collapse if it did not have a mass of consumers capable of absorbing its products. In some traditional societies the upper 5 percent of the population may have fifteen to twenty times as much income as the lower 50 percent. In highly industrialized societies this ratio is closer to four or five to one. Distribution of income is not tied solely to the level of development, but this is the most important single factor. Distribution of income in a "capitalist" United States is similar, then, to that of "socialist" societies in Western Europe, whereas in a "socialist" Soviet Union distribution of income is relatively more unequal and resembles that in other societies at its level of development.

This complex of changes constitutes a process sometimes referred to as social mobilization—the transfer of the main focus of commitment for most individuals from community to society and from the local to the national sphere. Social mobilization follows from the physical migration of the bulk of the population in a modern society from its traditional rural habitat. It also follows from the people's heightened awareness, through vastly expanded means of communication, of a national sphere of interest and of a much larger world beyond. In modernizing countries the flow of domestic mail relative to foreign mail tends to increase significantly; similarly, domestic commerce plays an increasingly more important role than international commerce in national income. Such trends, although they are by no means uniform for all countries, appear to reflect the increasing mobilization of resources and skills at the national level in terms of culture, political loyalties, economic interest, and social dependence, as well as a corresponding weakening of ties to both the local and the international spheres. The political significance of social mobilization is that it promotes the formation of a consensus at the national level by encouraging nationalism and economic and social integration, strengthening, in the process, the hold of the national community over all of its citizens.

Psychological. The psychological aspect of modernization is of fundamental importance, for in the last analysis it is on the perceptions of individual human beings that everything depends. The manner in which an individual adapts to his environment is a result of the conditioning received in the early years of life in the home setting and also of influences in later life that may be sufficiently powerful to affect the firmly set pattern established in childhood. In a typically stable traditional society a child is able to model itself after adults whose behavior follows reasonably predictable patterns. Within the local community children learn the range of problems they will face in later life and the accepted manner of handling them. When they reach adulthood, most individuals cope with life's problems in accordance with the age-old customs of the locality, and under these circumstances the range of initiative and original behavior is narrowly restricted.

The rather rigid social structure of traditional societies also tends to inhibit individualism. Most peasants never expect to change their occupation, and the relatively small numbers of large landowners, warriors, merchants, priests, and rulers, constituting narrow strata within the society, also tend to remain within the confines of their inherited status. The sense of achievement inspired by a desire to get ahead or to gain new privileges is consequently limited. The relatively static life of most members of a traditional society likewise protects them from the need to adapt themselves to peoples and situations not encountered in childhood, and few have any conception of the larger world beyond the mountains or even across the river. One should not, of course, exaggerate the static quality of traditional life. As each person went through the life cycle the pattern of his relations with others constantly changed. In all ages each individual lived in a state of balanced tensions, both between his conscious and unconscious strivings and between himself and others. Yet in a relative sense the traditional world was socially stable, with patterns of behavior tending to remain constant from generation to generation, even during periods of war and migration.

The fundamental problems of human nature and relations do not alter as societies modernize, but they are dealt with in a different environment. The essential difference is that the relative stability of traditional society is lacking under modern conditions. The norms by which parents live may be out of date by the time children grow up, and behavior patterns are constantly changing as a result of altered social conditions and the influence of foreign ways of life. The social fluidity underlying these changes also affects the relationships of individuals in adulthood. In circumstances under which peasants move in masses to the cities, artisans become managers, and privileged elites must compete with the formerly underprivileged for a multitude of new jobs, the qualities that make for success are adaptability, initiative, and empathy. Young people tend to imitate their peers rather than their parents, and individualism has a higher value than conformity. Opportunities for upward mobility are available to a large proportion of the population that in a traditional society would never have thought of changing occupation or residence, and man is emancipated from the vast accretion of customs and beliefs that in traditional societies tend to smother individuality. Possibly at some future time a new plateau in the growth of knowledge may permit a new stability, but that time is not in sight. Indeed, the advanced societies are today undergoing more profound and rapid changes than ever before.

In traditional societies individuals are normally involved in relations principally with the family, the local community, and the functional group to which they belong. They tend to look upon others in terms of the narrow viewpoint, bred by the restricted range of acquaintances, in which their personal security is invested. Having little ability to see other points of view or appreciate different ways of doing things, they regard all alien persons and customs as hostile. Moreover, individuals in traditional societies have little expectation of change in their status and believe that the age-old social order is divinely ordained and unchangeable. Clearly in all ages there have been widely traveled and sophisticated individuals, as well as a measure of innovation and social change; and revolts and migrations of various types have testified to the presence of unrest. From a relative point of view, however, traditional societies are static, closed, and quiescent.

The Agony of Modernization

This rapid and rather impressionistic review of the main differences between tradition and modernity has purposely stressed the elements of expansion and amelioration, and may have conveyed the idea that mankind has benefited greatly from this process. This is certainly the case up to a point; indeed, it has often been asserted that an era of "progress" has arrived in which the benefits of man's new knowledge can be made available to all. A variety of utopias have been conceived of, in which it is anticipated that all manner of human ills will be overcome; even serious students of society with less utopian goals discuss the possibility of a world rid of war and poverty within a foreseeable future. Yet it is well known that modernization has been accompanied by the greatest calamities that mankind has known. Now that man has perfected weapons capable of destroying all human life, it is unavoidably clear that the problems modernity poses are as great as the opportunities it offers.

Of these problems, one of the most fundamental has been that the construction of a new way of life inevitably involves the destruction of the old. If one thinks of modernization as the integration or the reintegration of societies on the basis of new principles, one must also think of it as involving the disintegration of traditional societies. In a reasonably well-integrated society institutions work effectively, people are in general agreement as to ends and means, and violence and disorder are kept at a low level. When significant and rapid changes are introduced, however, no two elements of a society adapt themselves at the same rate, and the disorder may become so complete that widespread violence breaks out, large numbers of people emigrate, and normal government becomes impossible—all of which has happened frequently in modern times.

Modernization must be thought of, then, as a process that is simultaneously creative and destructive, providing new opportunities and prospects at a high price in human dislocation and suffering. The modern age, more than any other, has been an age of assassinations, of civil, religious, and international wars, of mass slaughter in many forms, and of concentration camps. Never before has human life been disposed of so lightly as the price for immediate goals. Nationalism, a modernizing force in societies struggling for unity and independence, easily becomes a force for conservatism and oppression once nationhood is achieved. Few political leaders have had the vision to place the human needs of their peoples above national aims. Too often the means for achieving modernization have become ends in themselves,

MODERNISATION - IMMEDIATE GOALS -

and are fought for with a fanaticism and ruthlessness that risk the sacrifice of these ends.

Systems of knowledge based on age-old principles have been undermined, and numberless individuals in the modern world have found no other basis of orientation than immediate needs and goals. Eternal truths, generally embodied in religious dogmas and in conceptions of divinity, have been unthinkingly discarded because they were expressed in a manner that had come to be regarded as old-fashioned. Not infrequently these truths were later rediscovered and proclaimed as the latest revelation of modern science. The paradox of the dual nature of man—simultaneously rational and irrational—which was well understood in earlier times, had to be reasserted by modern psychology after several generations during which learned men had advocated the cult of reason. The desire to be modern has often led to the glorification of the transitory and to the frequent rejection of fundamental values as expressed in traditional institutional forms.

The process of political integration and centralization has been particularly destructive of men and institutions. National histories celebrate the success of rulers in defeating regional and local authorities, in bringing the church under control, and in winning prized pieces of territory from neighbors. Each of these acts may have contributed to the strength and integrity of the country, hence to its ultimate ability to forge a modern society, yet they involved not only a great deal of slaughter but also the destruction of institutions and organizations that had functioned successfully for generations. Frequently, after drowning in blood an entire network of local officials, the central authorities have had to find other people—usually less capable and experienced—to perform the same functions.

An inherent contradiction in the process of modernization is the tendency toward the concentration of authority at the level of politically organized societies and at the same time toward the integration of most aspects of human activity within a much larger framework, in some cases embracing all of mankind. When for the first time systems of knowledge of universal validity have been developed; when societies are increasingly dependent for their security on factors that

CONTRADICTION — INDEPENDENCE & INTERDEPENDENCE IN MODERNISATION

extend far beyond their boundaries; when systems of production require raw materials, markets, and skills that no one society can provide; when social relationships and cultural institutions overlap national confines; and when the orientation of the individual is developing toward acquiring values that know no national frontiers— at this very time the effect of organizational controls within which all aspects of human activity must operate is being concentrated increasingly at the level of national states, of politically organized societies. This growing contradiction between independence and interdependence at the present stage of modernization lies at the heart of the contemporary international crisis.

One sometimes thinks of the modern age as being especially conducive to internationalism, but this has not thus far been the case. In traditional societies diverse peoples often have shared common religions, enjoyed fluid political allegiances and economic ties within large and loosely knit empires, and in a few cases employed languages recognized to some extent as universal. Today the inexorable requirements of modernization have been concentrated to such an extent at the national level that international organizations vital for national security can be formed only on the condition that they be forbidden to intervene in matters that are essentially within the domestic jurisdiction of member states. Intervention is permitted only if there is a threat to peace so grave that the great powers are willing to compromise their differences and take appropriate measures to prevent a major war.

Another source of unrest characteristic of the modern age has been the threat that the developing modern integrated society has posed to traditions and values evolved at a time when these were nurtured by a relatively small group of privileged leaders. The problem has led serious students to question whether education of a high quality can survive if everyone must be educated, whether ideas and standards will not erode if they must be presented in a form in which everyone can understand them—indeed, whether democracy is workable if everyone can make his influence felt. To some extent such fears no doubt are present among the former privileged leadership groups, which resent the necessity of sharing their privileges. Yet the problems of maintaining quality in an integrated or mass society cannot be said to have been solved. When a national budget must be approved by persons representing innumerable discordant interests, and when literature and art must be adapted to a mass audience at the risk of losing financial support—to cite only two examples—the problem is real.

Other social concomitants of modernization are equally grave. In many undeveloped countries, where the birth rate has remained high long after the death rate has declined, the growth in population may outstrip by a considerable margin any possible expansion in the output of food and manufactured goods. In these cases, even though agriculture and industry are stimulated by local efforts and foreign aid, production per capita may decline. The reluctance of the peoples of these countries to adopt methods of birth control is due to traditional values and behavior patterns that in their rate of change lag far behind medical care. In India, which has a serious population problem, not only are birth-control methods not employed but the many millions of Hindus refuse to eat the cattle that wander uncontrolled and often damage crops, or to kill the monkeys that devour enormous quantities of fruit and nuts. In such a case traditional scruples take precedence over human needs, and millions suffer.

The population problem is further compounded by the fact that in the early stages of economic growth, consumption on the part of the bulk of the population must be kept stable in order to provide the necessary investments. But how can this be done when the population is already growing faster than the production? In the more acute cases the answer has not yet been found. In the relatively developed countries, such as Britain in the mid-nineteenth century and Russia in the twentieth, the real income of wage earners appears to have declined absolutely for a generation or more before the benefits of the new industrial production became widely available. These countries started their growth at a much higher level than that of the newer states, however, and enjoyed more favorable conditions of development.

The effects of modernization on the stability and identity of personality have also been serious. The relatively stable personality characteristic of traditional societies is formed by an environment in which the elders are the unquestioned trustees of a cultural heritage that has changed only slowly through the centuries. Children are brought up within the immediate family in an atmosphere of emotional security, and enjoy face-to-face relations with the members of their community in relative isolation from peoples of a different heritage. This environment and set of relations make for a strong sense of identity and self-assurance, which for the overwhelming majority of members of traditional societies is never strained by confrontations with conflicting norms and values.

Although the fundamental psychological problems of individual adjustment may not change through the ages, and the incidence of aggressive and passive personalities and of neurotic and psychotic individuals may vary little, the environment in which these adjustments are made is greatly altered in the course of modernization. The traditional cultural heritage, rapidly undermined, gives way to a fundamental uncertainty as to norms and values. The environment in which children are raised and the norms that govern their upbringing are directly affected by a number of trends. Urbanization alters the family structure, and the local community dissolves as rural inhabitants desert the villages for cities and not infrequently for foreign countries. Changes in the relations between men and women attendant upon the mechanization of labor profoundly affect the centuries-old patterns of identity that have distinguished masculine and feminine roles.

The individual is less under the domination of his environment in modern than in traditional societies, and to this extent he is freer, but at the same time he is less certain of his purpose and in times of great unrest is prepared to surrender his freedom in the interest of purposeful leadership. This is what is meant by the loss of identity characteristic of individuals in societies undergoing rapid social change. The modern environment tends to atomize society, depriving its members of the sense of community and belonging without which individual fulfillment cannot be satisfactorily achieved. Many regard personal insecurity and anxiety as the hallmarks of the modern age, which can be traced directly to the profound social disintegration that has accompanied modernization.

This disintegration of traditional norms and values is apparent in the many forms of pathology that characterize modern societies. It is generally believed, although it is difficult to prove, that all categories of social disorganization—crime, delinquency, divorce, suicide, mental illness—have seen an increase in frequency as societies have become more modern. Underlying this trend is the circumstance that the close ties of individuals to others in the immediate environment are loosened as individuals by the millions migrate from rural to urban areas and the conformity to norms and effectiveness of sanctions characteristic of traditional societies are weakened. In a general sense this isolation of the individual is referred to as alienation.

At the heart of alienation is the impersonality of the societies in which the entire life of an individual—work, home, nourishment, health, communication, recreation—is managed by a variety of bureaucratic organizations that tend to treat individuals as numbers, bodies, or abstract entities. People may live in apartment houses where they do not know their neighbors, work in offices or factories where their colleagues change every few months, prepare food purchased from or delivered by unknown persons, eat among strangers in restaurants, enjoy entertainment either transmitted by electronic devices or seen in theaters or stadiums filled with persons one has never seen before, worship in churches where ceremony, clergymen, and congregation are unfamiliar, and grow up as children without close relations with parents and in environments where danger lurks in the street, and trees and animals are rarely seen. Indeed, individual social and spiritual needs receive more attention in modern armies than they do in the ever-growing metropolises in advanced societies. In terms of the relations of individuals to their environment this impersonal way of life in a modern metropolis—perhaps somewhat overdrawn for emphasis, but not untypical of the way many millions live—lies at the opposite extreme from life in the closely knit communities of traditional rural societies. No large numbers of individuals have been able thus far to adjust satisfactorily to the modern environment, and forms of social organization conducive to healthy personal adjustments have yet to be developed.

Related to these changes, in ways that are not entirely clear, is the increase in violence that has accompanied modernization. Painstaking but inevitably inconclusive worldwide estimates for the period 1820–1949 indicate that large wars have become more frequent and have taken a toll of 46.8 million lives. By comparison, 2.9 million lives have been lost in the same period from minor forms of group violence, and 9.7 million lives have been lost in murders involving one to three persons. One may gain some comfort from the fact that the increase in loss of life through violence has not exceeded the growth in world population. It nevertheless seems clear, although comparable statistics are not available for earlier periods of history, that the loss of life due to violence is significantly greater in proportion to population in modern than in traditional societies.

Some of this violence may be attributed no doubt to the willful malevolence of political leaders, but most of it can be explained by the radical character of the changes inherent in modernization. Involving the totality of human behavior patterns, these changes are correspondingly unsettling in terms of the identity and security of individuals and institutions. Traditional functions and institutions must be changed, but they do not surrender without a struggle. At the domestic level violence has taken the form of efforts to consolidate national authority, to suppress revolts, and to overthrow governments. The transition from traditional to modernizing political leaders has invariably involved violence and not infrequently civil wars of considerable intensity and duration. At the international level the dissolution of multinational empires, the liberation of subject peoples, the unification of territories to form new states, and the preservation of the national security of states both new and old have likewise been fraught with violence. Much of this violence has centered in the European and English-speaking societies that were the first to modernize, and it is possible that the inventiveness and vigor that enabled these peoples to develop modern knowledge and apply it to human affairs may be accompanied by an unusual bellicosity. It remains for the societies of Latin America, Asia, and Africa to demonstrate that they can achieve a comparable level of modernity with less violence.

The more modern societies are not freer than traditional societies from the problems inherent in personal and social relations; nor are they more civilized in any general or absolute sense. Modern societies, with a greater understanding of their physical and human environment, have a greater capacity for assuring the material welfare of mankind; yet at the same time, they face more complex personal and social problems and possess a greater capacity for violence and destruction. It is the task of the modern societies to make the best of their opportunities and to safeguard themselves as best they can against the destructive capabilities of their power.

2. Comparative History

The Comparative Method

Comparative studies play such a fundamental role in the formulation of generalizations about mankind that the use and abuse of this method deserves particular attention. It is interesting to note in this connection that recent studies of the machinery of the brain have demonstrated that the process by which we store, organize, and recall information in our human computers is based on a system of association and interconnection that is essentially comparative in character. In one form or another comparison is the most widely used method for organizing the great diversity of data represented by man and nature. All descriptive terms embracing more than one instance, whether general terms such as "tree" or "man," or more specialized ones such as "king," "slave," or "machine," are generalizations or models of varying complexity that are applicable to many thousands or millions of individual cases. Such terms, derived from the observation of similarities and differences, in this sense are based on the comparative method. Whether or not they realize it, even those most dedicated to the unique would find it difficult to write a sentence that does not contain generalized terminology in some form that is applicable to and based on the observation of more than one case.

The concern here, however, is not the general significance of comparison in thought and logic. It is, rather, the specific use of comparison as a method of historical research. In this context comparison serves two interrelated purposes, the first being the organization and classification of complex materials. Even in discussing a small community it is impossible to describe separately each one of its members and all aspects of their social relations. The individuals must be described in terms of groups based on uniformities arrived at through comparisons that are implicit as often as they are explicit. In the writing of history of groups as large as several nations or of mankind as a whole, the resorting to general concepts such as "Islam," "nationalism," or "peasantry," which reflect the uniformities found in many different cases in each category, becomes even more important. For purposes of organization and generalization, one must stress the uniformities represented by these categories and discuss the variations primarily as examples that serve to define the limits of the term.

The second purpose of comparisons is explanation, which employs the same principles of comparison as organization. Whereas the latter is concerned with completed events and has a static quality, explanation is concerned with change and with the dynamics of history. The principal difference is not in the method but in the entities compared. Organization is concerned with institutions and forms, while explanation is concerned with causes and functions. To this extent explanation is much the more precarious of these two uses of comparison. The nature and identity of institutions can be ascertained with relative ease. The study of functions and causes, on the other hand, involves the comparison of chains of events and of constellations of forces and motivations, the identification of which depends to a considerable extent on the insight of the scholar and calls for a much greater effort at objectivity. The desire to explain is often aroused by some pressing contemporary problem, and the pressure for an answer may lead a scholar to formulate a premature hypothesis, which then serves to distort his research. The continual interaction between hypothesis and evidence that characterizes scholarship requires great detachment even when one is dealing with matters remote from one's personal interest. When the scholar is motivated by a desire to find in history answers that may affect the solution of contemporary problems, the pressure to formulate a premature hypothesis may become unbearable—indeed, historians have not infrequently succumbed.

If comparison is so fundamental to the generalizations that serve to organize and explain the materials of history, why is it frequently regarded with such suspicion? The principal objection to the comparative method in history seems to arise from a belief in the uniqueness of historical events. Individual human beings may be readily compared, because the features common to all are so extensive that the variations can be accounted for with reasonable assurance. The situation is reversed, however, when it becomes a question of groups of individuals, sometimes numbering many millions, acting and interacting in complex situations over a considerable period of time. The variations among such groups are likely to be great and the elements of universality limited to rather general patterns that may not at first seem to have a great deal of explanatory value.

The view that stresses the uniqueness of historical events—sometimes referred to as "objectivism"—has attracted an increasing number of supporters in the course of a generation in which the number of historians has grown rapidly and the subjects of historical research have tended to become increasingly fragmented. The development of archives and other source collections has encouraged this tendency to the point where entire books may be written on the events of a few days or on a single decision. In earlier generations, when the study of history was emerging from theology, it was not uncommon for historians to think in terms of the whole of mankind and of universal history. Today, more often than not, universality is left to prophets, encyclopedists, and textbook writers, while historians in their capacity as professional scholars take pride in their specialized knowledge. There is much of value in this attitude, insofar as it stresses accuracy, detail, and rigorous use of evidence—virtues that form the foundations of professional history. Yet it often conceals a timidity and lack of imagination, as well as a desire for the intellectual security afforded by the mastery of a limited area of knowledge and adherence to accepted views.

This belief in the uniqueness of historical events and the concern for detailed and accurate knowledge are doubtless also in considerable degree reactions against the excesses of those who have maintained that laws of more or less universal validity can be derived from the study of history. These lawgivers, assuming the universality of patterns of development before they have been studied, carry that assumption to the point of believing that these patterns can with assurance be projected into the more or less indefinite future. These deterministic interpretations have built universal systems on the limited foundation of an ancient model, on the national characteristics of a particular country or ethnic or religious group, or on some social relationship, such as class conflict, judged by the author to be crucial for the human experience. These narrowly based conclusions, generalized to the point of absurdity, more often than not are harnessed to the messianic aim of both explaining and solving the problems of mankind. This type of determinism, unsound in theory and unsuccessful in practice, has naturally alienated serious scholars and contributed to the neglect of comparisons in history. At best the great historical lawgivers have been inspired by high-minded motives and have contributed valuable insights as a by-product of their work. At worst they have produced reckless generalizations that have captivated the minds of the unsophisticated and brought into disrepute the degree of understanding that historical scholarship is capable of providing.

Even when the lawgivers have had the modesty to recognize the limited value of their generalizations, such modesty has not generally been shared by their disciples. What was originally only a hypothesis, or even a metaphor, becomes in the hands of the disciples an immutable law. When carried into politics, this faith in historical laws has at times served as the excuse for liquidating thousands or even millions of human beings who are considered to be obstructing the implementation of the "law." When the claims of a nation, race, class, or party favored by a system of historical determinism are believed to be supported by the experience of all past history, as interpreted by the faithful, even the most extreme means of implementation have been justified.

The comparative method certainly has its pitfalls, but this should not be a deterrent to making greater use of this fundamental tool of historical writing. In an age in which mankind as a whole is for the first time being taken seriously as a basis of political, economic, and social organization—and also as a basis of organized destruction—one cannot fail to accept the challenge of making the broader generalizations that depend for their validity on comparisons. The question is not whether to use the comparative method, but how to use it in such a way as to avoid its pitfalls and take advantage of the opportunities that it offers.

Whether comparisons are used as a basis for organizing generalizations or in the search for causal explanations, the problems involved in making valid comparisons are the same. They can be examined in four categories: (1) relationship in time, (2) definition of the entities compared, (3) use of evidence, and (4) formulation of generalizations.

1. Civilized societies have been in existence for some seven thousand years, and imaginative historians have been tempted to draw on the entire range of human experience in the search for comparable materials. Clearly, though, there is much greater value in comparing contemporary events and institutions than those that are widely separated in time. The comparison of societies or smaller groups that are concerned with reasonably similar problems is more likely to lead to satisfactory conclusions than comparisons between societies existing many centuries apart. It is no doubt legitimate, if one is studying political leadership or slavery, to compare examples of these institutions taken from ancient Egypt and Greece with those in modern Arabia and the United States. The trouble with such comparisons is that since any aspect of a society is largely dependent on its total culture, the uniformities tend to be more nominal and the variations more real as the time-span increases.

At the same time, contemporaneity also has its problems. No two societies are at the same level of development at a given point in time, even though they may share many common traits and influences. Should the Soviet Union be compared with the United States of today, when the two societies match each other in important respects; or with the United States of a generation ago, when per capita production of most products, the balance between agriculture and industry, and the availability of secondary education were more nearly alike? Can valid comparisons be made between Nigeria and any country that is not at a similar level of political integration and of economic and social development? The legitimacy of a comparison depends on the definition of the selected problem, and its explanatory value is greatly enhanced if the entities compared have enough in common to make the differences significant.

2. The value of historical comparisons also depends on a careful definition of the entities being compared. The more specific and limited the basis of comparison, the more precise will be the results. Comparisons of provisions for human rights or of rules of parliamentary procedure will lead to more precise generalizations than comparisons of whole civilizations. The value of generalizations is directly proportional to the concreteness of the events being compared. In making generalizations about mankind, the question of the units of comparison is critical. The units must be large enough to yield conclusions of general import, for one would not expect to learn much about mankind as a whole from comparing systems f municipal government. Yet they must be sufficiently concrete to be capable of valid comparison. This is the difficulty encountered by the historians of mankind who use "civilizations," "cultures," "cultural-historical types," or "socio-cultural systems" as the basis for their comparisons. These large entities are usually defined in terms of a predominant religion or value system, more often than not combined with some degree of political hegemony. Yet such civilizations are by no means self-evident, and there is considerable disagreement among historians as to how they should be delineated and, indeed, how many there are. Since the outcome of the comparison depends to a con-

siderable degree on the configuration and number of the civilizations being compared, the definition of these entities is a matter of no little import.

To the extent that the changes characteristic of the modern era have taken place within a framework of political action, politically organized societies—states, nations, polities—offer a much more satisfactory basis of comparison than the more vaguely defined "civilizations" and "cultures." Even these relatively concrete entities nevertheless have some serious shortcomings as bases of comparison. Not the least of these limitations is the fact that politically organized societies vary widely as to structure and homogeneity. They range from small, relatively homogeneous societies with a long tradition of political stability (such as Denmark or Thailand), to large and complex groupings of subsocieties united by conquest or persuasion into a common political structure (such as China, the United Kingdom, the United States, India, and the Union of Soviet Socialist Republics). At the same time, some small societies (such as Lebanon) have a mixed population from an ethnic and religious standpoint, whereas some large ones (such as Japan) are quite homogeneous. In some instances societies have experienced in modern times vital changes in size, structure, political allegiance, and even geographical location. In other cases they have established offshoots in overseas territories that have retained the culture of the metropolitan society even though they have gained independence and have frequently merged with other societies. Again, many societies embrace such a wide variety of regional differences that it is difficult to make sound generalizations for the society as a whole. Yet one would have to turn to the individual human being to find an indivisible unit of analysis, and even some human beings have split personalities.

Although there exist shortcomings in using the politically organized society as a basis of analysis, it nevertheless offers distinct advantages for the study of the modern era. The modern era is one in which national feeling and goals have played a significant role, and our information about it is to a considerable extent of political origin. The laws, statistics, programs, and achievements characteristic of the modern era have been expressed in great measure in political forms, and trends of thought have been expounded more often than not with reference to the problems of specific societies. Moreover, the full complexity of modern society is probably best reflected in political ideas and programs, problems and institutions. "Civilizations" and "cultures" may have some use as a framework for consideration of earlier times, but they are not the framework within which modern societies conduct their business. No "culture" or "civilization" has ever passed a law or raised an army. Dealing with them is like trying to knit with spaghetti, for they tend to separate whenever they are placed under pressure.

Comparisons useful for the study of mankind as a whole can also be made at a level lower than that represented by the national state. The valuable comparisons that have been made of such institutions as slavery, feudalism, despotism, imperialism, and revolutions are likely to produce sounder results than those involving larger and less precise entities or series of events. These middle-range comparisons are nevertheless concerned with limited aspects of mankind's affairs, and their explanatory value is not intended to extend beyond these limits except insofar as they may offer insights in regard to related matters.

3. The third category of problems concerns the use of evidence in making comparisons. This is a question that has assumed particular significance in recent years as social scientists in many disciplines have sought to make comparative studies on a worldwide basis. Comparisons based on statistical data relating to the size and populations of countries, the extent of urbanization and literacy, the distribution of religious, linguistic, or ethnic groups, or of gross national product or industrial production often rest on shaky foundations. Population statistics even in the most advanced countries have a margin of error of about 5 percent, and in some countries it is much larger. In the case of China the margin of error may be as much as plus or minus 50 million people. Yet these are probably the most accurate statistics available.

Much more problematic are statistics bearing on gross national product, where there is still much disagreement among specialists as to what is being measured. Many of the elements that go into the calculation of gross national product are only a rough approximation. The approximation becomes much rougher when one converts the currencies of the world into U.S. dollars, rates of exchange being what they are, and the calculation is not made more accurate by averaging estimates made in two different currencies. The inaccuracy is further compounded when these estimates are expressed on a per capita basis for population figures that are themselves only rough approximations. When one sees neat rows of figures expressing GNP per capita down to the last dollar, or the construction from such figures of annual rates of change expressed in fractions of 1 percent, the innocent historian should definitely be on his guard. Such figures may be no further from reality than the subjective judgments that political scientists and historians often use in making comparisons, but they should be handled with caution. Moreover, statistics of reasonable accuracy are available for relatively few countries and then only for the last few decades.

The comparison of institutions, as long as they are carefully selected, is fraught with fewer dangers. Comparisons may be made of executive and legislative institutions, of political systems, of bureaucracies, and of the role in society of the police or the army. Such institutions take a variety of forms in different societies, but they are in most cases readily identifiable and can serve as the basis for the collection and comparison of data. When one proceeds, however, to compare societies on the basis of vaguely defined criteria such as political stability, ideological orientation, political enculturation, interest articulation, or interest aggregation—terms as to the meaning of which even scholars sharing the same outlook have difficulty in reaching agreement—the results are not likely to be fruitful.

4. The final category of problems concerns the way in which the comparative method is used in formulating generalizations. In theory one may seek uniformities in any series of events, however different in character or separate in time, but in practice one should seek to juxtapose uniformities and variables within a limited frame of reference. A frequent weakness in historical comparisons is the search for

uniform causes of similar events or institutions in several societies. This usually follows from a priori reasoning in which the common cause is assumed or established on the basis of research relating to only a few cases, and then applied to all cases of the same class. This tends to result in a neglect of all the factors except those that the historian is looking for, and the outcome is frequently an analogy rather than a comparison.

A significant distinction in formulating a comparative problem is that between functions and structures, or institutions. It is not always easy to identify functions and structures, and the distinction is more obvious in biology than in human society. The common functions of feeding, breathing, circulation, excretion, growth, and reproduction are performed by all living creatures, from the lowly amoeba to the majestic elephant, but the structures—or organs—by means of which these functions are performed vary enormously. As applied to human societies, speech and communication are functions, and language is a structure; the representation of interest groups is a function, and professional organizations and political parties are structures; the maintenance of order is a function, and bureaucracies and legislation are structures. Not all problems are amenable to study in terms of functions and structures, but when they are, it can be a most fruitful approach.

Another device in formulating a comparative problem is the use of a model or ideal type as a basis of comparison. This in effect involves a comparison in two stages. The first stage involves the definition of a model—"parliamentary government," for example—that is based on a comparison of the existing cases in this category. The second stage involves the use of this model as a basis for comparisons designed to investigate the extent to which this model stems from common origins, reflects a common environment, and so on, in the various cases in which it occurs. It is possible to discern a structure of dependent and independent variables, of correlations and covariations, that serves to organize one's data with reference to the selected problem and in appropriate cases to reach conclusions of explanatory and predictive value. By whatever means the problem is formulated, it is essential that the entities being compared be carefully identified at each stage and that the relationships between constants and variables be clearly defined.

Philosophers, when they discuss problems of historical explanation, are inclined to take sharply defined positions in favor of the particular, the relative, and the unique, on the one hand, or the general, the absolute, and the covering law, on the other. This polarization of approaches may be useful in philosophical argument, but it does not correspond to the experience of practicing historians. The latter are concerned with both the particular and the general—and the particular is never so particular that it cannot be described in terms applicable to more than one case, nor is the general so general as to be capable of formulation in a hierarchy of interlocking generalizations such as those that have been elaborated in the natural sciences.

For the practicing historian it is not a question of whether or not, but to what extent—and the extent depends on the criteria of comparison employed. The limits imposed on the historian are not of logic but of sources. The materials with which historians work are infinitely more complex than those of any of the natural sciences or of all the natural sciences combined, and most of the information needed for fully satisfactory generalizations is permanently lost. Even the records available for contemporary history, which are voluminous, represent only a fraction of what one would have to know to make explanations and generalizations comparable to those that are possible in the natural sciences. There can be no question of reproducing on the basis of historical materials the type of generalizing laws that the natural scientists have provided.

The pitfalls of the comparative method and the limits within which sound generalization is possible should nevertheless not be permitted to inhibit the broadening of the study of modern history to include mankind as a whole. It was not so long ago that historians hesitated to generalize about Europe and concerned themselves only with individual countries. The time has now come to formulate generalizations about the whole of mankind in modern times. We have many models of the approaches that should be avoided: histories that offer a genealogy of competing civilizations from the beginning of time, histories that view the whole of the human experience as the working out of a single idea, histories that see the modern world simply as the extension to all other peoples of the institutions developed in Western Europe and in the English-speaking countries.

Yet there are other types of generalizations that are likely to yield significant results. These could be based, for example, on comparisons of the historically evolved traditional institutions of the more than 130 separate states into which mankind is now organized, on comparisons of the patterns that the confrontations between traditional and modern institutions and functions have taken, and on comparisons of the different ways in which traditional institutions have adapted to modern functions. Whether the entities being compared are politically organized societies, or institutions, or processes, or systems of ideas is not important as long as these entities have historical reality. Such generalizations should not be expected to answer all questions about the past, present, and future, but they will enable historians to contribute much more to an understanding of the modern world than if they limit themselves to a study of the unique.

Modernization as a Process

It is useful to think of modernization as a process by which traditional institutions are adapted to modern functions, as long as the problems inherent in the functional approach are adequately appreciated. Functionalism is most commonly employed as a means of analyzing the workings of a system and of explaining the interrelationships of its parts in terms of the functions that they perform. The value of this approach in the study of modernization is that it sees societies as systems, in a sense analogous to living organisms, the institutions, or organs, of which may be viewed according to the ways that they serve to maintain the viability of such systems. The study of societies as a set of institutions and functions raises a wide variety of problems, capable of being empirically studied, that serve to clarify the complex interrelationships characteristic of human behavior.

The employment of the functional approach also faces some

serious problems. To the extent that such an analysis has the purpose of explaining the functions requisite to the maintenance of a system, it has an inherent bias in favor of equilibrium. There is no objection to this if one is analyzing the operation of a mechanism designed to regulate the heat of a house by means of a furnace and a thermostat. The circularity of the explanatory logic in such a case corresponds to a functional circularity. When it is a question of human affairs, however, where change is of the essence, the bias toward equilibrium represents a serious shortcoming. Functionalism in the behavioral sciences also runs the risk of exaggerating the intellectual and teleological aspects of human affairs at the expense of those aspects that are either irrational or so embedded in the traditional way of doing things as to be relatively immune to rational manipulation or control.

This bias toward equilibrium and even circularity in the functional approach to the study of societies is due in large measure to the neglect of the element of change. The analysis of a society in equilibrium must of necessity lead to limited results, because societies are never in equilibrium. They are constantly in the process of change, and it is the most characteristic feature of the modern era that change has been more rapid and thoroughgoing than in any other period of history. The ultimate source of this change is the growth of knowledge, the immediate impact of which bears on the functions that institutions perform. The dynamic quality of the intellectual innovation, political integration, economic growth, social mobilization, and personality adjustment, all of which represent in most general terms the characteristically modern functions, requires fundamental adaptations on the part of the diverse institutions that were in existence when man's greatly enhanced capacities gradually began to make themselves felt in recent centuries.

It is significant that functions can change rapidly and may even be profoundly affected by a single person—an innovator who revolutionizes a production technique, discovers a new secret of nature, or develops a new conception of human affairs. It takes few people to establish the fact that the earth is round, that steam engines can do the work of many horses and men, that it is not dangerous to eat pork if it is properly cooked, or that methods of birth control can be made effective and inexpensive. There is no correspondingly simple means, however, of changing the patterns of belief and behavior of millions of people.

It is sometimes thought that charismatic leaders, individuals endowed with a superhuman authority, can carry whole peoples along with them. It takes a great many tons of charisma, however, to move a society a single inch. It may be centuries before the teachings of such leaders are internalized to form the unconsciously accepted way of doing things, and even this gradual acceptance is achieved only as a result of innumerable and often significant compromises with previously existing beliefs. One has only to think of Christmas, with its association of Santa Claus with the birth of Christ, and of gift-laden fir trees adjacent to crèches in an environment of semitropical flora—or of Easter, when the Resurrection and the birth of spring are celebrated together in a setting of rabbits, eggs, lambs, and tulips—to appreciate how a palimpsest of practices and beliefs may form a harmonious whole no matter how incongruous it may appear to the uninitiated or the literal-minded.

Functional change depends on the few, and may often be rapid and easy. Structural change depends on the many, and is slow and painful. It is the task of leaders to mediate between function and structure—between the new knowledge and the old customs—and this is never easy. All institutions adapt to change in some degree, and some may change radically over the years. The family in undeveloped societies may be the primary unit for virtually all production, education, and social security, whereas in modern societies its functions may be limited to the socialization of the young. Some traditional institutions readily adapt to modern functions—as the bureaucratic autocracies have to modern centralized government. Others, such as tribal institutions, can hardly be expected to survive.

However great the institutional change, the very fact of adaptation means that many features of the traditional institutions survive. In varying degrees, depending on the institutions, the diverse features of traditional institutions remain characteristic of modern societies. The most obvious, and perhaps the most extreme, example of this is language seen as an institution performing the function of communication. Traditional Chinese and English culture developed many fundamentally different and mutually incomprehensible conceptions —almost as different, if such things can be compared, as the differences between the two languages in grammar and vocabulary. As the two cultures have modernized, their understanding of the world around them has tended to converge, until the point is reached at which the universality of modern knowledge permits relatively complete and accurate translation of ideas from one language to the other. The structures of the two languages may also change, at least to the extent that as a result of borrowing, identical terms are used to describe certain typically modern objects. Such structural change is likely to be slight, however, and as languages, Chinese and English are about as far apart as they were several centuries ago.

This is no doubt an extreme example, for in most cases institutional change is a good deal greater than that which the Chinese and English languages have undergone, but it is equally rare for traditional institutions to be altered as completely as are their functions. Families, political systems, religious values, literary symbols, have proved to be adaptable to a wide variety of functional changes over the centuries. For this reason the process of modernization may within the foreseeable future lead to a convergence and perhaps a universalization of functions, but not of institutions as long as the 175 societies in the world retain their relative discreteness as systems. There is much evidence that Japan and France, the United States and the Soviet Union, or Mexico and Poland are becoming more alike functionally, but there is no comparable convergence in institutional structure. What they do is becoming more similar, but the way they do it remains different in significant respects.

The Comparison of Modernizing Societies

The comparison of politically organized societies, or polities, in the process of political modernization involves problems of a political character as well as the more abstract ones of methodology. Societies do not exist simply as abstractions, nor do they have as discrete an existence as plants. They maintain relations with one another, populations migrate from one to another, and they can be partitioned and rearranged in a variety of ways. Indeed, it is not unlikely that at some future time politically organized societies, as we know them today, will tend to become absorbed into larger entities.

Societies in the process of modernization must therefore be considered both as independent entities, the traditional institutions of which are being adapted to modern functions, and also as societies under the influence of many outside forces. Indeed, the outside influences are so powerful that modernization is sometimes thought of primarily as acculturation—the adoption of the culture traits of another society. The distinction between the domestic process of change and the role in this process of models represented by more advanced societies is a vital one in comparing modernizing societies. The models adopted by modernizing leaders, except in the societies that were the first to modernize, are always derived in a considerable degree from outside their own society. The problems they face, however, are domestic and in essential ways unique. It is necessary, then, to be concerned simultaneously with comparisons on two levels—comparisons of the ways in which domestic traditional institutions adapt to modern functions and comparisons of the models of modernity that serve as a basis for this adaptation.

A related problem, in discussing the process of change in a large number of societies with widely varying traditional institutions and at different stages of development, is that of the extent to which one should employ terminology that is nominally general in its application but is useful only within the framework of the historical context within which the original meaning was formed. The alternatives seem to be either to employ such terms only in the strictly defined sense or to abandon them in favor of more abstract terms or even of neologisms to which meanings can be attributed that are relevant to a wide variety of situations.

The words "capitalism" and "socialism" were once thought to have fairly distinct meanings, but time has dulled their cutting edge.

If "capitalism" means the use of property to produce wealth, then the Communist countries are as capitalist as any; but if "capitalism" means the private ownership and control of the means of production, then there is a variety of mixtures of state, corporate, and private control in none of which is the role of direct state participation much less than one-fifth or one-quarter. If "socialism" means state ownership of property used for production, there are certainly some societies where in principle this is carried much further than in others. If "socialism" is taken to mean the distribution of wealth per capita in real terms, however, then the most highly industrialized societies tend to be the most socialist. It would be easy to demonstrate that Sweden, the United Kingdom, or the United States, for example, is in a significant degree more "socialist" in this sense than the Soviet Union or any other country that is "building communism." Under the circumstances, it seems best not to refer to capitalism and socialism but to describe in functional terms the role of private or state ownership or control and related aspects of the various political and economic systems.

A somewhat similar situation exists with the term "democracy," which started out to mean government by the people in a system in which the prevailing political culture, as well as the practical guarantees of human rights, makes it possible for political leaders to respond closely to the wishes of the majority. The proponents of this system undermine the integrity of the term, however, when they refer to "economic democracy." This conception is self-contradictory unless it means literally that economic as distinct from political matters are determined in a democratic fashion, and in fact it is intended to mean simply economic egalitarianism. The fact that nondemocratic societies are also non-egalitarian in terms of the distribution of the wealth produced does not seem to have impeded the continued use of this concept. The term "democracy" has been further diluted by its use as a general term to denote all governments not held "captive" by Communist parties. When used in this sense, it embraces quite a remarkable variety of governments. To confuse matters further, Marxist-Leninist ideology has adopted "democracy" to mean Communist-controlled, in contrast to "imperialist," and uses such terms as "national democracy" and "people's democracy" to denote degrees of Communist political influence. Clarity in this case is perhaps best served by describing governments in terms of the degree and type of representation, number of competing parties, means of reconciling the interests of conflicting groups, and pattern of human rights.

The description of the component groups of a society in terms of "classes"—whether the Marxist categories of "proletariat" and "bourgeoisie" or the various typologies of "upper," "middle," and "lower class" often preferred by social scientists—is another relic of an earlier era that has ceased to serve a useful purpose. In prerevolutionary France, for example, the States-General traditionally met as three separate estates—the nobility, the clergy, and a third estate representing lawyers, businessmen, merchants, artisans, workers, and peasants. The ultimate victory of the third estate destroyed this traditional system, but the custom survived of classifying populations into a few large groups that were assumed to have identities comparable to those of the estates. The more influential members of the third estate were now considered to have formed a new "middle class," or "bourgeoisie," and the rapid urbanization accompanying industrialization soon resulted in the creation of a new "working class," or "proletariat."

There are two objections to such classifications. One is that, as empirical studies have shown, societies are in fact divided into quite a number of subgroups—occupational, religious, organizational, political—which combine in a wide variety of patterns with reference to specific interests and decisions. These patterns depend to a large extent on how the members of these various groups identify their own roles and interests and on the various ideologies or interpretations of reality that prevail. The other objection is that the term "classes" has become so identified with the oversimplified classifications characteristic of nineteenth-century liberal and socialist thought that it is difficult to employ the word without becoming entangled in these earlier accretions of meaning. Here again, the best procedure seems to be to discard the older terminology and to use the more refined conceptions of occupational categories, social strata, and interest groups, which have been developed in recent years by behavioral scientists.

In making the distinction between a modern and a traditional society, one starts with a general conception of the nature of change in recent centuries. In a comparison of whole societies and individual aspects of societies, there gradually emerges a refinement not only of one's conception of what is in fact modern but also of which societies share these characteristics and to what degree. This newer conception of modernity is one that is of necessity based on the experience of the relatively few societies that have been most influenced by developments in science and technology, to the extent that this can be ascertained with some accuracy. One should therefore take into account the possibility that what appears to be "modern" in these countries may be due more to idiosyncrasies of their development than to universal characteristics and that the experience of later-modernizing societies may alter our views in significant respects. Earlier students assumed that representative government was a general characteristic of modernity because the most advanced countries had developed it. But the experience and research of the past generation have led many to question this conclusion. It is possible that representative government may be a modernization of the methods by which the feudal estates represented their interests and that societies with other traditional political institutions may modernize in a different direction.

Although the problems raised by generalization from a rather narrow base must be acknowledged, the definition of modernity takes the form of a set of characteristics believed to be generally applicable to all societies. This conception of modernity, when thought of as a model or ideal type, may be used as a yardstick with which to measure any society. The major phases of emphasis that confront societies in the process of modernization, discussed in the third chapter, may likewise be thought of as models or ideal types. Like modernity, they are uniformities based on the comparison of the experience of the relatively few advanced societies. In the fourth chapter all the societies in the world are compared in the light of these two models or ideal types—modernity and the phases of modernization—as a means of conveying an impression of the level of development of these societies at the present time. The implications of this situation for international relations and for the future are discussed in the fifth and sixth chapters.

A contrast between modernity and tradition is only the most elementary means of defining these concepts. It will, of course, be clear that in this sense both tradition and modernity are abstractions, for in reality no two societies are entirely alike and all are in a continual process of change. This conception of process—indeed, the whole problem of modernization—calls attention to the need for a greater use of logical modes of thought on the part of historians and social scientists. It is natural that social scientists should have such a great fixation on static models, since their first task as members of a relatively young discipline has been to analyze and generalize about the most readily available data on contemporary societies before making the comparisons in time that would be necessary to study change. Historians, although problems of change are their primary concern, have also tended to focus either on relatively static situations or on extremely simple conceptions of change.

Modernization must be thought of not as a simple transition from tradition to modernity but as part of an infinite continuum from the earliest times to the indefinite future. This essay examines only a limited portion of this continuum, and when abstractions such as tradition and modernity are used they should be considered only as single frames in the motion picture of history that have been enlarged for purposes of study. This form of abstraction from a continuum of variables is in fact a risky procedure, for it tends toward an artificial polarization of alternatives. Generalizations about democracy and dictatorship, leaders and followers, order and movement, rightism and leftism, are the simplest possible description of continua in terms of two poles. Such generalizations should be counterbalanced by an emphasis on the great variety of relationships between central authority and popular control in the more than 130 sovereign governments, by the fine gradations in degrees of leadership from a few influential individuals to those who are totally devoid of initiative in any realm of human activity, and so on. Game theory, factor analysis, and systems analysis, for example, have made significant contributions in related disciplines.

When one considers modernization as a process, therefore, one thinks of it as a continuous series of changes accompanying the growth of knowledge and its effects on man's ways of getting things done. As a means of bringing a degree of order to the great complexity of human affairs, one may think of traditional societies as a pattern of inherited institutions or structures that is relatively static at the time that modern knowledge makes its initial impact on it. The effect of modern knowledge is to change the functions that traditional institutions must perform, and this in turn affects the institutions themselves. It is in this sense that the impact of modern functions on traditional institutions lies at the heart of the process of modernization.

3. The Politics of Modernization

Politics and Modernization

The worldwide diffusion of modernity is so complex a process that one should not attempt in brief scope to do more than point out its complexities and suggest ways of organizing and examining them. If one approaches modernization in terms of the five aspects already suggested—intellectual, political, economic, social, and psychological—a degree of clarity is achieved only at the sacrifice of many essential interrelations. No two aspects exert influence at the same rate or in a similar manner, nor do they necessarily bear the same relationship to each other in different societies.

Knowledge and ideas normally find their way around the world rather easily. In the natural sciences and related disciplines, in particular, communications are so well organized that the publication of an important discovery in one country is today soon conveyed to scholars in other parts of the world. Similarly in other fields, statements of leaders, especially of political leaders, rapidly become known to other interested persons. Even before the introduction of modern means of communication, there was considerable intellectual intercourse among educated persons. Whether ideas thus diffused are accepted is another matter. Yet even alien views have a tendency to become a part of one's thinking and to influence it in ways that are not always appreciated. Indeed, despite the variety of peoples and societies, there are everywhere groups of educated individuals who are in continual communication with their colleagues around the world and who share similar values. Moreover, in the realm of ideas, individuals may undergo rapid transformations. The child of an ignorant peasant or shepherd may be educated at a great university and become within a relatively short time as much at home in the world of modern ideas as anyone else.

The diffusion of other aspects of modernization is neither so rapid nor so general as in the realm of knowledge. The influences may be felt, but they fall on a wide variety of soils and produce many varieties of fruits. The only certainty is that no society among the later modernizers will reproduce a pattern of modern institutions quite like those of the societies that modernized first. Some find it easy to develop centralized political institutions, whereas others do not; some adapt themselves rapidly to the industrial way of life, whereas others must overcome major obstacles presented by traditional beliefs and practices. In at least one case, that of China, the traditional way of life had such a powerful hold on the minds of leaders that modernity was successfully resisted for many generations. In this particular instance, one of the most sophisticated of the traditional societies was for a long time one of the most reluctant to modernize.

Politics in the broadest sense is the conceptualization and implementation of plans of action, and the growth and diffusion of modernity can best be understood in terms of its political aspect. Political developments, relatively easily determined, provide the most readily available framework for analysis, comparison, and periodization. Although each aspect of modernization may be expected to reflect in some degree all of the others, since they represent different approaches to the same phenomenon, it is politics that provides the organizational basis for a society. Political struggles are struggles for the power to put into effect programs derived from the working assumptions of one or another group of leaders. Such programs often embrace wide areas of human experience, and occasionally in revolutionary times may seek to effect sweeping changes in all aspects of a society. It is customary to employ such political adjectives as Napoleonic, Victorian, Meiji, Kemalist, or Stalinist to describe not only the law and government but also the educational system, architecture, literature, and even the behavior patterns of politically defined periods, and there can be no question that a political regime frequently stamps an entire culture with its own characteristic style. Politically organized societies are the most satisfactory basis for the study of modernization. Despite certain limitations, they are the framework within which the process of modernization in all its complexity unfolds.

One may take as a starting point the more than one hundred politically organized societies constituting the United Nations, and there are a number of others equally well defined that for one reason or another have not joined that organization. Beyond this, there is an element of arbitrary choice. Societies under foreign rule that seem clearly on the way to independence or substantial autonomy are considered here for comparative purposes as independent societies, as opposed to those that appear for the time being to form integral parts of more complex societies. It is here that one has to make difficult—and somewhat arbitrary—choices. It must also be recognized that the number and identity of states are never entirely stable. The forces that served to unite Germany and to unite Italy in the nineteenth century are now at work in the Arab world, in Southeast Asia, and perhaps also in Africa as well. A number of politically organized societies may suddenly dissolve into one, and occasionally they also regain their individuality after a period of uneasy cohabitation.

Despite the shortcomings of the political approach, other ways of looking at the subject suffer greatly by comparison in terms of specificity and accuracy. Attempts to study the development of societies in economic and social terms must navigate a veritable quicksand of data. For most countries of the world there are few reliable statistics except for the contemporary era. To approach the problem of modernization primarily from an economic or social point of view is to limit oneself either to generalities, or to only a few countries in depth, or to the most recent period. Skilled social scientists have been able to make very imaginative and thought-provoking use of the available data, and their work is essential to an understanding of the interaction of modernity and tradition, but it is to politics that one must turn for a more comprehensive understanding of its course and problems.

Change is the essence of history, and the debates, struggles, and compromises that have characterized modernization are well reflected in the correspondence, speeches, reports, legislation, and other documents that serve as the basis for political history. Change may be viewed within the framework of the conception that a society evolves with reference to the problems that it faces. This conception is reflected in its religion, ideology, "style," and value system, and permeates all modes of expression. A society's understanding of itself and its problems—its sense of identity and purpose—is the principal binding force that integrates the members of that society and enables them to act effectively in common to solve their domestic and foreign problems. This is a profoundly conservative force, and properly so. The welfare and security of all the members of a society depend on its effectiveness, and they cannot lightly abandon beliefs, practices, and institutions that past experience has proved to be reliable.

At the same time, a society's conceptualization of itself and of its problems is constantly being challenged. It is being challenged first of all from within. Catastrophic droughts, floods, earthquakes, and various forms of pestilence may fundamentally undermine the assumptions of a society about its immediate environment, which may lead to a profound reorganization of its way of life including, perhaps, migration to a new land. Learned men in their monasteries, libraries, and laboratories are always turning up new ideas that call into question accepted beliefs. These are not often so profoundly disrupting as the discovery that the earth is round or that it is not the center of the universe, or that the powerful forces contained by the atom can be released, but even small revisions of an accepted idea endanger the certainty that has been achieved by such great effort. Technical innovations likewise challenge stability when they set in motion changes in the conditions of work that necessitate a rearrangement of the social order. Members of a society may travel abroad, or become acquainted at home with foreign travelers, books, and machines that suggest different ways of doing things. Foreign influences may also be more forcefully introduced by foreign invasions that threaten the existence of a society that cannot meet the challenge or by a prolonged occupation, sometimes lasting for several centuries, during which a society may be completely reshaped under foreign tutelage.

In these and other ways societies are confronted by challenges and have to deal with them. In the most elementary sense societies may be said to meet the problem of change by concentrating their efforts alternatively—or simultaneously, if one thinks in terms of component elements of a society—on defending the existing conceptions and adapting them to an altered conception. It is not by chance that political struggles have come to be expressed in terms of an incumbent government and an opposition, the ins and the outs, conservatives and liberals, parties of order and parties of movement. This fundamental choice between inflexibility and adaptation—which in some cases may be a choice between the tried and the untried, the known and the unknown—may ultimately take the form of a simple polarization at the highest level of society, but it reflects the accumulation of an infinite number of smaller choices that it is virtually impossible to trace in full detail and few of which in isolation would present clear-cut issues.

Analogies are a weak reed to lean on, especially in historical matters, but it may help to think in terms of the evolutionary process by which over many millions of years gases turned to earth and later to water, water provided the environment for elementary life, and life developed more complicated forms until there emerged the human being who makes and writes history. The difference between man and elementary life, water, rocks, or gases is incalculably greater than that between the modern and the traditional or even the earliest ages—yet this vast difference was bridged by infinitely small adaptations and combinations over many hundreds of thousands of years in a manner that is not yet fully understood. Historical change is of this order of complexity—but with this significant difference that when these changes accumulate in such a way as to have an important effect on human affairs, society can mobilize itself to deal with them. Some historians have discussed change in terms of challenge and response, or of cycles—such as growth, florescence, and decline; faith, reason, and fulfillment; intuition, rationality, and materialism—but these approaches do not do justice to the complexity of the problem. In this respect the social scientists have come closer to reality when they have sought to group the variables into hierarchies and clusters of functional problems in a manner sufficiently complicated to do justice to the subject yet also capable of being understood and put to practical use.

Societies can grapple with these accumulations of changes, but they do not necessarily succeed in adapting to them. It is one of the favorite hobbies of some historians in their spare time to plot the rise and fall of civilizations, and many large volumes have resulted from this effort. It is a form of "do it yourself" history in which, since civilizations have not identified themselves as clearly as have modern states, historians are relatively free to describe and arrange them in a variety of patterns to suit themselves. The difficulty is that these analogies with the human life-span rely too much on the discrete identity of civilizations and neglect the fact that their human inhabitants survived and may even have prospered after their civilization had "fallen" or "died." Civilizations and politically organized societies—as we are calling national states—may indeed be ephemeral, as are the individual human beings who inhabit them. The aggregate of human beings nevertheless survives as a social organism and reorganizes itself in new ways to meet new problems. Rather than worrying so much about the larger structures, whether real or artificial, one should pay more attention to the individuals that make up society. A number of empires, and perhaps a "civilization," "fell" at the end of the First World War. Yet their peoples have survived—after some intervening difficulties—to enjoy much more prosperous and hopeful times. This form of adaptation is of greater concern to the study of modernization than is the fate of civilizations.

Political Leadership

The discussion thus far has been primarily in terms of generalized trends evolving through the centuries and of the politically organized societies within the framework of which so many of the activities of mankind are conducted, yet one must not forget that it is individuals who make history and through whom these trends and activities are expressed. Political leaders are those who make or actively aspire to a share in making the policy decisions of a society. In studying political leadership it is useful to think of politics as including not only government in the conventional sense but also decision-making in all spheres of public policy. Political leadership may be exercised on the international, national, or local level; and it may be concerned with the representation of interest groups, the exercise of formal functions of government, or the determination of policy in nongovernmental spheres. Political leadership must be thought of in terms not of the few leaders who make the headlines but of the thousands of individuals in every society who play a prominent role in policy decisions. In a relatively static society political leaders normally come from a small number of oligarchic families, or are selected and trained by well-established procedures. In periods of rapid change, however, political leaders tend to show a much greater diversity of origin. All societies undergoing change are involved to some extent in the transfer of political power from old hands to new. The source and nature of the new political leadership become a central issue in the study of change.

The term "elites" is employed—principally by anthropologists and sociologists and by political scientists with a penchant for behavioral terminology—to describe those persons or positions that command the greatest authority or respect in any group. More frequently than not, this term is used to denote those who occupy the highest ranks in a system of stratification by virtue of birth or status. It is also sometimes used to describe a position achieved by merit. In either case one may think of a single elite embracing all privileged persons in a society or group of societies—such as the aristocracy in eighteenth-century Europe; one may distinguish among more specialized elites such as those concerned with the religious, artistic, social, intellectual, military, political, or other matters in a given society; one may differentiate geographically between international, national, regional, provincial, urban, and village elites; or one may employ a combination of these criteria. "Elites" is a more narrow and discipline-oriented term than "leadership," and it is not generally used in those disciplines the principal concern of which is the study of political power. One thinks of elites more commonly with reference to traditional societies than to modern. As long as they are properly defined, however, one may use such terms as "political elite" and "power elite" as synonymous with "political leadership" without loss of meaning.

"Intelligentsia," a more specialized term than "elites" and "political leadership," is used in a variety of ways. Generically it refers to those who work with their intellects, and it is often defined to include all those with a higher education or with equivalent informal training. In the Soviet Union today this term is used to describe the entire "white-collar class," as distinguished from industrial workers and peasants. It is also widely used in a sense virtually synonymous with "elites," and in this sense one might perhaps refer to a "political intelligentsia." More properly, however, "intelligentsia" or, alternatively, "intellectuals" denotes those who work creatively with their minds, regardless of their profession. The intelligentsia in this more limited definition is of particular interest in that it constitutes one of the important groups in a society that is concerned with political leadership.

The central problem in political modernization is the process by which a society makes the transition from a political leadership wedded to the traditional system to one that favors thoroughgoing modernization. In traditional agrarian societies, where a relatively small group of privileged families wield political power, one can truly speak of a "power elite," even though the structure and composition of this elite may vary greatly from one society to another. Political power in these societies is generally closely associated with land-ownership, military strength, and religious influence. In a few instances—as in the oriental despotisms—the state bureaucracy was able to assert its dominance over all other sources of power. In most cases, however, local political leaders have tended to be stronger collectively than those at the center of the political system. Political leaders in general, whether local or central, wielded relatively little authority in comparison with those of modern states. In a modern society the government has far greater responsibility and authority than ever before. Through taxation and a myriad of other controls and services, it influences in unprecedented degree the lives of all its citizens. It is also significant that in an advanced society, in which all citizens are literate and a large number have had at least a secondary education, real power in all the various forms in which it is expressed is much more diffuse than in traditional societies. It is no longer a question of a small oligarchy confronted with the problem of organizing a large peasantry. A large bureaucracy is now required to mobilize the diversified resources of a dynamic population, and it cannot be controlled readily by a few families.

Leadership in political modernization may come from two general sources. The first source is the incumbent traditional leadership itself, members of which may out of conviction or necessity decide that the system that they inherited from the past is out of date and that a drastic change to modern policies is necessary. This is a rather common occurrence, in fact, especially in the societies that were the first to modernize, and it is a matter of regret that the fascination that so many historians have had with revolutions has barred them from devoting more attention to the emperors, kings, and bureaucrats who have undertaken fundamental modernizing reforms. At the same time, it must be recognized that this type of reformer is rarely prepared to go all the way, for sooner or later he comes to realize that he is reforming himself, his family, and his friends out of the position that they have traditionally enjoyed and that he is setting in motion a process that is bound to undermine the basis of that position. These reforms, though often far-reaching, are likely to be of a limited, protective, defensive, and patrician character.

The second source of leadership, derived from those who are dissatisfied with the incumbent traditional leaders, may in turn be thought of in terms of two categories. One comprises dissident members of the traditional political leadership itself. In this category one finds persons who have become alienated from the old way of life and who are convinced that modernization is desirable even if it means a loss of their privileges. This category also includes those who espouse modernization for tactical reasons: younger sons of kings and princes seeking advancement, lords who have been slighted, local leaders desiring national prominence, and many others. In the other category are members of the legal, medical, and business professions and of the new armies where rank is based on merit, and intellectuals from various walks of life. Members of this second category, not members of the traditional ruling oligarchy, believed that they did not have influence on public policy commensurate with their substantive contribution to society and had a kind of "no taxation without representation" motivation. It is significant in this connection that modernizing leaders, even those advocating extreme revolutionary programs, were almost never peasants, artisans, or laborers. From Cromwell, Washington, and Robespierre, to Lenin, Atatürk, Mao, Ho, Nehru, Nasser, and Castro, revolutionary leaders have normally been well-educated individuals who would have made a respected place for themselves in the existing society if they had not become alienated.

Given the commitment of incumbent traditional leaders to their way of life and to their personal stakes, it is not surprising that they cede their power only under duress. Traditional political systems normally do not make provision for fundamental reforms by constitutional means, and a change in leadership that involves a displacement of the traditional oligarchy cannot be made without violence. Modern states may well be able to set their colonies on the road to independence without bloodshed, although this is the exception rather than the rule, but the transition from traditional to modern leadership has generally been violent. Between the seventeenth and the nineteenth century Great Britain, France, the United States, Germany, and Italy were all wracked by major revolutions and internal wars, and there is little reason to believe that the states modernizing later will be able to avoid violence. Violence or at least the threat of violence is inherent in all political relations, but in modern times it has become endemic. To say this is not to justify or to advocate violence. It is merely to note the fact that violence—as is the case with other forms of social disorganization—has become increasingly common in modern times. People tend to cling tightly to the traditional way of doing things, identifying their personal security with the culture with which they were indoctrinated in childhood, and the scale of violence can be reduced only when, under firm leadership, people become convinced that change is necessary.

The violence accompanying political modernization takes many forms, but the most familiar of these is revolution. It is not easy for modernizing leaders to overthrow a traditional government, for the latter initially controls the instruments of coercion and is backed by most politically active citizens. Popular discontent may break out in the form of agrarian *jacqueries* or urban riots, but such disorders can usually be suppressed. Indeed, incumbent traditional governments cannot be overthrown until they have already been seriously weakened from without or from within. More often than not, the defeat of the government in a foreign war gives the opponents their opportunity. Especially if such a defeat is at the hands of a more modern country, the advantages of modernity will have been demonstrated, and significant segments of the traditional army and bureaucracy may be prepared to transfer their allegiance to more modern leaders. In extreme cases a victorious foreign army may occupy a country for a number of years, install a government of its own choosing, and use its own troops as the local instrument of coercion. In the absence of military defeats, revolutionary situations may also develop when incumbent governments delay modernizing reforms for so long that the contrast between theirs and neighboring countries becomes glaring. In such cases the example of more modern states is impressed daily on the traditional bureaucracy as well as on its modernizing opponents, and the balance of opinion shifts to a point where the incumbent government becomes fatally vulnerable.

The dependence of historical change on the vital role of individual leaders, who in great crises may alone be responsible for choices between alternative policies involving the efforts of entire societies, exposes these societies to the possibility that the removal of the leader may vitally effect its destinies; for contingency in history is essentially a question of the fate of individuals on whom a great deal depends. An accidental death or the withdrawal of a leader for personal reasons may exert a decisive influence on the course of events. Not often do great decisions depend on the presence of one particular leader alone, and decisions in history are usually shared by a large number of individuals who are not personally indispensable. Yet as the many small choices accumulate to form great issues, the nature of the culminating choice may depend to a great extent on the presence and character of an ultimate decision-maker. In this sense the contingencies of life and death, and less dramatically of the entire life experience that has developed the character of individual leaders, may play a vital role in the development of events and may affect the destinies of entire peoples for many generations.

Phases of Modernization

All aspects of modernization have been fraught with strife, and its politics has been particularly susceptible to crises arising from the struggles of contending leaders to assure the acceptance of their policies. The stakes are high, the pressures are powerful, and the conflict has been intense. The issues have been posed in a great variety of ways in the more than 170 politically organized societies that constitute today the organizational framework of mankind, but it is possible to distinguish certain critical problems that all modernizing societies must face: (1) *the challenge of modernity*—the initial confrontation of a society, within its traditional framework of knowledge, with modern ideas and institutions, and the emergence of advocates of modernity; (2) *the consolidation of modernizing leadership*—the transfer of power from traditional to modernizing leaders in the course of a normally bitter revolutionary struggle often lasting several generations; (3) *economic and social transformation*—the development of economic growth and social change to a point where a society is transformed from a predominantly rural and agrarian way of life to one predominantly urban and industrial; and (4) *the integration of society*—the phase in which economic and social transformation produces a fundamental reorganization of the social structure throughout the society.

The central problem faced by modernizing political leaders is that of adapting the particular traditional culture of their own society to a way of life commensurate with the opportunities afforded by modern knowledge, and politics is the struggle for the power to implement the programs that they advocate. The substance of the competing programs nevertheless embraces the aggregate of the problems confronting a society, and the crises of political modernization reflect intellectual, economic, social, and psychological problems, as well as political ones. The discussion of political crises, then, calls for a consideration of the entire process. One could doubtless achieve the same result by discussing the course of modernization in terms of any of its other aspects, but since politics is primarily concerned with public policy and with the organization of society, it provides the most convenient framework for discussing the entire complex development. Although in a sense modernization is accompanied by a continuing crisis, the four phases discussed here mark major problems calling for concentrated effort in the development of nations, and are often designated by national holidays, monuments, constitutions, legislative acts, and treaties. The peaks of these crises are also the periods when domestic or international violence is most likely to occur. Between these crises, on the other hand, there may often be extended periods of relative stability in which the previous gains are digested.

The Challenge of Modernity

When traditional societies are initially confronted by modernity, and when some of their prominent members become the advocates of a new and challenging way of life, the incumbent leaders may adopt one of a variety of courses. They may combat the new ideas and persecute the innovators as heretics; or they may discuss them, accept some, and reject others; or they may find them to be valid and attempt a fundamental reorganization of their institutions accordingly. Usually some combination of these reactions occurs, and the combination is rarely the same in any two cases.

In most respects the societies that were the first to modernize had the easiest time of it, for they were able to digest the new knowledge and technology over a considerable period of time and to absorb the impact gradually. England did this so successfully that despite a revolution and subsequent violence in several forms, the ruling oligarchy—substantially renovated—managed to survive until the second half of the twentieth century. In the westernmost countries of Europe the process was likewise quite prolonged.

The origins of modern knowledge may be traced to the significant new scholarship and technological innovation in the Middle Ages commonly referred to by historians as the renaissance of the twelfth century. Modern ideas and techniques emerged decisively in the fifteenth century, and by the sixteenth and seventeenth centuries a full-fledged scientific revolution was in progress. Rapid economic growth, urbanization, and social mobility were by now well under way, and the need for a more effective organization of human resources led to the development of new methods of communication and business, and especially to political consolidation. Kings began to exert greater authority at the expense both of local lords and of the Church, and practices of administration and taxation were revised to meet the demands of the new situation.

The initial growth of knowledge, as well as the related technology, was largely the work of the traditional elite—a small circle of large landowners, churchmen, merchants, and artisans—and was at first regarded as a useful and acceptable development. As the consequences of early modernization began to become apparent, however, and as the fundamental assumptions of traditional societies were increasingly challenged, the process of transforming the traditional order became increasingly turbulent. The trial of Galileo by the

Inquisition in 1632 because of his heretical view that the sun did not rotate around the earth, and his recantation, was only the most dramatic of many confrontations between the new knowledge and the traditional culture.

Despite the wide acceptance by the end of the seventeenth century of the scientific attitude and its many and diverse consequences, the modern way of life had not yet penetrated deeply into society. The rulers now accepted the need for reform, and as "enlightened despots" they generally championed the interests of merchants, manufacturers, and townspeople against those of the provincial and country magnates who had an agrarian base. They kept the reforms within the traditional framework, however, and expected to preserve the privileges and wealth that the oligarchy had always enjoyed. The modernizing reforms of the enlightened despots were defensive or preventative, in the sense that they were calculated to satisfy the demands of a rapidly changing society without destroying the traditional privileges. This policy was not the result of greed so much as of a deeply ingrained belief that the traditional division between leaders and followers was divinely ordained and indispensable to any well-ordered society. Not until the English, American, and French revolutions had run their course was the oligarchic framework of traditional society finally broken.

The relatively small number of European countries where modernity had first emerged had begun in the meantime to exert their worldwide influence from the beginning of the modern era. By the end of the fifteenth century they had discovered America, explored much of the African coastline, and developed much more intensively the ancient contacts with eastern Mediterranean and Asian societies. To this extent, and in this early form, the challenge of modernity was a universal one almost from the start. Yet the modern made contact with the traditional only at its peripheries, and it was not until the eighteenth and nineteenth centuries that the influence of modern ideas and institutions began to penetrate more deeply into political, economic, and social affairs.

The societies immediately adjacent to those that modernized first, the Muscovite and the Turkish, possessed governments that were sufficiently strong to control direct Western influences within their territories and sufficiently farsighted to foresee that they must adopt Western methods if they were to retain their independence. Starting at the end of the fifteenth century in Russia, and somewhat later in Turkey, a systematic policy was adopted of employing Western technicians and specialists to modernize the army and the bureaucracy, to build fortifications and public buildings, to establish factories, and to develop natural resources. This policy reached its most active form in Russia under Peter the Great and in Turkey under Mahmud II. These were classic cases of defensive modernization, in which much of the traditional system was deliberately strengthened— especially the part that involved the strict regulation and taxation of the agrarian sector—against more general modernizing influences exerted directly from without and indirectly from within, through the reorganization of the administrative system.

The Consolidation of Modernizing Leadership

The most dramatic of the crises of political modernization are those concerned with the transfer of power from traditional to modernizing leaders. "Transfer of power" is perhaps too colorless a phrase to describe these events, for they involved in every country political struggles of the first magnitude. We know now, and many were confident then, that the modernizers would in the end be victorious—but the leaders of the old regimes fought bitterly and often skillfully to maintain their positions.

This struggle may be thought of in terms of three essential features. The first is the assertion on the part of political leaders of the determination to modernize. This assertion may take the form of revolution by disaffected members of the traditional oligarchy or by modernizing leaders representing new political interests. Occasionally the traditional oligarchy itself initiates the process. There is typically a generation or more of political struggle before a program of modernization gains sufficiently wide acceptance to provide a secure basis of support for a modernizing leadership.

The second feature is an effective and decisive break with the institutions associated with a predominantly agrarian way of life, permitting the transition to an industrial way of life. In the case of societies with a relatively closed agrarian economy, this break frequently takes the form of a dramatic emancipation of the bulk of the population from traditional agricultural institutions. In other societies it may come about more gradually as a result of the commercialization of agriculture, changes in the ideology, or other institutional changes.

Finally, the creation of a politically organized society in those cases where one did not exist in the initial phase is also essential. Many societies have encountered difficulties in working out a viable form of political organization, which is so essential to the process of modernization. In other cases whole peoples migrated to new lands, sometimes previously uninhabited, and established offshoots of older societies. In still others the early modernizers extended their political authority over societies in an early stage of modernization and remolded them along modern lines.

The revolutions that bring modernizing political leaders into power vary greatly in their character, but all may be said to have at least two dimensions: they are violent or nonviolent, and they are internal or external. The well-known revolutions—such as the English, the American, the French, the Russian, the Turkish, the Yugoslavian, the Chinese, the Vietnamese, the Cuban, and the Algerian—were all violent and internal. They were internal in the sense that domestic revolutionaries bore the main brunt of the fighting, even though they often received substantial foreign aid. It is also significant that in all of these cases the task of the revolutionaries was not to overthrow firm and vigorous governments but to topple them after their stability had already been undermined. Frequently the traditional government is defeated before the revolution occurs, in the course of a foreign war—as was the case in Russia, Turkey, Yugoslavia, China, and Vietnam; or else it may become so corrupt as to alienate most of its supporters before the onset of the revolutionary crisis—as in the case of England, the American colonies, France, Cuba, and Algeria. Some of the revolutionary movements—such as the American, Vietnamese, and Algerian, and many others in different parts of the world—have had the dual goal of independence and social change. Indeed, these two motives are often so intertwined as to form a single goal.

Revolutions may also be imposed from without, and have at the start little internal support. A foreign army may overrun a country and establish an entirely new set of institutions after destroying the former government. The French did this in many countries of Western and Central Europe in the course of the Napoleonic wars, as did the Soviet Union in Eastern Europe and North Korea after the Second World War. A revolution is no less a revolution for being imposed from without, and many turn out rather well.

Nonviolent revolutions are relatively rare, although some of the most successful have been of this type. The overthrow of the Tokugawa regime in Japan in 1868 was essentially bloodless, and it ushered in a period of fundamental modernizing reforms that have widely been regarded as a model of peaceful change. Similarly the emancipation of the serfs in Russia in 1861 led to widespread reforms and rapid industrialization by the 1890's, and is recognized by both Russian and Western historians as a main turning point in the history of the country.

The second criterion for evaluating the transition to modernizing leadership is the reform of land tenure to permit the most effective use of agriculture in the great economic transformation that was under way. Land ownership has varied greatly in traditional societies, and an equally wide variety of solutions has been applied. The aim of these reforms is to increase the productivity of agriculture in order to feed the growing cities, to provide agricultural goods for manufacturing, and indirectly to furnish further capital for investment in industry.

Agriculture, the principal source of income until modern times, formed the political, economic, and social basis of traditional societies. It was naturally the most conservative sector of society, and efforts to change systems of land tenure and methods of cultivation were bound to be major political issues. In England, where landowners and merchants provided the modernizing leadership, agricultural reform was stimulated by the enclosure of formerly common lands by the landowners so that they could apply modern methods to improve production. The situation in England was the exception rather than the rule, however, for in most parts of the world the large landowners have been opponents of modernization and have not devoted their incomes to economic growth.

In these countries the purpose of agricultural reform was to break up the large estates, either by distributing land to the peasants or by organizing it in some other way so that its surplus could be devoted to industrialization. In places where the landowners opposed modernization, agricultural reform became a crucial issue; because the landlords were the main support of the traditional government, any reform in agriculture involved a thoroughgoing political revolution. This was the case in most countries of Latin America, the Near East, and Asia.

The third criterion for judging whether the transition of modernizing leaders to power has taken place is the creation of a national state with an effective government and a reasonably stable consensus on the part of the inhabitants as to ends and means. It is one of the most striking features of this process that of the 133 independent states in existence today, no more than twenty had approximately their present territory before the accession to power of modernizing leaders. These countries—such as England, France, and Switzerland among the earlier modernizers and Russia, Iran, China, and Japan among those that made the transition somewhat later—already had a distinct national identity before the modern era. They were able to go forward with the work of modernization without having to do more than defend their existing frontiers under conditions in which they generally had an advantage over the aggressors. These countries had many other problems, but at least they did not have this problem.

For all the other countries of the world—as well as for the thirty to forty that are now waiting to be born—the creation of a national state has been a central issue that overshadowed almost all others. The underlying ideology of the modernizing leaders maintained that they could not reform, tax, educate, and build until they were free from the foreign lords who discriminated against them and impeded their efforts. This costly process of nation-building took many forms. With Germany and Italy it involved the unification of smaller states, principalities, and other territories into single national states in the course of over half a century of domestic and international wars. In the case of Austria-Hungary and Turkey, it involved the breakup of great multinational empires so that new states could be formed by the component peoples. The countries of the two Americas, Africa, and Asia were with few exceptions formed after long and bitter struggles with the tutelary powers.

In all of these instances nationalism was not an end in itself but a means to an end—modernization. Yet the struggle for independence was in many cases so long and costly, and the emotions aroused were so powerful, that nationalism frequently came to overshadow modernization and to divert it from its main course. The struggle for independence had absorbed so much in lives and effort, and the resources required to defend the frontiers and maintain an independent status were so great, that other matters came to play a secondary role. The powerful appeal of nationalism was, moreover, frequently used by conservative leaders to prevent reforms, and the nationalism that was generally linked with liberalism before independence became more often than not a force for conservatism. Nation-building was essential to modernization, because it was the most effective way to mobilize the efforts of the peoples concerned, but it also caused some of modernization's most difficult problems.

The manner in which these essential categories of change have occurred—political revolutions, agricultural reform, and nation-building—has varied widely in different societies. They have occurred in all possible sequences, and have been combined to form a variety of complex challenges to political leadership. In a few countries other problems may have loomed larger than these three. All were nevertheless essential to the effective mobilization of the efforts of the peoples concerned, and the transfer of power from traditional to modernizing leaders cannot be said to have taken place until solutions to all three sets of problems have been found.

Economic and Social Transformation

The phase of economic and social transformation, as understood in the present context, represents the period between the accession to political power of modernizing leaders and the development of a society to the point at which it is predominantly urban and the focus of mobilization of the great majority of the population is toward the society as a whole rather than toward local communities and specialized groups. Among advanced countries this phase may be considered to have extended from 1832 to 1945 in England, from 1848 to 1945 in France, and from 1865 to 1933 in the United States. Among countries that modernized somewhat later this phase may be thought of as having started in 1917 in Russia, in 1923 in Turkey, in 1930 in Brazil, in 1949 in China, and in 1952 in Egypt, and as still continuing. In many other societies modernizing leadership is still consolidating its position, and the phase of intensive economic and social transformation lies ahead.

If the consolidation of modernizing leadership is a period of dramatic political change—of coups, revolutions, and wars of national liberation and unification—it is nevertheless one of relatively superficial developments that affect the nationality, citizenship, and legal status of the average person more than they affect his daily life. Empires have come and gone for centuries with relatively little effect on the personal affairs of the great majority of their peoples, and the initial impact of the accession to power of modernizing leaders is in most cases no greater than these earlier changes. Economic and social transformation, on the other hand, is less dramatic but much more profound. The change in values and way of life of the average person in the more advanced countries has been greater between the mid-nineteenth and mid-twentieth centuries than between ancient Mesopotamia, Egypt, or China and the early modern period. This has been a period of transformation in all realms of human activity that is unprecedented in history.

Underlying this rapid transformation has been the dramatic growth of science and technology. In the early nineteenth century the natural sciences were poorly differentiated from philosophy and from one another, and a single individual could specialize in or keep abreast of a considerable variety of fields. Goethe, to take only one example, although obviously an exceptional one, could do original work in law, drama, and the novel, as well as in anatomy, botany, geology, and physics. A century later even scholars within the same disciplines had difficulty understanding one another's work because of the degree of specialization that had been attained. Virtually all of modern science has developed in this period, and at its start technology was just at the beginning of its greatest development. The steam engine was just being harnessed, and the development of electricity, metallurgy, and electronics, not to mention nuclear power, still lay ahead. It is the myriad of applications of science and technology that has led to this great transformation in human affairs.

The concentration of effort required by economic and social transformation is focused primarily at the level of the politically organized society, the national state or polity, rather than at the local or the international level. Typical of this transformation were the German customs union of 1837 and similar movements in other countries designed to eliminate local barriers to trade, to establish national currencies and postal systems, and the like. The implementation of these developments leads to a corresponding concentration of policy-making, both public and private, at the national level. This preoccupation with national affairs tends to weaken the international as well as the local ties of a society. Societies become less cosmopolitan during this phase, and more self-centered. The security and identity of the individual becomes linked to a much greater degree with the national community than with the local or the international.

The political consequences of this concentration of effort at the national level are reflected not only in administrative centralization but also in a significant intensification of nationalism. In the preceding phase nationalism is concerned with independence and unification, and reflects a spirit of freedom from traditional restraints and an anticipation of new opportunities. In the period of economic and social transformation nationalism comes to represent a jealous concern of almost psychotic proportions for the security of one's own society and, at the same time, a systematic attack on loyalties of a local or ideological character that might threaten national cohesion. In France the development of theories of integral nationalism, the long struggle between republicanism and clericalism, and the dramatic confrontation in the Dreyfus case between cosmopolitanism and chauvinism are characteristic of this phase. The French seem to have had a particular capacity for dramatizing these controversies, but they occurred in all societies. Even value systems with a strong international commitment, such as Christianity and socialism, have been overwhelmed by a nationalism that derives its emotional force from the extensive investment of personal security in politically organized societies.

The intellectual and political aspects of this transformation are probably clearer in retrospect than they were at the time, but the economic and social changes were apparent to all. Indeed, their impact was so great that social theorists have been unable to resist the temptation to stress them at the expense of the more profound features of modernization. In the most general sense, the scope of these changes is reflected in the transfer of more than one-half of the work force of a society from agriculture to manufacturing, transportation, commerce, and services, and of an even larger proportion of the population from a rural to an urban environment. The proportions of this transformation have varied a good deal from one country to another. The share of agriculture in national product and in the labor force was already below one-half in the United States and in many countries of Western Europe in the first half of the nineteenth century, but much of the manufacturing was still of a rural character and did not have the profound social impact of the later urban industrialization. In the countries of Asia, Latin America, and Africa the agrarian component has been much higher at the start of this phase and the impact of the transformation is likely to be more profound. There are many statistics that one could cite to describe the economic transformation that occurred, but suffice it to say that in the advanced countries virtually the entire industrial plant and communications system as we know them today were built during this phase.

The social aspects of this transformation brought many benefits, but also heavy burdens. This phase is one of rapid growth in secondary education and medical care, the benefits of which were extended to the great majority of the population. The shift of the work force from agriculture to manufacturing, transportation, communications, and services is accompanied by a significant change in the relationship of social strata to one another and to the exercise of political power. At the start of this phase the individuals directly concerned with political power constitute no more than a fraction of the population, and the great majority are peasants or rural and urban workers who have no political role. In the course of this period there is a rapid growth in the management and service cadres, following upon the development of education. There is also a considerable broadening of the base of the ruling group as the sources of recruitment change from landownership to business, commerce, and areas of activity requiring university-trained specialists. The executive, managerial, and service strata may come to embrace as much as one-half the population of a society.

The burdens of this transformation are borne by the large numbers of peasants who desert the villages that they have inhabited for many generations and move to cities in larger numbers than can be accommodated. While the evidence is not so complete or reliable as one would wish, it appears that in some countries for as much as a generation there may have been an absolute decline in the standard of living for significant segments of the population. In those societies where the labor force was made up largely of immigrants, as in the United States and Canada, such a decline does not seem to have taken place. In others, where the shift of the labor force occurred under great government pressure, the burdens on the labor force have been particularly heavy. Much depends on the circumstances under which a country modernizes and on the policies of its leaders. In the West European countries it took thirty to fifty years to shift as much as one-quarter of the labor force out of agriculture as compared with less than half this time in the Soviet Union, and in general in the countries that developed earlier the tensions of this transformation were more attenuated.

The policies under which this transition from agriculture to industry is made constitute one of the key distinctions between liberal and statist policies. The tightly centralized direction of the Soviet state resulted in a rapid transfer of the labor force, but this dynamism was purchased at a high price in human suffering. It has been estimated that not until the 1950's did the Soviet level of real wages and per capita purchases reach that of 1928. This latter level, in turn, was about the same as that of 1913. The hardships of the peasants and industrial workers, however, were not the result only of Soviet policies. Both the administrative centralization and the pressure on the common man were also characteristic of tsarist methods, and Soviet policy intensified them without altering their essential character. This is only one example of many that one could cite regarding the variations in the policies under which economic and social transformation is implemented. Yet despite these variations, societies in this phase of development share certain fundamental uniformities.

Value systems always seem to lag somewhat behind economic and social developments, and the assumptions and outlook of leaders in this phase remain under the strong influence of the traditional agrarian and rural frame of reference. Indeed, the work force itself, as it moves from the countryside to the cities, retains many of its rural modes of thought and life. Village traditions are carried over into the cities, and the deference of peasant to landlord is transmuted into the respect of the poorly educated for the technically trained. Similarly minority groups retain many of their disabilities throughout this phase despite the actual changes in their status and the cosmopolitan goals of the society. A kind of agrarian cushion protects the bulk of the population from the hardships of urban life, but at the same time delays the fulfillment of their expectations.

The Integration of Society

The stage of development represented by this fourth phase of modernization has been variously referred to as the achieving society, the advanced society, the communist society, the developed society, the free society, the great society, the industrial society, the integrated society, the mass society, the mass-consumption society, the mobilized society, the modern society, the new society, the organic society, the rational society, the reasonable society, the socialist society, the technological society, and the urban society—to list these designations alphabetically. These terms all refer to the same general phenomenon, but reflect a diversity of assumptions, emphases, and expectations. Of these terms, "integrated society" is the most satisfactory. The essence of this phase is that the great movement of peoples from the countryside to the city transforms the structure of society from one of relatively autonomous regional, organizational, and occupational groupings to one that is highly fragmented and in which the individual is relatively isolated.

The concept of integration as used in this connection means in particular that the individual's ties with local, regional, and other intermediate structures are reduced at the same time that his ties with the larger and more diffuse urban and industrial network are strengthened. This shift in relationships gives the individual the advantages of greater opportunities in a more flexible society and a larger share in the distribution of resources in terms of education, consumer goods, and a variety of services. It deprives him, however, not only of the support and consolation offered by membership in a more autonomous community but also of the relative stability of employment and social relations that agrarian life provides in normal times. The urban environment offers the ultimate hope of a greatly enriched way of life, but the agrarian provided the reality of social warmth and personal security.

A society that reaches this stage of integration can make much more efficient use of its human resources—if one may refer to human beings in such an impersonal manner. It has consumer production for a mass market, a high per capita national income, a high level of general and specialized education, widely available provisions for social security, and adequate organization for leisure. This is the case, however, only if the society is well organized and things are working well. The more highly a society is mechanized, the more susceptible it is to paralyzing forms of disorganization. In times of disorder and economic depression, it is plagued by the possibility of large-scale unemployment and attendant social unrest. In less integrated societies there is also extensive unemployment, or perhaps more accurately underemployment, but it is in considerable measure cushioned and even concealed by the agrarian sector. The urban workers in less developed societies have not usually broken their ties with the rural community and can return to it for support in time of need. In an integrated society the individual is atomized—torn from his traditional community moorings, isolated from all except his immediate family, and left to find his way alone among the large and impersonal public and private organizations that provide him with his employment, medical care, social welfare, and pension. It is under these circumstances that loneliness, insecurity, and the weakening of close human relationships deprive the individual of an environment suited to psychological stability.

There are many indexes by which one can judge the integration of society, although the point at which one sets the beginning of integration is of necessity somewhat arbitrary. If one takes as the central criterion the movement of population from the countryside to the cities, the most satisfactory index of integration is the proportion of population engaged in manufacturing and services as distinct from agriculture and other forms of primary production. It is also often the practice to rank countries by gross national product per capita as a gauge of development. It is readily apparent that other indexes of development—literacy, enrollment in educational institutions, urbanization, health, and availability of means of communication—tend to follow these trends in occupational structure and per capita product. On the basis of these standards one may identify fourteen countries as having entered the phase of social integration since the First World War: Australia, Belgium, Canada, Denmark, France, Germany, Luxembourg, the Netherlands, New Zealand, Norway, Sweden, Switzerland, the United Kingdom, and the United States. In the course of the next generation another dozen or more will enter this phase, including the Soviet Union and Japan, the countries of southern and eastern

Europe, and the more advanced Latin American countries, such as Argentina, Uruguay, and Mexico.

Integrated societies differ from those in the preceding phase of economic and social transformation in their structure of political power. Personal power tends to become institutionalized through bureaucratization, and the exercise of power is divided into many specialties and shared by many people. This corresponds in considerable measure to trends in social stratification, according to which those concerned with the direct exercise of political power are recruited to an increasing extent through university education and are much more numerous than in earlier phases. At the same time that the ruling groups are being enlarged, and come to depend more on merit than on privilege, the number of those at the opposite end of the social scale is reduced.

As societies become more productive, wealth tends to be more evenly distributed and the standard of living of rural and urban workers tends to approximate that of salaried employees. Now four-fifths or more of the relevant age group completes secondary education to age nineteen and as many as one-third may continue to higher education. It also becomes increasingly possible for individuals to rise, and descend, in the social scale without regard to social origins. The result is a great enlargement of the middle ranks of society—salaried employees in a wide range of occupations— recruited from families originally employed as rural and urban workers. This tendency toward the equalization of income and status of the great majority of the members of a society is the inevitable result of economic development. Mass production cannot be maintained without mass consumption. It would be an economic impossibility, even if a ruling group desired to do so, for a society to maintain a high rate of growth of per capita national product without distributing production to the consumer.

The end of this process is not easy to foresee, but as automation reduces the labor force required to sustain economic growth it is not unlikely that a substantial proportion of the work force of an integrated society will be guaranteed an income regardless of whether or not they work. Under these conditions a radical redistribution of employment and leisure becomes normal, and appropriate arrangements are made to adapt societies to it. The wealthy have never been seriously embarrassed by light employment and leisure, and as societies become more affluent the opportunities and problems of a shorter work day will be extended to greater numbers.

When societies reach this phase there is also a much greater consensus than ever before among interest groups regarding the policies of modernization that should be followed. Conservatives, liberals, and socialists can still engage in lively political struggles, but differences in policy regarding major issues are greatly reduced. The degree of integration is such that the pressure for the common welfare predominates over interest groups, and the wide range of theories prevalent in earlier phases regarding policies of modernization tend to be reduced to a substantial agreement as to what is feasible and desirable. In Western Europe socialists and conservatives have more in common today than ever before. If there is not an end to ideological controversies within integrated societies, at least the range of controversy is greatly narrowed.

This type of society has frequently been referred to as a mass society, and a great deal has been written about it. The central concern of this literature is the fear of "massification"—that the atomized individuals will form an undifferentiated "mass" that can be swayed easily by demagogues and turned to destructive ends; that the gradual weakening of intermediate political structures and social organizations will result in the national government's accumulating all power; that the only culture able to survive will be that which appeals to the instincts and understanding of the lowest common denominator, which is usually calculated to be on a par with that of early adolescence; and that the creative minority that has been responsible for the flowering of modern knowledge will sink into and be suffocated by the popular quicksand.

Much of the writing on totalitarianism has had a similar tendency. The concentration of all political power in the hands of an authoritarian government, at the expense of political power formerly exercised by formal and informal local and associational groups, is sometimes seen as an inevitable consequence of massification. This is not the case. All but one of the totalitarian political systems, in fact, have arisen in societies that were still in a relatively early stage of economic and social transformation. In some cases, as in Soviet Russia and Communist China, totalitarianism has represented in significant degree a modernization of traditionally authoritarian or despotic political systems. This is not to say that these societies necessarily had to evolve into totalitarian systems, but rather that the weight of tradition predisposed them to extreme forms of centralization in the absence of vigorous political movements favoring more liberal policies of modernization. In other societies, such as North Korea and the Communist countries of Eastern Europe apart from Yugoslavia, totalitarian regimes were imposed from outside by military force and were not congruent with local traditions. In a few countries—in Germany in 1933, in Yugoslavia during the Second World War, and in North Vietnam in 1954—totalitarian systems arose for domestic reasons in response to political and economic collapse. Of these countries only Germany of the 1930's represents a society on the threshold of social integration, and it should not be equated with the Soviet Union or with other Communist societies if one is interested in the social origins of totalitarianism. Fascist Italy and Franco Spain are also sometimes considered to be totalitarian, but they in fact resemble traditional authoritarian regimes much more than modern totalitarian systems—and they too were still in a relatively early stage of economic and social transformation when these regimes were established.

Germany is, then, a unique case where a failure to meet problems of social integration led to a sharp decline of public morality of an extreme variety, and its origins should be sought more in local than in general conditions. A dozen countries have moved as far or further along the road to integration without resorting to totalitarianism and mass murder. The way in which a society reacts to the crisis of integration depends a great deal on whether it has had a pluralistic or an authoritarian political tradition, whether representative institutions and the legal protection of individual liberties had deep roots, and whether an oligarchy had normally held untempered power. The character of the leadership is also a vital factor. There are not many Hitlers, and this particular man might well have been struck down by a vehicle or a disease before he achieved power. Chance plays a considerable role in these matters.

The circumstances under which modernizing leaders take power also cast a long shadow over the later development of a society. If the transfer of power from the traditional leaders is achieved with considerable bloodshed, it may lead to the glorification of violence for many generations.

"Massification" is a characteristic problem of the modern integrated society, but it is not its principal characteristic. In the advanced societies that have achieved integration with reasonable stability, a vital role in maintaining social order has been played by religion, ethnic loyalties, and other traditional binding forces that have survived modernization without loss of vigor. The Jewish and Catholic religions and the many Protestant sects have maintained their vitality in most integrated societies and are able to offer solace in life's crises and a framework of social action that helps to counterbalance the dangers of atomization and massification.

The central problem, then, is that individuals in modern integrated societies are torn from their relatively autonomous communities and are brought into contact in the urban context with a wide variety of unfamiliar people. Many problems of human relations that at an earlier stage were avoided or compromised on some local basis now have to be met frontally. The institutions of advanced societies are not yet fully understood, and the means of controlling them in the interest of social stability are still being formulated.

The integration within a single society of peoples of widely differing religious, social, and ethnic backgrounds is also baffling. It is not by chance that the term "integration" is used in the more specialized sense of the desegregation of Negroes in the United States, or that the problem did not become acute until a century after their emancipation from slavery. During most of this period the Negroes lived in the relative autonomy of agrarian life, and were not competitively involved to any great extent with the dominant white majority. Students of this subject have nevertheless noted that during each of the periods of rapid economic growth Negroes have been increasingly drawn into the modern urban centers. The point is finally reached where the inequalities of treatment under which they have lived can no longer be tolerated, and American society has been forced to seek a solution. This is an example, although a particularly acute one, of the crises the integration of society provokes. Those who are discouraged by the slow pace of racial integration in the United States may gain solace from the realization that this is the first time in world history that peoples of such disparate backgrounds have sought to solve the problem of living together in an advanced society.

This description of the course of modernization within societies in terms of four phases is not intended to convey the impression that these are watertight compartments. Indeed, there is a sense in which all of these critical problems continue in some degree throughout the modern period. Modernity represents a recurring challenge long after its underlying principles have been understood and accepted, and traditional ideas and institutions have an extraordinary staying power. Modernizing leaders must struggle to retain their initiative long after their accession to political power. Economic and social transformation is a continuing process, at varying rates, both before and after its period of greatest dynamism. Societies move toward integration gradually over many decades and even centuries.

It is rather a question of successive periods of concentration of effort on individual phases of this complex and interacting process. When a society first becomes cognizant of the challenge of modernity, it must concentrate its efforts on formulating a response to this challenge—whether it comes from within or from without. Modernizing leaders do not gain the ascendancy, in turn, until after the challenge of modernity has engaged a society for a considerable period of time. Similarly economic and social transformation cannot be implemented in a dynamic fashion before leaders who regard this as their primary task come to power. And finally, the integration of society does not become a critical problem until economic and social development has reached a high level.

To distinguish among these four phases is nevertheless not to say that all societies pass through them at the same pace. The countries that were the first to modernize could afford to be more leisurely, and the proportion of their economy devoted to manufacturing, transportation, commerce, and services was much greater in the early nineteenth century than it is in many countries of Asia, Latin America, and Africa today. Nevertheless as each successive society enters the phase of economic and social transformation it does so in an increasingly dynamic environment of more developed societies.

In the European countries where national liberation or unification formed a part of the modernizing leaders' struggle for power, independent statehood was achieved at the end of this phase when these countries were already well on the road to economic and social development. In the later-modernizing societies, on the other hand, modernizing leaders come to power in newly independent states at the beginning of the phase of political consolidation. Their accession to power marks not the end of a long domestic struggle but rather the beginning of one in which they still have to win recognition of their authority on the part of local and regional leaders and a variety of associational groups. At the same time, they are also at an early stage of economic and social development. Indonesia in 1949, for example, or Nigeria in 1960 was nominally at the same stage of political development as Germany in 1871 or Poland in 1919, yet in real terms one would have to go far back in European history to find the type of political organization or the level of economic and social development that the new states of Asia and Africa represent.

The logic of these four successive phases must be seen in the context of wide divergencies of levels of development, and the modernization of each society must be understood in terms of its own traditional heritage, resources, and leadership. A comparison of many societies in terms of these phases is useful as a means of visualizing modernization as a worldwide process, but this does not mean that any given society can gauge its course by the experience of those that have preceded it except in general terms.

Societies in the Process of Political Modernization

An attempt to identify characteristics of political modernization that are intermediate between those that are true of all societies and those that are unique to each will of necessity lead to conclusions that are general and suggestive rather than clearly delimited and precise. They therefore run the risk of being misunderstood by the literal-minded. It is nevertheless desirable at this stage to list the societies of the world in terms of the phases of political modernization discussed in this chapter and the patterns of modernization described in the next.

The phases themselves are only generally defined, and are in fact phases of emphasis on one of a number of concurrent developments rather than distinct stages. Similarly all societies do not fall neatly into the seven patterns—Ethiopia, Israel, Liberia, Nepal, and South Africa, among others, are in significant ways exceptional. Moreover, any periodization based on political events or decisions is open to dispute, and of all the dates that one can cite, perhaps 1789 is the only one that is relatively free from controversy as a milestone in the modernization of a society.

Yet as long as these limitations are understood and taken into account, there is no reason not to suggest specific dates for the various phases of modernization for all the societies in the world. The phase called the challenge of modernity is of necessity more generally defined than the others, and does not need to be detailed on this table. The societies are ranked first by pattern* and within each pattern chronologically. The chronology is based on the beginning of the consolidation of modernizing leadership (1776 for the United States, 1789 for France, 1803 for Germany, 1861 for Russia, 1868

* The nature of each pattern is described in the next chapter, beginning on page 95.

for Japan, 1964 for Malawi, and so on), with countries that have completed the consolidation of modernizing leadership listed ahead of those that have not.

It will be clear to those who have followed the argument so far that the periodization and typology set forth here are concerned with political modernization rather than with the other aspects of this process. As already noted, intellectual developments are too amorphous to be amenable to comparable categorization. Reasonably accurate information regarding economic and social changes is available only for recent decades, and our understanding of the psychological aspect is still rather rudimentary. At the same time, the available information regarding comparative levels of development of societies tends to show that the other aspects of modernization are reasonably correlated with the political. The bases of resources and skills of traditional societies nevertheless vary so widely that one cannot draw conclusions regarding the general level of development of a society without knowing a great deal more about it than what appears in this table.

Patterns of Modernization

	Consolidation of Modernizing Leadership	Economic and Social Transformation	Integration of Society
First Pattern			
United Kingdom	1649–1832	1832–1945	1945–
France	1789–1848	1848–1945	1945–
Second Pattern			
United States	1776–1865	1865–1933	1933–
Canada	1791–1867	1867–1947	1947–
Australia	1801–1901	1901–1941	1941–
New Zealand	1826–1907	1907–1947	1947–
Third Pattern[a]			
Belgium	1795–1848	1848–1948	1948–
Luxembourg	1795–1867	1867–1948	1948–

Third Pattern (cont'd)	Consolidation of Modernizing Leadership	Economic and Social Transformation	Integration of Society
Netherlands	1795–1848	1848–1948	1948–
Switzerland	1798–1848	1848–1932	1932–
Germany	1803–1871	1871–1933	1933–
Italy	1805–1871	1871–	
Denmark	1807–1866	1866–1945	1945–
Norway	1809–1905	1905–1945	1945–
Sweden	1809–1905	1905–1945	1945–
Spain	1812–1909	1909–	
Portugal	1822–1910	1910–	
Austria	1848–1918	1918–	
Czechoslovakia	1848–1918	1918–	
Hungary	1848–1918	1918–	
Greece	1863–1918	1918–	
Poland	1863–1918	1918–	
Finland	1863–1919	1919–	
Ireland	1870–1922	1922–	
Iceland	1874–1918	1918–	
Bulgaria	1878–1918	1918–	
Romania	1878–1918	1918–	
Yugoslavia	1878–1918	1918–	
Albania	1912–1925	1925–	
Fourth Pattern			
Uruguay	1828–1911	1911–	
Brazil	1850–1930	1930–	
Argentina	1853–1946	1946–	
Chile	1861–1925	1925–	
Mexico	1867–1910	1910–	
Venezuela	1870–1958	1958–	
Bolivia	1880–1952	1952–	
Costa Rica	1889–1948	1948–	
Puerto Rico	1898–1952	1952–	
Cuba	1898–1959	1959–	
Paraguay	1841–		
Colombia	1863–		
Ecuador	1875–		
Haiti	1879–		
Peru	1879–		
Dominican Republic	1881–		
Guatemala	1881–		

Fourth Pattern (cont'd)	Consolidation of Modernizing Leadership	Economic and Social Transformation	Integration of Society
Panama	1903–		
Nicaragua	1909–		
Honduras	1919–		
El Salvador	1939–		
British Honduras (U.K.)	1961–		
Fifth Pattern			
Russia	1861–1917	1917–	
Japan	1868–1945	1945–	
China	1905–1949	1949–	
Iran	1906–1925	1925–	
Turkey	1908–1923	1923–	
Afghanistan	1923–		
Ethiopia	1924–		
Thailand	1932–		
Sixth Pattern[b]			
Algeria	1847–1962	1962–	
Cyprus	1878–1946	1946–	
Taiwan	1895–1945	1945–	
Philippines	1899–1946	1946–	
Korea	1910–1946	1946–	
South Africa	1910–1962	1962–	
India	1919–1947	1947–	
Pakistan	1919–1947	1947–	
Ceylon	1920–1948	1948–	
Israel	1920–1948	1948–	
Lebanon	1920–1941	1941–	
Syria	1920–1941	1941–	
Iraq	1921–1948	1948–	
Malta	1921–1961	1961–	
Mongolia	1921–1950	1950–	
Egypt	1922–1952	1952–	
Indonesia	1922–1949	1949–	
Tunisia	1922–1955	1955–	
Burma	1923–1948	1948–	
Jordan	1923–1946	1946–	
Jamaica	1924–1962	1962–	
Sudan	1924–1956	1956–	
Guyana	1928–1966	1966–	
Morocco	1934–1956	1956–	
Hong Kong (U.K.)	1936–		

Sixth Pattern (cont'd)	Consolidation of Modernizing Leadership	Economic and Social Transformation	Integration of Society
Cambodia	1949–		
Laos	1949–		
Vietnam	1949–		
Libya	1952–		
Trinidad and Tobago	1959–		
Malaysia	1963–		
Yemen	1963–		
Saudi Arabia	1964–		
Maldive Islands	1965–		
Singapore	1965–		
Bhutan			
Guadeloupe (Fr.)			
Guiana (Fr.)			
Kuwait			
Macao (Port.)			
Martinique (Fr.)			
Masqat and Oman			
Nepal			
Réunion (Fr.)			
Somaliland (Fr.)			
South Arabia Fed. (U.K.)			
Surinam (Neth.)			
Timor (Port.)			
West Indies (U.K.)			
Seventh Pattern[c]			
Liberia	1847–		
Ghana	1957–		
Guinea	1958–		
Cameroon	1960–		
Central African Republic	1960–		
Chad	1960–		
Congo (Brazzaville)	1960–		
Congo (Léopoldville)	1960–		
Dahomey	1960–		
Gabon	1960–		
Ivory Coast	1960–		
Malagasy Republic	1960–		
Mali	1960–		
Mauritania	1960–		

Seventh Pattern (cont'd)	Consolidation of Modernizing Leadership	Economic and Social Transformation	Integration of Society
Niger	1960–		
Nigeria	1960–		
Senegal	1960–		
Somalia	1960–		
Togo	1960–		
Upper Volta	1960–		
Sierra Leone	1961–		
Tanzania	1961–		
Burundi	1962–		
Rwanda	1962–		
Uganda	1962–		
Western Samoa	1962–		
Kenya	1963–		
Malawi	1964–		
Gambia	1965–		
Rhodesia	1965–		
Zambia	1965–		
Angola and Cabinda (Port.)			
Basutoland (U.K.)			
Bechuanaland (U.K.)			
Equatorial Guinea (Sp.)			
Mauritius (U.K.)			
Mozambique (Port.)			
Portuguese Guinea (Port.)			
South-West Africa (S. Af.)			
Swaziland (U.K.)			

a Also includes Andorra, Liechtenstein, Monaco, San Marino, and the Vatican City State.

b Also includes the Bahama Islands (U.K.), Bermuda (U.K.), Brunei (U.K.), Comoro Archipelago (Fr.), Ifni (Sp.), Netherlands Antilles (Neth.), Persian Gulf States (U.K.), Protectorate States (U.K.), Seychelles (U.K.), Spanish North Africa (Sp.), Spanish Sahara (Sp.), Virgin Islands (U.S.).

c Also includes American Samoa (U.S.), Cape Verde Islands (Port.), Fiji (U.K.), French Polynesia (Fr.), Guam (U.S.), New Caledonia (Fr.), São Tomé and Principe Islands (Port.), Tonga (U.K.), Trust Territory of the Pacific Islands (U.S.), and the islands administered by Australia and by the Western Pacific High Commission (U.K.).

4. Comparative Modernization

Criteria of Comparison

A consideration of the characteristics of modernization common to all societies is useful in setting forth the broad nature of this process, but individual cases vary so greatly that such generalizations are of only limited help in understanding the problems of particular societies. To consider separately each of the more than 170 politically organized societies, however, would take one far beyond the limits of this chapter or even of this book. It would require a work of encyclopedic character, prepared by a large number of scholars in many fields of knowledge. As a manageable compromise between generalizations embracing all societies and an analysis of each, one may explore the principal variations that emerge from an examination of groups of societies. No two societies modernize in quite the same way—no two have the same base of resources and skills, no two have the same heritage of traditional institutions, no two are at the same stage of development, and no two have the same pattern of leadership or the same policies of modernization. It is nevertheless possible to distinguish among types of societies that have shared the main problems and policies of modernization, without losing sight of the individuality of each.

The usefulness of a typology depends on the relevance of the criteria on which it is based to the problems it is designed to clarify. The purpose of the typology set forth here is to compare societies according to the characteristic political problems that modernizing leaders have faced in gaining power and in implementing their programs. More particularly, it is based on considerations of (1) whether the transfer of political power from traditional to modernizing leaders in a society occurred early or late relative to other societies; (2) whether the immediate political challenge of modernity to traditional leaders in a society was internal or external; (3) whether a society enjoyed a continuity of territory and population during the modern era or underwent a fundamental regrouping of lands and peoples; (4) whether a society was self-governing in the modern era or experienced a prolonged period of colonial rule; and (5) whether a society entered the modern era with developed institutions that could to a substantial degree be adapted to the functions of modernity or with essentially undeveloped institutions that had to give way extensively to those borrowed from more modern societies.

1. Priority in the transition from traditional to modernizing political leadership and institutions is a critical criterion because of the fundamental influence exerted by the more modern on the less modern societies. One may acknowledge that later-developing societies may have provided the environment for vital contributions to the evolution of modern ideas and institutions, but such contributions could generally not be fully implemented except in societies where the political leadership was fully dedicated to modernization. In stressing the vital importance of chronological priority in modernization, one calls attention not to an absolute uniqueness of the modernizing efforts of the societies that developed earlier but to the relative originality of these efforts. This need for originality in the absence of foreign models was in most respects a blessing in disguise, although the disguise was no doubt often impenetrable at the time. The advantage of this enforced originality was that the early-developing societies were more inclined to consider issues on their merits and to

seek solutions in terms of specific problems of adaptation, without the distracting and often misleading examples of foreign models. This was a slow and difficult effort, fraught with mistakes and misconceptions, but it was an empirical process that more often than not led to stability.

The societies that developed later had before them the successful—as they appeared more often than not to be—efforts of their predecessors. The leaders of these societies perceived their own problems in terms of these models, and a vast polemical literature grew up in these countries over the question of the applicability of these models to the local situation. The apprehensions in regard to foreign influences expressed by Rammohun Roy, Ralph Waldo Emerson, Aleksandr I. Herzen, Djamal al-Din al-Afghani, K'ang Yu-wei, and Kanzo Uchimura, among many others, were all part of a great debate over the relevance and applicability of foreign models that has raged for two to three centuries. Opinions have tended to polarize around such general issues as the wholesale acceptance of foreign models versus a complete rejection of them, and a belief in the universality of the institutions evolved by the early-modernizing societies versus a selective adaptation of native institutions to the functions of modernity.

The advantages of lateness were obvious enough in the purely technical sphere, where the machines and techniques developed as a result of great effort in the early-modernizing societies could be purchased or copied in their most advanced forms. In the realm of institutions, which involve the values and mores of the masses of the people, however, the widespread introduction of foreign models incongruent with traditional institutions often led to extensive dislocations and sometimes ended in complete failure. The stimulation of foreign models is an intense and vitalizing force in the later-modernizing societies. Yet unless the leaders of these societies have the wisdom to distinguish between the generally applicable functions of modernity and the institutional forms derived from alien traditions, the influence of foreign models is likely to divert them from empirical experimentation and to interfere with a more discriminating consideration of the adaptability to modern functions of the native traditional heritage of ideas and institutions.

2. The significance of whether the political challenge of modernity is internal or external lies in the nature of the struggle between traditional and modernizing leaders, the length of time required to consolidate modernizing leadership, and the extent to which stable modern institutions are established. Although no society develops in the absence of extensive foreign influences, there are a number of countries (the first, second, and fifth patterns discussed below) where the consolidation of modernizing leadership was essentially a domestic process. In these countries, in the absence of a decisive confrontation on native soil with foreign occupying forces, the struggle between traditional and modernizing leaders is one in which ideology plays the central role and the lines between distinct groups of leaders are less sharply drawn. Typically in these countries the modernizing leaders come from the traditional elite, and the recruitment of new leaders from strata that have not formed a part of this elite is relatively gradual even when these societies have undergone revolutionary convulsions. Since the modernizing leaders come largely from the traditional elite, changes in leadership take place through a series of compromises in which traditionally minded leaders often preserve a substantial influence over a period of many generations. The adaptation of traditional institutions to modern functions is correspondingly gradual, and institutions are likely to be more stable because of the deliberate manner in which they are adapted and their greater congruence with the traditional political culture.

In the societies where political modernization has been a more or less direct result of invasion or colonialism (the third, fourth, sixth, and seventh patterns discussed below), the process of transition in leaders and institutions is likely to be much more abrupt and discontinuous. The critical difference lies in the role of foreign leaders in precipitating drastic change and in introducing foreign models in a decisive and often violent fashion. Under these circumstances domestic leaders from strata other than the traditional elite are likely to gain influential positions, and issues arising from the confrontation with foreign intruders and from the politics of invasion and colonialism tend to confuse and complicate the ideological controversies over policies of modernization. Under these conditions the adaptation of traditional institutions to modern functions is significantly more disjointed, arbitrary, and violent than in the societies that modernized without foreign intervention, and modern institutions typically bear a much sharper imprint of foreign models and hence are less congruent with native traditional institutions and are likely to be less stable.

3. It also makes a profound difference whether a society enjoys a continuity of territory and population during the modern era or undergoes a fundamental regrouping of lands and peoples. Relatively few societies have experienced such continuity (the first and fifth patterns), and they had the advantage of being able to devote greater attention to problems of domestic development. Although these societies encountered weighty issues of foreign policy, and were among those that devoted the largest proportion of their wealth to military expenses, they did not face the fundamental adjustments of nation-building and consensus-forming that occupied so much of the attention of the newly formed and reorganized societies. However great the burdens of national security imposed on Great Britain and France or Russia and Japan—or even Turkey and China, which were subjected to a significant degree of foreign intervention—these were problems that they faced from a basis of common experience that had deep roots in the traditions of the past.

Most societies (those in the second, third, fourth, sixth, and seventh patterns) did not have the advantage of this degree of continuity and cohesion. Indeed, the process of political modernization in these societies was one that necessitated a fundamental regrouping of lands and peoples. This complex adjustment involved in a variety of combinations the amalgamation of small polities that were drawn together by common traditions and interests, the dissolution of multinational dynastic empires, and the liberation of minority peoples from alien rule. Reorganizations such as these could not be made without a series of internal and external wars that sapped the strength and disoriented the value systems of the peoples concerned.

Even after the achievement of independent statehood, the animosities aroused in the course of nation-building left a disturbing legacy of problems. Internally these societies were deeply divided over the adoption of one or another program of nation-building, form of government, policy of economic and social development, and degree of emphasis on national defense. To the normal range of controversies common to even the most stable and cohesive societies were added those differences that stemmed from the multiplicity of backgrounds and experiences of the diverse peoples forming the new nations, varieties and degrees of bitterness inherited from the wars of liberation and unification, and a confusing heritage of institutions often derived from several layers of earlier political systems.

Some of the new states brought together, often for the first time, peoples of the same language and tradition that had lived in the past under different sovereignties. These states had a better chance of formulating coherent policies. Others, however, united peoples of profoundly different traditions, even though they might share in some degree a common cultural heritage. In these countries the problems of assimilation and homogenization have been added to the normal and not inconsiderable controversies aroused by modernization, and not infrequently the obstacles to consensus have appeared almost insuperable. Some societies were in effect dual or even multiple in character. By means of policies that involved both assimilation and compromise through a variety of legal concessions, the English welded their Welsh, Scottish, and Irish territories into the United Kingdom; the United States absorbed its ethnic minorities and coerced its regional dissidents; the Soviet Union succeeded in appeasing or coercing its fifteen major and more than fifty minor nationalities; and China was able to hold together a congeries of territories that include a major Moslem minority and numerous smaller national groups. Others have had a more difficult time of it. Yugoslavia's three major and a half a dozen minor nationalities have lived together in peace only under the domination of powerful leaders. Israel's minority of Arabs is not resigned to its position. In Cyprus the Greek majority and Turkish minority harbor apparently irreconcilable differences. In Latin America a number of countries have not yet granted effective citizenship to the Indians and mestizos, who form a majority of their populations. In South Africa and Rhodesia the dominant European minority, constituting 13 percent of the population in the former and 5 percent in the latter, seeks permanent subjection of the African majority against odds that to an outsider must appear insuperable.

To these internal burdens are added special problems of foreign policy. Each of the newer nations was established in some degree at the expense of one or more of its neighbors, and in many cases it was by no means obvious where the boundaries of the new states should be. Some countries—Poland, Yugoslavia, Bulgaria, Pakistan, Ethiopia, Somalia—have had continuing border problems with all of their neighbors. The creation of new states has also in a more general sense tended to upset the existing political arrangements and balance of power, necessitating readjustments and causing resentments that have often taken many years to reconcile. In these and other ways newly formed states are distracted from their central concern of economic and social development by the peculiar burdens of foreign policy that accompany nation-building.

As a means of overcoming the divisive legacies of nation-building, many societies have sought to foster consensus and national pride by evoking memories of a heroic past. The Chinese and Japanese were among the few that could do this without seriously tampering with the historic record. The Egyptians, Greeks, Italians, Iranians, and Israelis had to overcome significant gaps in the continuum of peoples and governments to claim their ancient civilizations as legitimate forebears. The British, by an imaginative leap of even greater daring, were able for a time to convince themselves that they were the heirs to the culture of the Greeks and the administrative skills of the Romans—and they educated their ruling elite accordingly. Charlemagne proved to be a useful multipurpose symbol, serving as honorary ancestor of both the French and the Germans in periods when they were intense rivals and later of the European Economic Community, in which France and Germany were close partners. The Turks, disregarding a legitimate past of modest glory in Central Asia, sought to manufacture a history that provided them, in the Hittites, with an ancestry that they claimed to have been the original source of all civilization. When the Gold Coast gained its independence from British rule, its new leaders borrowed the name of Ghana from a tenth-century principality of local fame located in Mali, several hundred miles to the northwest of the new state. Incongruous as they may seem to uninvolved observers, these were serviceable inventions that gave newly formed or reorganized nations artificial roots in the past that helped them to survive the whirlwinds of modernization.

4. The course taken by modernization in a society is likewise affected by whether it is self-governing in the modern era or has experienced significant periods of colonial rule. The problems the self-governing countries face, and these are numerous and burdensome, are matters of domestic concern. The controversies that they provoke are among leaders and peoples that share a common citizenship and a common goal of nationhood. Many countries have lived briefly under foreign rule, and in critical phases of their nationhood—the countries of Central and Southern Europe overrun by the armies of Napoleon, and China, Turkey, Iran, and Ethiopia under a variety of forms of partial occupation and intervention by foreigners—but these periods of foreign rule were of relatively short duration and more often than not served as incentives for intense stages of national revival and reform.

The experience of the countries that underwent more thoroughgoing forms of colonial rule was very different. It had significant positive aspects, in that the metropolitan countries introduced, sometimes at their own expense, political and judicial institutions; railroads, highways, and port facilities; crops and industries; and institutions of health, sanitation, and education that were much in advance of what the colonial countries themselves might have achieved by their own efforts.

Yet the benefits of colonialism generally affected only limited sectors of societies and at an early stage of their development, and were accompanied in the long run by shortcomings of a fundamental nature. The central problem is that modernization, as it develops beyond the initial levels, involves profound and costly, and generally violent, changes that can be implemented only by indigenous leaders. The metropolitan countries, having undertaken their colonial responsibilities with limited economic or strategic objectives in mind, had neither the resources nor the personnel to supervise the transformation of the colonial societies from an agrarian to an industrial way of life. On the contrary, they wished to achieve their aims with the smallest possible commitment of budget and manpower, and they were generally inclined to rely on and strengthen the traditional leaders and institutions as a means of preserving the status quo. Even when they sought on occasion to introduce their own institutions, especially in the realm of justice, finance, and education, it was only in restricted forms that did not affect the bulk of the population.

5. A final criterion for classifying countries in the process of modernization is whether their traditional institutions were sufficiently developed to be adaptable to the functions of modernity. The modern institutions of the advanced countries have been formed by the adaptation of their traditional institutions to modern functions, and a majority of the world's population (all but the seventh pattern) lives in societies with institutions that are more or less capable of such adaptation. In order to have a language that can express modern ideas, one must start with a written language capable of being developed through accretions of meaning and the borrowing and inventing of new terms. What is true of language is also true in varying degrees of religious, legal, and political institutions. Even in the realm of abstract knowledge, the eastern Mediterranean and Asian societies have traditions of research and speculation that have contributed to the evolution of modern ideas and provide a link with modern knowledge.

At the same time, there are some societies (the seventh pattern) where the level of development of traditional institutions is on the whole not adequate to provide a basis for adaptation. When societies do not have a written language or evolved political, legal, or religious institutions, adaptation encounters apparently insuperable problems. In these cases the solution is to borrow institutions wholesale from more advanced societies. Most African countries use European languages for official matters and have adopted systems of law, education, and government that have no significant links with their own traditional past. This approach is sensible and expeditious, and it is probably in the long run the only solution. It nevertheless involves an extensive discontinuity between tradition and modernity and leads to a very different course of development from that of societies where modern institutions are more congruent with the traditional.

There are, of course, many different kinds of criteria that can be employed to compare and categorize modernizing societies. The criteria that have been suggested above, for reasons already noted, are cast in a framework of historical development, nation-building, and international relations. At the same time, this classification serves to group societies in considerable measure on the basis of cultural, economic, and social criteria as well. This is natural, since the chronological arrangement and the emphasis on the sources and nature of modernizing influences tend to bring together countries of a similar character. The early-modernizing societies of Western Europe and their offshoots have a uniformly higher per capita gross national product, level of urbanization and education, proportion of population engaged in nonagricultural occupations, and degree of social mobilization than those that modernized later. Similarly the societies in the seventh category—the undeveloped societies modernizing under tutelage—are generally the least developed in these areas. Even within individual categories the chronological order of a society corresponds more often than not to its level of economic and social development. This classification also groups most of these societies together in terms of their historical culture. Societies of Western, Central, and Eastern Europe and their offshoots in the New World are in the first four categories; and those of the Arab world, sub-Saharan Africa, and South and Southeast Asia, for example, are likewise grouped together in the sixth and seventh categories. To this extent the classification on the limited criterion of political modernization reflects in large measure ties of common experience with which these countries are normally associated.

This general correlation of political, economic, and social characteristics applies to a much lesser degree, however, to the fifth category—Russia, Japan, China, Iran, Turkey, Afghanistan, Ethiopia, and Thailand. What these societies have in common from the point of view of political modernization is the fact that their traditional governments were sufficiently effective to resist formal submission to colonial rule, and the modernizing role of their governments was thus very different from that of the later-modernizing societies that became colonies. There are in fact many striking parallels among the members of this category in the political aspect of modernization, despite the considerable diversity among them in culture and historical experience. The Russian traditional culture is European and Christian; that of Turkey, Iran, and Afghanistan is Central Asian and Islamic; that of China, Japan, and Thailand is East Asian and Buddhist; and that of Ethiopia is Amharic and Coptic. In terms of economic and social development Russia and Japan are relatively advanced and in important respects rival or surpass many of the societies in the first four categories, whereas the remaining societies in the fifth category are separated from them by a significant gap. Indeed, if it were not for the primarily political purposes of this typology, there would be reason to dissolve this category and to place these countries in the other six patterns. The process of political modernization in these societies is nevertheless so distinctive that their consideration as a separate pattern is well justified.

The arguments supporting these criteria of classification are closely related to the historical framework of this study, and if this subject were approached from the point of view of other disciplines, different criteria might well be adopted. Anthropologists would give greater attention to traditional cultures, family structure, or linguistic or religious groupings; political scientists would be inclined to stress constitutional forms, party systems, articulation of interest groups, and distribution of political power; sociologists would emphasize systems of stratification, social mobility, urbanization, literacy, and communications media; economists would be concerned with patterns of resources, gross national products, rates of industrial and agricultural growth, and systems of savings and investment.

Interesting patterns combining a variety of criteria have also been formulated. These are based on the rather high correlation that has been found between such variables as literacy, gross national product per capita, and levels of education, health, and communications media, and facilitate the construction of typologies based on levels of development that are quite enlightening. Criteria of classification based on the characteristic political problems faced by modernizing leaders have a particular value in a historical context, but in other contexts typologies based on alternative criteria would have to be elaborated.

Seven Patterns of Political Modernization

First Pattern

The first pattern of political modernization is formed by Great Britain and France, which were the earliest countries to modernize and which in their different ways set the pattern to a significant degree for all other societies.

The English revolution came so early, and the subsequent restoration was so prolonged, that it is often lost to sight as a germinal stage of political modernization. Students have long debated the significance of the seventeenth-century revolution, and considerable disagreement regarding its relationship to earlier and subsequent political and economic trends still remains. Yet a substantial and well-documented body of scholarship now sees in Puritanism a critique of traditional authority and a search for new values that are modern in their essence. There are significant common elements among Puritans, Jacobins, and Bolsheviks, for instance, in the social origins of their leaders, in their emphasis on order and discipline, and in their efforts at a rational reappraisal of the old order. The Puritan phase of English politics was to be absorbed in subsequent developments more fully than was the case with most revolutionary ideologies, and its identity to a considerable extent disappeared, but there emerged in the eighteenth and nineteenth centuries a distinctively British policy of modernization.

The originality and influence of the French revolution is generally recognized, and even after innumerable subsequent revolutions in many parts of the world over a period of more than 175 years it remains the classic example of the initial transfer of political power from traditional to modernizing leaders. What is distinctive about the French revolution is the example that it set for those that were to follow. The direct influence of modern British institutions has been limited to other English-speaking countries and to societies in Asia and Africa that came under British rule. The American revolution can claim primacy in implementing the theory of the sovereignty of the people in a constitutional form that defined and institutionalized the executive, legislative, and judicial powers. The American constitution, and the process by which it was formulated, had a wide influence in Europe at the time and has contributed important elements to the constitutions of a considerable number of new nations in the nineteenth and twentieth centuries. This influence has been limited and indirect, however, since the intellectual and social environment that produced the American revolution has few counterparts in other parts of the world.

The French revolution, on the other hand, contributed both ideology and institutions that were widely imitated. Throughout Northern, Central, and Southern Europe, French ideas and institutions were introduced directly by the armies of Napoleon. French republicanism was the model for modernizing leaders in much of the Moslem world as well as in Latin America. The societies of Southeast Asia and

Africa that came under French rule have also relied heavily on the French model. An indirect influence of modern French institutions has also been exerted in Asia and Africa through Dutch and Belgian rule. Jacobinism as a generalized ideology is in the twentieth century the leading alternative revolutionary doctrine to Marxism-Leninism, and has been a primary source of inspiration for such revolutionary leaders as Atatürk, Nasser, and Ben Bella in the Near East, Sun Yat-sen, Nehru, and Sukarno in Asia, and Cárdenas and the pre-1960 Castro in Latin America. Each of these leaders had his own individuality, and no doubt each came under many other influences, but the distinctively Jacobin cast of their thinking gave them a common bond with the French revolutionaries.

In addition to sharing this distinctive priority in the theory and practice of the transfer of political power from traditional to modernizing leaders, Great Britain and France are distinguished from other societies by the extent to which the challenge of modernity was an internal one, by their continuity of territory and population in the modern era, and by the adaptability of their traditional institutions to modern functions.

Several consequences have flowed from this pattern of development. One is that in Great Britain and France the adaptation of traditional institutions to modern functions evolved more slowly than in the countries that modernized later. Although both countries experienced the upheavals of revolution and restoration—France in a much more dramatic fashion and on several occasions—substantive change in the political, economic, and social spheres took place only gradually. In the case of Great Britain one may consider the transition from traditional to modernizing leadership as having taken place between 1649 and 1832. The political problems of economic and social transformation were encountered between 1832 and 1945. In France, from 1789 to 1848 and from 1848 to 1945 may be considered the comparable dates.

This relatively slow pace of change—in comparison with most later-modernizing societies; and the fact that it was to such a large extent internalized (that is to say, free from radical foreign intervention and therefore dependent primarily on the juxtaposition of domestic interests)—resulted in a relatively orderly and peaceful adaptation of traditional institutions to modern functions. In Great Britain this process was so gradual that not until the twentieth century did national political institutions correspond more or less fully to the economic and social changes that had been taking place over many generations. In France, after the initial upheaval, the modern institutional framework that the Napoleonic Code established in 1802 provided the basis for a development that was orderly in substance despite much political unrest.

The two countries also resemble each other, despite significant superficial differences, in the way that political leadership was transformed. In Great Britain this transformation was so gradual that even in the mid-twentieth century graduates of a few universities fill most important positions. Students were recruited from an increasingly wide range of strata, but their education was so strongly oriented toward a national consensus that attitudes changed slowly through the decades. Even the Labour party drew to a significant extent from the same sources of leadership as the Conservative. In France the same degree of consensus was never achieved, and there has remained to the present time a profound division between politically active Frenchmen who are adherents of a multiparty parliament and those who are supporters of strong personal leadership. There have also been periods of political instability, such as that after 1945 when there were twenty-five prime ministers in thirteen years. With this apparent instability, France has nevertheless undergone at the administrative level a relatively gradual and stable transformation under many generations of skilled civil servants trained in the *grandes écoles.*

The role of Great Britain and France as the first countries to modernize, combined with their long experience as trading and colonizing countries, gave them an initial position of international influence that was beyond their capability to maintain in the long run. London and Paris were until the First World War the capitals of the world in virtually all realms of human endeavor, and Great Britain and France were the two countries with the largest overseas possessions. These possessions, the most populous of which were, to be sure, under British rule, had a total of some 420 million inhabitants in 1914. This position of predominance did not survive the First World War, and indeed both countries have seen their international fortunes decline since that disastrous conflict. What was nevertheless unusual was not this eclipse but the earlier period of disproportionate influence, which could not have been maintained unless the rest of the world had stood still. If one judges these two countries in terms not of world power but of per capita development, they can be seen to have achieved a level of attainment that is still among the highest and that depends only on the ingenuity of their political leaders for continued growth.

Second Pattern

The offshoots of Great Britain and France in the New World may be considered to form a second pattern of political modernization. The term "offshoots," which appears again in connection with the fourth pattern, is employed here to mean countries that are settled by peoples of the Old World who become politically and culturally dominant in the new societies even though they may on occasion form only a minority of the population. These offshoots usually started as dependencies, but they differ from other colonies in that the dominant population was the same as that of the mother country. The United States, Canada, Australia, and New Zealand, with a total population of 225 million, are the societies that form this pattern.

Insofar as the dominant populations of these societies were inhabitants of their metropolitan countries of origin until the seventeenth century, they too may be said to have faced the immediate political challenge of modernity as an internal problem and to have entered the modern era with developed institutions adaptable to the functions of modernity. In other respects, however, they have differed from their societies of origin. The transfer of political power from traditional to modernizing leaders took place somewhat later and under different circumstances, they underwent a fundamental regrouping of lands and peoples, and they experienced prolonged periods of colonial rule.

The accession to political power of modernizing leaders in these societies was associated, for reasons discussed earlier, with the attainment of political independence. These colonies could in theory have been made integral parts of the mother country, as France had done with some of its overseas territories, but their interests were in the long run very different from that of a Great Britain that was profoundly involved in European affairs, and they were too distant and ultimately too large and populous to be coerced.

The struggle between traditional and modernizing leaders took its most dramatic form in the United States, where it may be said to have extended from 1776 to 1865. The war of independence has generally been thought of as having a rather limited revolutionary content, but it has been demonstrated that in proportion to the population the number of émigrés was four or five times greater than that in revolutionary France and that the value of émigré property confiscated was proportionately not much less than in France. The Civil War, which led to the final defeat of slaveholding (hence traditional policies), was a conflict of greater proportions than any in the world between 1815 and 1914. In domestic violence this phase of American history rivals that of any other country, and the problems that provoked this violence—independence, national unity, and emancipation of slaves—were characteristically modern issues.

In Canada, Australia, and New Zealand the process was more gradual and less violent. The populations of these societies were more homogeneous and more closely tied by commerce to the mother country, and it was a long time before they were sufficiently robust in terms of number of inhabitants and diversity of economy to embark on an independent course. This process may be considered to have taken place between 1791 and 1867 in Canada, between 1809 and 1901 in Australia, and between 1826 and 1907 in New Zealand, the terminal date in each case marking the achievement of dominion status.

The most significant characteristic of this pattern of political modernization is that these societies left the traditional social structure behind in the mother country. They undertook the process of economic and social transformation not from a base of long-established and relatively closed strata of peasants, artisans, and landowners, but with a fluid social structure that was much more readily amenable to change. This fluidity was greatly enhanced by the presence of large and undeveloped frontier regions where land and other resources were abundant and the authority of the state was weak. Canada, the United States, and Australia are the second, fourth, and sixth largest countries in the world in area, but they (and New Zealand) have among the smallest populations in the world in proportion to agricultural land. The availability of these frontier regions served not only as a source of wealth but also as a safety valve for the social problems of the more densely populated areas. Individuals and groups that sought redress of grievances, or that failed to make a satisfactory living, or that wished to give effect to unconventional views could move into the frontier regions rather than face compromise or possible defeat at home.

Along with these opportunities, the frontier brought problems. Of these the most important was that the abundant resources could not be developed without labor, and the large influx of peoples that this involved presented unique problems of assimilation. In the nineteenth century alone, many millions immigrated to the United States, Canada, Australia, and New Zealand. The problem of assimilation was confronted in the most extreme form in the United States, for in the other three countries factors of circumstance and policy resulted in a more gradual and homogeneous immigration. In the United States public education for several generations was devoted to producing a consensus of ideas and values in what was commonly referred to as a "melting pot" of ethnic and religious groups.

If this assimilation was a matter of concern to the politically active leaders who were predominantly English-speaking and Protestant, it also presented many difficulties to the immigrants themselves. Members of the first generation, if they were not English-speaking, remained in large measure aliens throughout their lives. The second and often the third generations faced a conflict of loyalties, in terms of language, culture, and other values, between the Old World and the New, under circumstances in which the latter could not in the end fail to win. Communities handled these problems in diverse ways, and not infrequently where religious and other cultural bonds were well knit a tolerable and often mutually reinforcing adjustment was reached between the two ways of life. There were also many cases, however, where a satisfactory adjustment was not made for several generations.

At the same time, neither the Europeans nor the relatively few Asians faced the frustrations of the Africans who were brought originally as slaves and who were emancipated in 1863. The values and institutions that they had brought from their homeland were not particularly adaptable to a modern environment, and adaptation was frustrated to the extent that they lived under a system of slavery that divided families and communities. Emancipation confronted the Negroes with the twofold problem of the absence of a developed native culture that might have assured social cohesion for a transitional period, and at the same time a massive resistance on the part of the rest of the population to their assimilation. The result was a widespread antagonism and alienation that did not develop into a direct confrontation so long as most of the Negroes were engaged in agriculture, but later became a major issue of public policy in the more closely knit relationships of an industrial society. The United States faced a dual problem of integration: the general problem confronting all societies when they become predominantly industrial and the special but directly related problem of integrating Negro citizens into a non-Negro society.

Some American historians have sought to generalize from the frontier experience and to see it as the principal stimulus of individualism, opposition to government regulations, and democracy. This may have been the case in the English-speaking societies, although the benefits of an abundant frontier region must be weighed against the problems that it brought. The comparative study of frontier regions is not yet a well-developed subject, but further research may well reveal that frontiers tend to encourage in a more extreme form the characteristics of the metropolitan areas. If the voluntarism characteristic of the English-speaking societies was given a wider scope in the frontier regions, so was the authoritarianism of the Russian government that undertook to develop Siberia in the nineteenth century.

By the 1930's, when the societies of this second pattern began to face the political problems of social integration, they had surpassed the European level of development and were by general agreement the most affluent societies in the world. They had benefited not only from the vast resources of the New World, and from the relative geographical isolation that permitted them to devote their major energies to domestic affairs, but also from the developed and liberal institutions that they had inherited from the Old World and from the skilled and energetic peoples that had come in many millions to seek a more satisfying way of life.

Third Pattern

A third pattern of political modernization comprises the societies of Europe in which the consolidation of modernizing leadership occurred after the French revolution and as a direct or indirect result of its impact. These societies undertook to adapt their political institutions to modern functions somewhat later than Great Britain and France; they also underwent a long and generally violent period of the regrouping of territories and peoples that was one of the most distinctive features of their experience. These societies were predominantly self-governing in the modern era, although the minority peoples of Eastern Europe, and also of Ireland and Iceland, were initially under a form of alien rule that in certain limited respects resembled colonialism. Like the societies in the first two patterns, these countries also had developed institutions in the traditional era that were readily adaptable to modern functions.

It is, of course, significant that many of the European societies had participated for several centuries in the development of modern ideas and institutions, and equaled or surpassed England and France or the countries of the New World in many fields of endeavor. The navigational skills of Spanish and Portuguese seamen; the commercial attainments of Dutch, Venetian, and Dalmatian merchants; the scientists of Polish, Bohemian, Magyar, and German origin; the scholars, artists, and mechanics of these diverse societies—and many others—made contributions of fundamental importance to the formation of a modern way of life. In the political sphere, however, these peoples did not break away decisively from the traditional mold until after the French revolution, and to this extent their political modernization was decisively influenced by the French model.

The collapse of the old regimes came as early as 1795 in Belgium, Luxembourg, and the Netherlands, in 1798 in Switzerland, and in the first decade of the nineteenth century in Germany, Italy, Denmark, Norway, and Sweden. In these countries modernizing political leadership may be said to have been consolidated between 1839 in the Netherlands and 1871 in Germany and Italy. In Eastern Europe the political transformation did not begin until somewhat later and was not completed until the destruction of the dynastic empires that culminated in the First World War.

The consolidation of modernizing political leadership in these countries was characterized not only by the decisive influence of foreign models, in many cases imposed or at least introduced by force of arms, but also by the prolonged and difficult process of nation-building. Few of the traditional states survived this process intact. The most complex of these territorial and political reconstructions involved the Holy Roman Empire, the constituent territories of which were reorganized a number of times before achieving a relative stability in 1871. Equally fraught with violence, although basically less confusing, was the dissolution of the Ottoman and Hapsburg empires as one by one their constituent nationalities gained their independence by gradual stages through war, revolution, and diplomacy involving a wide variety of negotiations, intrigues, maneuvers, and compromises.

Apart from the many fundamental differences among the societies sharing this pattern in the traditional heritage of institutions, as well as in the contingencies of political leadership, the most characteristic feature was the human expense of nation-building. To a significantly greater extent than was the case in Great Britain and France, and in their offshoots in the New World, the energies of the political leaders and the emotions and resources of their peoples were devoted to defending the newly acquired frontiers and to preparing for the liberation of adjacent or related territories still under alien rule. In Central Europe a precarious stability was achieved in 1871, but further east the passions of nationalism continued to smolder until they ignited the great conflagrations of 1914–1918 and 1939–1945. Although nationalism was only a means to an end—self-determination to permit societies to modernize free from the discriminatory rule of alien peoples—it became for several generations an end in itself. On the altar of nationalism were sacrificed many of the human rights that modern societies are capable of affording; there were also significant and frustrating delays in economic and social development. In its extreme form, in Hitler's Germany, this perverted sense of values was responsible for the most inhuman brutalities that history has known.

The most rapid phase of economic transformation in these societies took place in the latter part of the nineteenth century and the first half of the twentieth. Switzerland and Germany were confronted with the problems of social integration by the 1930's, and eight other societies reached this stage after the Second World War. These societies are among the most advanced in the world, rivaling and not infrequently surpassing in various respects the countries that modernized earlier. A dozen others, however, principally the societies of Eastern and Southern Europe, have not yet developed a predominantly industrial way of life. In some cases this slow development has been due to the shortcomings of the resource base, but it is more generally the result of policies that have given a higher priority to political security, stability, and consensus than to economic and social transformation. Spain and Portugal are prime examples of this relative lack of concern for modernization on the part of political leaders.

Fourth Pattern

The offshoots in the New World of the European societies in the third pattern may be considered as forming a fourth pattern of political modernization. The societies in this pattern are the twenty-two independent countries of Latin America, with a combined population of some 230 million. These societies differ from those in the second pattern, also populated predominantly by immigrants from the Old World—apart from differences in their bases of resources and skills—in that modernization came later, was to a much greater degree under foreign influence, and was influenced in particular by those societies of the third pattern that were inclined to place the least emphasis on modernization.

The achievement of national independence in Latin America did not result in the accession to power of a modernizing leadership, but rather in the establishment of a form of neocolonialism that tended to perpetuate the traditional way of life. Even in those countries inhabited predominantly by Europeans—Argentina, Costa Rica, and Uruguay—the position of modernizing leaders was not consolidated until almost a century after their emancipation from European rule. This can be explained in part by the agrarian wealth of these countries, which inhibited the development of an urban population, but it seems to have been due primarily to the values of the politically active inhabitants. Their declarations of national aims and the forms of government that they established were based on the liberal European model, and their rhetoric drew heavily on that of the French revolution, but in content their political systems did not for several generations begin to resemble modern institutions of citizenship and statehood.

Political modernization in a majority of the Latin American societies has been severely inhibited by the fact that the inhabitants of European extraction were in a minority and were disinclined to share their political power with the mestizo and Indian inhabitants—and in some cases with immigrants from Africa—who formed the majority of the population. The situation in these societies differed significantly in this respect from that in the United States, where the Indian population was negligible and the Africans constituted some 10 percent of the population. In the United States the non-European population was sufficiently small so that it could be largely ignored until pressures of social integration, starting in the 1930's, brought the problem inescapably to the forefront of public policy. In a majority of the Latin American societies, in contrast, the size of the non-European population inhibited the extension of effective citizenship and led to a widening gap between a few wealthy inhabitants of European extraction and a mass of relatively impoverished semi- and non-Europeans. The social effects of this gap were enhanced by the practice of the dominant minority of investing their wealth abroad rather than at home.

Mexico was the first country of predominantly Indian and mestizo inhabitants where effective citizenship was extended beyond the limits of the European population. This political broadening was accomplished through the revolutionary constitutional reforms in 1917 that extended citizenship to all inhabitants, effected a land reform, and fostered systematic economic and social development under government guidance. The achievement may be explained in part by the preparatory work of Juárez and Díaz, who established a tradition of liberal reform combined with political discipline, and in part by the proximity of the United States, which through commerce, investments, and example has exerted a powerful influence. The central and indispensable source of the Mexican achievement, however, without which the other influences would have been inconclusive, was the presence of vigorous leaders inspired by an ideology that was both revolutionary and liberal.

By the middle of this century modernizing leadership had been consolidated in about one-half of the countries of Latin America, and these were in the process of rapid economic transformation. Judging from the evidence of recent efforts to rank countries by correlated indexes that measure achievement in a variety of economic and social fields, such countries as Argentina, Uruguay, and Venezuela have achieved a per capita level of development roughly comparable to that of the Soviet Union, Italy, Japan, and the more advanced countries of Eastern Europe. Others, such as Brazil, Chile, Colombia, Costa Rica, Cuba, Mexico, Panama, and Puerto Rico, are clearly in the process of rapid transformation. Others yet, however, such as Bolivia, Haiti, and Paraguay, are still among the least developed countries in the world.

Fifth Pattern

Those societies that modernized without direct outside intervention, but under the indirect influence of societies that modernized earlier, represent a fifth pattern of political modernization. The relatively few societies constituting this pattern are Russia, Japan, China, Iran, Turkey, Afghanistan, Ethiopia, and Thailand, inhabited by some 1.2 billion people. What these societies have in common is the fact that their traditional governments were sufficiently effective, because of long experience with centralized bureaucratic government, to enable them to resist direct and comprehensive foreign rule for a prolonged period in modern times. In contrast to most other societies, they modernized essentially at their own initiative and with a significant continuity of territory and population. The ability of these societies to preserve their independence may be explained by a variety of circumstances. In China, Iran, and Turkey the balance of power—or, more crudely, the divisions among their more modern rivals—was doubtless a more vital factor than military strength in protecting their independence. In Afghanistan, Ethiopia, and Thailand inaccessibility and isolation also played a role. Russia and Japan, on the other hand, relied for their independence primarily on their own military strength. The ability to take advantage of the balance of power, however, as well as to maintain a significant military establishment, stemmed in the long run from a tradition of organized government sufficiently effective to meet the foreign challenges that these countries faced.

The pattern of political modernization represented by this group of societies may also be considered in terms of the problems that they have not had to face. They have not had to cope in modern times with the creation of new nations out of disparate territories under foreign rule. This is a deeply divisive experience that, especially in the later-modernizing European societies, has occupied much of the attention and energies of political leaders at the expense of the economic and social problems of modernization. It is one of the most enduring characteristics of the societies in the fifth pattern that they established the territorial and human base of their states before—and in China, Japan, and Iran many centuries before—they encountered the challenge of modernity. These societies have also not had to face the problems of direct foreign rule characteristic of colonialism. All have experienced some degree of foreign intervention in modern times—periods of foreign occupation in parts of their territory (in Ethiopia five years under Italian rule), preferential treatment for foreigners in the form of capitulations, and extensive reliance on foreign loans and advisers. These various kinds of intervention were nevertheless a very different experience from the direct and prolonged foreign tutelage represented by colonialism. The leaders of these societies may have been humiliated in varying degrees by the extent of their reliance on more modern societies, but with the exception of relatively short periods of occupation, it was a question of dependence rather than subjugation.

In this group of societies the traditional governments themselves—in Russia under the Muscovite and Petrine traditions, in Tokugawa Japan, in Ch'ing (Manchu) China, in Ottoman Turkey, in Persia under the Kajar dynasty, in Ethiopia under Theodore and Menelik II, and in Siam under Chakri rulers—took the initiative in meeting the challenge of modernity. This bureaucratic tradition may have evolved in response to particular problems of irrigation and communication or may have been due more generally to factors of geography, political environment, and the contingencies of leadership—matters on which scholars disagree—but it is significant that in many respects they matched Great Britain and France in the continuous and gradual character of their transformation from old regimes to new.

The traditional governments were strong enough to prevent their countries from being overrun by more modern societies—for the challenge of modernity was essentially a foreign challenge, even though modern knowledge was to gain adherents within these countries as a domestic challenge—and also realistic enough in the long run to know that unless they introduced modern reforms they would ultimately succumb to foreign rule. They therefore initiated what might be called programs of limited or defensive modernization, designed to preserve the traditional society and protect it from the more intensive and thoroughgoing changes that might have resulted from the success of foreign or domestic modernizers. Such were the reforms of Peter I and Nicholas I in Russia, of the later Tokugawa shoguns, of Mahmud II and Abdul-Medjid I, of the statesmen of the late Ch'ing period, of Mongkut and Chulalongkorn in Siam, of Shah Nasir ud-Din in Afghanistan, and of Emperor Menelik in Ethiopia. These reforms were concerned with providing modern training and equipment for the bureaucracy and army, improving transportation and communications, and establishing institutions of higher education. Foreign specialists were invited to train native scholars and artisans, and native leaders went abroad to study modern techniques.

It was an essential feature of these reforms, however, that they were designed not to transform the traditional system but to strengthen it against foreign pressures. The agrarian economies and the way of life of the peasants, who constituted over four-fifths of the population, were virtually unaffected by limited modernization, and the elites retained their traditional privileges. By these means the challenge of more modern societies was at least temporarily met and the transition to political leadership favoring programs of intensive modernization was delayed for several generations. The essentially conservative nature of these governments was nevertheless matched by a purposefulness that prevented them from losing touch with reality, and they came to recognize that intensive modernization was in the long run inevitable. This realization was achieved as a result either of the shock or threat of military setbacks or of a recognition under less dramatic circumstances of the advantages of modernity.

What is significant, in any event, is that in these countries the fundamental break with the past was made not as a result of a revolution by domestic forces outside the government, or of occupation by a foreign power, or of a national uprising against foreign rule, but by the traditional leadership itself. The decisive breaks with the past were represented by the emancipation of the serfs in Russia in 1861, the overthrow of the shogunate in Japan in 1868, the replacement of the Chinese classics by modern learning in 1905 as a requirement for admission to the bureaucracy, and the establishment of forms of constitutional government in Persia in 1906, in the Ottoman Empire in 1908, in Afghanistan in 1923, in Ethiopia in 1924, and in Siam in 1932. These acts, marking the end of the old regimes, were taken at the initiative of either the ruling sovereigns, as in Russia and China, or leaders who were high-ranking members of the incumbent bureaucracies. The last four cases are usually called "revolutions," but they were revolutions only within the ruling elites and did not closely resemble those in Great Britain and France, and in much of the rest of Europe.

Even though the initiative in both the limited and the intensive forms of political modernization in these societies was taken by incumbent rulers and bureaucrats, they were unable to sustain this initiative over a long period. Only in Japan was the political power of a modernizing leadership consolidated by 1945 without the revolutionary overthrow of the dynasty—although the military revolts in the 1930's and 1940's and the American occupation were in a sense revolutionary in content. In the other countries the consolidation of modernizing leaders involved more decisive revolutions—such as the establishment of the Provisional Government in Russia in February-March 1917, followed by the Bolshevik revolution in October-November; a succession of revolutions in China led by Sun Yat-sen in 1911, Chiang Kai-shek in 1927, and Mao Tse-tung in 1949; and the revolutions as a result of which the incumbent dynasties were overthrown by Mustafa Kemal in Turkey in 1923 and by Riza Khan in Persia in 1925. The modernizing leadership that took the initiative in Afghanistan in 1923, in Ethiopia in 1924, and in Thailand in 1932 cannot yet be said to have been consolidated.

At the same time, the cohesion and sense of identity of the traditional cultures that enabled the societies in this pattern to preserve their integrity in the face of powerful modernizing pressures from abroad served also in various ways to delay the process of transformation. The most extreme example is China, the most ancient and sophisticated of the traditional societies, which had the greatest difficulty in adapting its institutions to modernity. Of the many explanations of this phenomenon that have been advanced, the most plausible is that the political and intellectual leaders were so strongly convinced that the traditional truths were correct that they could not bring themselves to abandon them. It was not until 1905 that modern knowledge replaced the traditional in the civil-service examinations, and even today most Chinese leaders retain a remarkably Sinocentric view of the world.

These societies, for reasons already noted, may properly be treated as a single pattern of political modernization, but in other respects they differ greatly. These differences are evident not only in their traditional ideas and institutions but also in their resource bases. Both Russia and Japan started with a strong agricultural base and by the end of the nineteenth century were among the most rapidly industrializing countries in the world. Different as they are in the patterns of their economic development in the twentieth century—and in the origins and institutions of their political leadership—their per capita level of economic and social achievement today is about the same as, or is above, that of most societies except those of the English-speaking world and Western Europe. On a comparable per capita basis, China, Iran, Thailand, and Turkey have made less progress, and Afghanistan and Ethiopia are among the least developed countries in the world.

Sixth and Seventh Patterns

The more than one hundred independent and dependent societies of Asia, Africa, the Americas, and Oceania that have experienced colonial rule may be divided into two final patterns of political modernization. The sixth pattern is composed of the thirty-four now independent and twenty-nine dependent societies, with a population of about 1 billion, the traditional cultures of which are sufficiently well developed that they could interact with those of the more modern tutelary societies in their adaptation to modern functions. Thus Islam, Hinduism, and Buddhism have faced problems of adaptation to modern knowledge similar to those confronting Christianity and Judaism. Arabic, Hindi, Urdu, and Malayan are being developed and enriched for the purposes of modern communication, as were English, French, and Italian in their day, and Russian, Japanese, Chinese, and Turkish somewhat later. Traditional forms of government in the Near East and Asia are adaptable to modern political needs, as were the feudal institutions of Europe and the bureaucratic systems of Russia, Turkey, Japan, and China earlier. The societies constituting the seventh pattern, however—the thirty-one independent and the approximately twenty dependent societies of sub-Saharan Africa and Oceania, with a population of 200 million—did not have religion, or language, or political institutions sufficiently developed, at the time that they faced the challenge of modernity, to be readily adaptable to modern conditions. Instead, they have found it more practical to borrow from more modern societies modern ideas and institutions that are more or less unchanged.

Common to these two patterns was the experience of colonialism, which had the effect of stimulating the initial phase of modernization, the challenge of modernity in a traditional society, but of delaying the next phase, the consolidation of political power by modernizing leaders. The younger and more aggressive leaders in the colonial societies, more often than not members of or related to the traditional elites, often obtained an advanced education in the metropolitan country only to return home and find their efforts at reform opposed by a coalition between their own traditional leaders and the colonial administrators. This was a profoundly frustrating experience for the forward-looking younger leaders, and consequently their modernizing programs often took a violently nationalistic and antiforeign form. Indeed, when the colonies finally gained their independence, it was not uncommon for their leaders to be antiforeign modernizers or, more specifically, anti-European Europeanizers. At the same time that they sought to introduce modern ideas and institutions, they resisted foreign influence and assistance even at the cost of slower rates of change. They wished to modernize rapidly, but they wished to do it by themselves and in their own way.

The interpretation that views colonialism primarily in terms of exploitation fails to take into account the complexity of the modernizing process in these societies. Exploitation indeed there was, especially in colonies with mineral wealth that could be easily extracted or with markets capable of absorbing the industrial products of the tutelary societies. To the extent that these activities brought an unusually high rate of profit, it is appropriate to consider them as exploitation. Although such exploitation made fortunes for a few Europeans, it did not impoverish the colonies in any fundamental way. They were too poor to produce much wealth per capita or to absorb large quantities of consumer goods. The great markets for the industries of the advanced countries, and the principal destinations of their investments, were at home or in countries at a comparable level of development.

The most ruthless pillaging of wealth and the greatest excesses of violence and bloodshed to which the developing countries have been subjected have resulted from the efforts of their own modernizing leaders, after the attainment of independence, to transform them from an agrarian to an industrial way of life. The colonial experience drew particular attention to the position of tutelage of these societies and to the frustrations of modernizing leaders in their efforts to achieve independence, but characteristically political violence and economic hardship appeared in their most extreme forms after the achievement of independence.

To a far greater extent than in the societies in the second and fourth patterns, colonies established in the New World as offshoots of European societies, these colonies were dependent on the tutelary power for their political cohesion. Only in exceptional cases did they have a historical basis for an independent nationhood, and their political configuration as colonies and later as independent states was due more to the political authority of the tutelary power than to their own initiative. India, perhaps the most extreme case, was a congeries of more than five hundred traditional sovereignties held together primarily by British authority. Most other colonial societies were similarly dependent on the political authority of the tutelary power. When the power finally withdrew, it left significant remnants of its authority in the territorial settlement, the terms of independence, and other arrangements.

Despite this often frustrating state of tutelage, the level of the traditional culture of these societies was such that they could participate to a considerable extent as partners in fostering modernization. Adaptation of native institutions and direct borrowing interacted to produce original and effective forms. They developed their own educational systems, established institutions of higher learning, trained cadres of leaders both at home and abroad, and were able even within the framework of tutelage to assume many of the responsibilities of self-government. While the challenge of modernity in these societies was represented by the initial impact of European ideas and institutions, the consolidation of modernizing leadership was begun under tutelage and was in most cases completed by the time of independence. Nuri as-Said, Nehru, or Sukarno may have felt frustrated before independence, but it cannot be said that the consolidation of modernizing leadership was accompanied by any greater violence than it was in Europe or in the New World. The tutelary powers have borne a heavy burden of criticism, but since their departure it has become increasingly clear that the obstacles to modernization in these societies should be sought primarily in the traditional heritage of resources and institutions.

While sharing in common with the sixth pattern many problems of political modernization, the societies of the seventh pattern are distinguished by the absence of a traditional culture sufficiently developed to be capable of adaptation to any significant degree to modern functions or of interaction with the cultures of more modern societies. Consequently they are confronted by two characteristic problems: they have not been able to take any substantial modernizing initiative during the colonial period, and after gaining independence they face within the environment of a relatively modernized world and in unprecedented conditions the entire range of problems that other societies have faced since the initial challenge of modernity.

In these societies as in those of the sixth pattern, the tutelary powers were pursuing limited objectives and did not see it as their task to make the great investments that would be necessary to overthrow traditional leaders, improve agriculture, establish industries, and develop education. The more developed colonial societies took the initiative themselves, often overcoming the initial opposition of the tutelary powers, and went ahead to create their own modern institutions. The native peoples of sub-Saharan Africa and Oceania did not have the capacity to take such initiative. It was this lack of initiative, rather than a discriminatory oppressiveness on the part of the tutelary powers, that accounts for the relatively static character of these societies under colonial rule. For them independence marked not the end but the beginning of the period of the consolidation of modernizing leadership, for it thrust upon their leaders for the first time the task of creating modern societies.

The unprecedented experience of the societies of the seventh pattern of starting virtually from nothing, relatively speaking, confronts them with problems the solution to which is not easy to foresee. The only outcome that can be foretold with assurance is that they will not have to retrace the steps of earlier-modernizing societies. They can acquire jet airplanes, modern factories, and programs of education without having to invent and develop them. At the other extreme, it seems equally certain that the lack of a developed traditional culture will not make it that much easier for them to acquire modern institutions through direct borrowing. If unlimited resources were available, such societies might acquire a full equipment of modern schools, hospitals, factories, farms, and cities, and there would only be the problem of training a new generation to use this equipment. This would be as true of a developed as of an undeveloped society, however, and the former would be much better able to use the equipment. It would appear therefore that in the long road ahead societies in which four-fifths or more of the population are rural and illiterate will be able to take only those short cuts available to all societies by acquiring to the extent of their means modern equipment from the advanced countries. Since their means are generally limited and they start at a low level of development, the course ahead will be long and hard.

5. Prospects for a Modern World

World Politics in the Modern Age

The process of modernization affects not only the domestic development of societies but also the relations among them. While many of the traditional forms of international relations have survived —alliances and war, conquest and colonization, cultural diffusion and propaganda—these forms have been infused with new meanings. What has dramatically altered in the modern era is the rate of intellectual, political, economic, social, and ultimately psychological, change. This rate of change has produced unprecedented types and degrees of instability with which politically organized societies have found it particularly frustrating to cope.

The central problem of maintaining international order is that, although each of the participants in the international system desires stability on its own terms, they are so diverse in size, influence, level of development, heritage of political culture, and perception of the international environment that it has been difficult to find common ground for cooperation. This is not to say that a permanent stability is possible, for all social systems—local, national, and international —will always be in a continual state of flux as long as human beings retain the capacity to think. The relationship between forces of instability and forces of order has been tense ever since societies were well enough organized to have relations with one another. What is characteristic of the modern era, however, is that the rapid growth of knowledge has had the effect of radically altering the quality and dimensions of the forces at work. The evolution since the seventeenth century of more orderly forms of diplomatic practice, conference procedures, international law, and international political and functional organizations has served to institutionalize these relations, but the failure of these institutions to regulate instability is reflected in the continuance of international disorder of many types and growing dimensions.

The developments that have increased the difficulty of maintaining international order deserve particular attention. Not the least of these is the growth in the number of participants in the system. The number of societies participating actively in the international system, through exchange of diplomatic representatives and membership in international bodies, has grown from 25 in 1815 to 40 in 1900, 60 in 1920, and more than 130 in 1965. The sheer physical effort of maintaining contact and exchanging opinions among such a large number of participants should not be underestimated. The deliberations at the headquarters of the United Nations in one year alone involve the production of no fewer than 90,000 pages of documents in six languages, which must be distributed in some 450 million copies. A further complexity is created by the great differences in the dimensions of the countries of the world. The members of the United Nations, for example, range in population from 500 million to 100,000, and in gross national product from over $700 billion to a few million dollars.

One of the most dramatic features of modernization has been its effect on the relative position of the societies that were the first to modernize. They were transformed in a few centuries from outposts of the Roman Empire to the greatest centers of influence that the world has known. As the initiators of modernization they were also cast in the role of its missionaries, and as aggressors they carried modern ideas and institutions to the ends of the earth. At the height of their influence (1900–1920) a half dozen European societies held no less than half a billion non-Europeans under their rule. This relationship of rulers to ruled engendered continuing strife, and modern practices were frequently rejected when imposed by the sword. It also fostered the phenomenon of anti-European modernizers, who simultaneously borrowed European practices and fought European rule. Yet in the long run the more modern societies also served as the tutors of other societies, bringing them the benefits of modern knowledge as well as its inescapable problems. Seen in this light, imperialism may be regarded as a modernizing force. When the ruled reached the stage of being able to reject the tutelage of the more modern societies, the worldwide political influence of the latter gradually declined.

The relative domestic stability of the early modernizers in Western Europe and the New World was due in no small part to the fact that they developed in a world in which they had few rivals and eventually became the most influential centers of political power and in many respects the avowed models for all other societies. In contrast, the later modernizers had to undertake the process not only under conditions of greater strife and instability but also under the urgent pressure of seeing before them models so much more advanced that the desired goal seemed almost unattainable. The juxtaposition of societies differing widely in degree of modernization cannot but exert a disruptive influence on less modern societies, although the extent of this disruption depends on the circumstances under which change is introduced. In any event, where the jet plane and the oxcart exist side by side, the strains of modernization are immeasurably greater than where the development of the various aspects of a society has been more gradual and balanced.

Although it is clear that later modernizers encounter profound problems, they also have distinct advantages. Imperialism is frequently seen only as a source of political oppression, but in fact it has served to diffuse the benefits of modernization at a cost that is, relatively speaking, quite modest. As a consequence of imperialism, many modern institutions and artifacts have been made available in their most highly developed form, relieving less modern societies of the costly experimentation that was originally required to create them. Early modernizers have at times found themselves surpassed by other societies that have benefited from their pioneering work. In machinery and production methods, and in creative thought and scientific research as well, the early modernizers have eventually found themselves equaled and even outdistanced on occasion by their former pupils.

On the whole, the diffusion of modern ideas and institutions through imperialism has tended to intensify the challenge of modernity; but it has also served to delay the accession to power of modernizing leaders. The tutelary societies wished to extend the benefits of modernization to the degree and in the particular respects that would serve their own needs, and they were not eager to see a thoroughgoing modernization that would eventually lead to the independence of the ruled and to the loss of such benefits as the rulers may have gained from the relationship. Indeed, thoroughgoing modernization is a revolutionary process requiring the mobilization of great human and material resources, and no tutelary society would embark on this task unless it were a matter of paramount national interest. France undertook the modernization of Algeria, as did Russia that of Central Asia, and Japan that of Korea and Manchuria, but these were exceptional cases. More commonly, as with the Dutch in Indonesia, the British in India, the Americans in the Philippines, and the Belgians in the Congo, the tutelary societies relied on the traditional oligarchies to maintain order. By doing so, they were able to preserve their authority with a minimum expenditure of resources, but at the cost of imposing great frustrations on the native modernizing leaders, who more often than not had been trained in the universities of the tutelary society.

It was noted earlier that one of the principal sources of tension characteristic of modernization has arisen from the fact that this process has tended to invest the governments of each society with increased authority while it has at the same time made them more interdependent. On the one hand, the increased authority of governments has been promoted by the need for societywide controls in the economic and social realm in order to establish the mobilization of resources, order, consensus, and institutional uniformity called for by the requirements of modernization. On the other hand, many forces —improvement of means of communication, the universality of modern knowledge, the expansion of the area within which goods and services are exchanged, the migration of many millions of people from one society to another, the emergence of international associations of functional groups, the economic specialization of regions and even of whole societies—have tended to make societies more interdependent. Economic and social transformation requires a range of resources and skills such as is rarely found within the limits of a single politically organized society. There are a few societies that are able, by virtue of their territorial extent and the variety of their resources and skills, to develop in relative isolation from their neighbors. Among these, the United States and the Soviet Union are, in their different ways, outstanding. They are exceptions, however, and the powerful forces tending simultaneously to strengthen and to undermine political authority have frequently resulted in an acute sense of insecurity on the part of modernizing societies.

Indeed, these forces have been so pervasive that one may properly interpret the various forms of imperialism, alliance relationships, wars, and experiments in political integration that have characterized international relations in modern times as a search for security that is significantly more urgent than in earlier times. Seen in this perspective, the imperialism that reached its climax in the last decades of the nineteenth century was an attempt on the part of more modern societies to enhance their security by extending their sovereignty over less modern societies and thereby gaining control over their resources and skills. It is clear that neither investments, trade, nor surplus population necessarily followed the flag and that the interest groups favoring imperialism in modern societies were motivated by many considerations. At the same time, there seemed to be good reason to regard empires as a reasonable guarantee of security, for there was a sufficient number of instances of imperialist states gaining advantages that they would not otherwise have had from their overseas possessions. As the benefits to be drawn from possessing certain territories could not always be calculated in advance, there was a strong inclination on the part of an imperialist state to seize them in order to prevent rivals from acquiring them. In addition, managing an empire often necessitated the acquisition of strategic positions for the purpose of protecting both the more valuable and the distant territories. A few modern states were able to extend their rule over other peoples living in contiguous territories and to incorporate them into the metropolitan society instead of ruling them as colonies: England incorporated Wales, Scotland, and Northern Ireland; Russia incorporated the Ukraine, the Baltic states, Transcaucasia, and Central Asia.

The expansion of the more modern societies came to an end about 1900, not because of a revolt on the part of their possessions, which did not occur until a generation or two later, but because there was no more territory to conquer. Modern societies now sought through alliance systems the security they had failed to achieve through imperialism. The alliance relationships that had previously been regarded as secondary bulwarks of security, to be sacrificed if necessary when overseas territorial gains were at stake, now became issues of the first importance. These relations were regarded as so vital that it was considered justifiable to risk general war to protect an ally, however small, if the alternative might be a weakening of the alliance system. Under these circumstances international conflicts became endemic; indeed, the First World War came about because of just such a crisis.

The First World War resulted from the inability of the European political system to adjust to the contradictory pressures of nationalism and interdependence. The peace settlement, moreover, did nothing to resolve this fundamental problem. Quite the contrary, it confirmed the forces that tended toward the strengthening of nationalism, statism, and economic self-sufficiency, and weakened the institutions and beliefs that worked for the reconciliation of differences among societies. Cultural nationalism and economic autarky became the order of the day, and proposals at the peace conference and later to strengthen arrangements designed to institutionalize the international pressures of modernization were defeated. The economic depression, unprecedented in scope, was greatly intensified as a result of economic nationalism, which also obstructed all efforts to relieve the crisis through international measures.

The First World War also had the effect of undermining the influence of Europeans over other peoples and of changing the international system by introducing not only a greater number of participants but also a wider variety of interests. As societies enter the phase when integration tends to take precedence over development as a main problem, there is greater concern for international order and less interest in foreign adventures that might lead to war. The more advanced countries were reaching this stage between the two world wars, and if it had not been for the disrupting effects of the world depression, they might have avoided a second conflict. Certainly since the Second World War European societies have been much more disposed to support orderly international institutions than ever before in their history. The societies associated with this approach have been nevertheless relatively few in number.

At the end of the war a much larger group of societies, with a majority of the world's inhabitants, were still concerned with the consolidation of modernizing leadership and the early stages of economic and social development. Many faced problems of nation-building that called for the annexation of neighboring territories, the breakup of dynastic empires, and the consolidation of disparate lands. When their territorial problems are resolved, countries at this stage of development frequently adopt policies that are isolationist and autarkic, and in a variety of ways designed to protect a still fragile independence in an international environment that is perceived as hostile. Such an attitude is not conducive to a stable international order. A further category of societies, with many millions of inhabitants, has been in a position of seeking independence from foreign rule. For them international order is the greatest enemy, for their principal hope for independence lies in the troubles of the tutelary powers. The two world wars in fact led directly or indirectly to the emancipation from foreign rule of seventy societies with more than a billion inhabitants, and another forty societies, with 27 million inhabitants, are still waiting restlessly for independence.

This disorderly intermingling of levels of development and varieties of national aims is perceived by the inhabitants of these societies in terms of several conflicting ideologies. Apart from the simple juxtaposition of haves and have-nots, and of innumerable nationalisms deeply embedded in the life experience of each society, and of many subsocieties, are more rational ideologies that have a long history in political thought and that represent serious efforts to generalize and abstract from human experience. These ideologies have their origin in Western Europe; they share many assumptions and beliefs, and have a common concern for the problems of modernization; yet they incorporate fundamental differences in values and outlook that make one system antagonistic to another, and they have become so interwoven with the ways in which each society conceives of its national interest that even countries sharing the same ideology may come into violent conflict.

Political scientists would probably distinguish at least three main categories of modernizing ideologies: liberal, Marxist-Leninist, and national-statist. Such a categorization would immediately have to be hedged with conditions, however, and broken down into numerous subdivisions. Suffice it for the purposes here to note that this profusion of antagonistic and contradictory ideologies, even though they are all pursuing the same general ends, is one of the major factors making for instability in the international political system. Moreover, all of these ideologies carry a heavy burden of outmoded assumptions, and none takes into full account the realities of the modern world. Ideologies must be reasonably stable, since one of their main functions is to sustain a consensus among a wide variety of people. Yet the modern environment to which these ideologies have reference is ever changing, and they find themselves continually outstripped by events.

In a world so burdened by conflicting institutions and ideologies, order depends on a consensus among the dominant participants in the international system that the costs of disorder and instability are greater than the possible benefits. The prospects for such an agreement lie in two factors: the development of a number of major states to a point where the demand for international integration outweighs the values of isolation and opportunism, and a revolution in military technology that immeasurably enhances the costs of major wars to the point at which these are entirely disproportionate to possible benefits.

It is no doubt a truism to say that order in the international system depends on a consensus among the principal participants. Nevertheless it is instructive to recall that in the eighteenth century, and again throughout much of the nineteenth, the international order that had its headquarters in Europe was administered by a concert of powers that kept conflict within reasonable bounds. This concert was shattered by the revoutionary wars of 1792–1815, resulting from forces of change that can readily be associated with the process of modernization. The concert was then re-established, and it served the purposes of maintaining international order rather successfully until the latter part of the century. This concert of interests was weakened by the revolutions of 1848, the Crimean War, and the wars of German and Italian unification, but when Europe faced a major crisis in 1878 the forces making for consensus were still strong enough to maintain order.

From the 1880's until 1945, however, there was no comparable consensus, and Europe and the rest of the world were wracked by the greatest wars that mankind has known. It is easy to say that the values that nations hoped to gain from wars were considered greater than the expected costs, and it must be recognized that both world wars produced substantial benefits insofar as they assured the security of a majority of the participants. This balance of costs and benefits, insofar as it has been a rational calculus, is only now being affected by the development of military technology. Not until the advent of nuclear weapons, and indeed not until the perfection of delivery systems in the 1950's, did the benefits that might be derived from major international wars come to be questioned. This is not to say that the political leaders of the dominant societies have formally agreed to refrain from using nuclear weapons—although this would be a good idea if there were monitoring by an adequate inspection system—or that there are no prominent military specialists who continue to regard the use of such weapons as justifiable. It is rather that the consequences of such use are now generally recognized to be immeasurably greater than were the consequences of wars waged with conventional weapons only a decade or two ago.

By vastly increasing the costs of wars in which nuclear weapons are employed, the revolution in military technology has contributed substantially to the formation of a consensus among the dominant societies that deliberate resort to nuclear weapons should be avoided. This attitude is a significant contribution to the maintenance of international order, and there is in fact less likelihood of general war today than at any time since the late nineteenth century. It is at the same time an ironic by-product of this stabilizing tendency of nuclear weapons that local wars in which conventional weapons are employed can now be undertaken at relatively less cost than earlier and with hopes of substantial benefits. Wars in Egypt, Algeria, the Congo, Kashmir, Vietnam and elsewhere have occurred in recent years, and have been kept within reasonable limits. Indeed, to the extent that societies possessing nuclear weapons are inhibited from using them, other societies have a relatively greater military potential than would otherwise be the case. In this sense nuclear weapons, while serving as a deterrent to major wars, have created an environment in which minor wars can be undertaken with less fear of major consequences than was the case a decade or two ago.

The world today is one in which a hopeful but still precarious international order is maintained by the dominant societies, partly because they realize that their ultimate security lies on the road to international integration and partly because they fear the costs of any other road in an era of nuclear weapons. These hopes and fears find their best, if imperfect, expression in the United Nations, which through its various organs reflects the degree of accord achieved so far and the types of international functions that seem most conducive to the development of an orderly system of relations. Within this framework of order, managed by the more developed societies, a great many less developed societies—and also some that are well developed—pursue ends that assume both the necessity of destabilizing change of a local character and the possibility of undertaking minor wars that do not appear to threaten the international order or to risk escalation to nuclear weapons.

Conceptions of a Modern World

The potential destructiveness of international conflict served to stimulate thought about the general organization of the world even before nuclear weapons confronted mankind with the possibility of universal destruction. Of the various conceptions of how a modern world society is likely to emerge from the anarchy of national sovereignties, two trends of thought deserve particular attention. Both had their origin in Europe, and indeed they have much in common not only for this reason but also because they have a common point of departure and strive toward a common goal. They nevertheless envisage different paths toward this goal. One trend of thought is that prevalent since the First World War in the West European and English-speaking societies, which took the initiative in forming the League of Nations and the United Nations and which have gained much influence in many parts of the world. The other trend of thought is that of the societies that have viewed the predominance of the West European and English-speaking peoples as a threat to their independence and development. Within this second trend, the views of the communist leaders are the most fertile and enduring.

The conception of the modern world prevalent in the advanced West European and English-speaking societies has assumed their initiative in the formation of international institutions, and the transformation of the world as a result of the widespread adoption of their values and institutions. This conception has its origins in the religious and social thought that was rooted in the medieval Christian Church, and in the eighteenth and nineteenth centuries a more or less realistic view of what the world is really like began to inform these theories. It was not until the catastrophe of the First World War, however, that this trend of thought can be said to have moved from the realm of speculation to that of practice.

The view of the modern world that has its roots in the experience of advanced West European societies and their overseas heirs may be considered in terms of a theory of development, an attitude toward other societies, and a plan. The theory of development places predominant emphasis on the political aspect of human activity. Historical change is seen in terms of a gradual transition from societies where the government is the master, through stages that vary somewhat from one theorist to another, to the final establishment of governments by the peoples themselves. This conception is firmly based on a constitutional experience that is described as "Western"—incorporating as it does a considerable variety of systems—and that considers this experience to be of universal validity. In this view, "Westernization" and modernization are virtually indistinguishable.

This theory of the ineluctable development of political systems from despotism to constitutional democracy reflects a predominantly diffusionist approach to political development. This approach maintains that the central problem is the transfer to the societies defined as "non-Western" of the political institutions already developed by the West European and English-speaking societies—collectively referred to as "the West." Just as the automobile and the jet engine can be made to work equally well in England or in Yemen, in France or in the Malagasy Republic, so the conceptions of individualism, civil liberties, and parliamentary government can be transferred from England and France to these other societies and can be made to work there. The necessary condition is that the political leaders in these societies must be helped to achieve the proper degree of enlightenment. The world is divided into "Western" and "non-Western" societies, and the correct—and indeed unavoidable—course for the latter is to adopt the political institutions of the former as rapidly as possible. It is recognized that their own traditional institutions may be adaptable in some degree to the norms of the West European and

English-speaking societies, but the chief emphasis is placed on the diffusion of "Western" political institutions to these societies. It follows that the various communist and statist systems are regarded not as alternative programs of modernization, but rather as temporary aberrations on the part of societies that are either not yet ready for political freedom or have come under the influence—through domestic revolution or foreign intervention—of wrong-headed leaders.

The plan of development envisaged by this conception involves the establishment of one form or another of democratic government in each of the new states and at the same time the formation of a worldwide organization of such governments. The establishment of an approved form of democracy and the international union of these governments are apparently regarded as the ends toward which mankind is moving. Economic and social change will continue, but within the more or less fixed framework of democratic national societies. These societies are seen as traveling on parallel tracks. Though some are far behind others, they will all in due course arrive at the same destination.

There have been many variants of this approach. Some saw the League of Nations as the final parliament of man. In a similar spirit, serious students of international affairs have seen the 1960's as the time when the United Nations should be transformed into a genuine world government, with powers of taxation, legislation, regulation, and coercion. More modest advocates have been prepared to wait longer and to permit a somewhat greater diversity of patterns of development. These alternative variants nevertheless agree that the modern world will bear an essentially "Western" imprint.

Seen in the light of this Westernizing approach, political developments in the twentieth century appear in an optimistic light. Except for three communist states in Asia, all of the more than seventy states that have gained independence since the First World War can be claimed as followers of the Western democratic goal in some general sense. Even among those that have at some stage in their political development been vociferously "anti-Western"—Turkey and Iran in the 1920's, Egypt and Indonesia in the 1950's—political leaders have drawn extensively on the European radical republican model and may be said to be seeking "Western" goals despite their deviation from the correct path of development. Contemporary world politics is seen as a civil war between "West" and "East"—the latter term encompassing even greater diversity than the former—in which the West has the advantage of greater resources, greater experience, and greater proximity to the ineluctable course of political development. The challenge, from this point of view, is that some societies still have so far to go that they may be enticed by false promises of short cuts to modernity.

Communist thinking about the form that a modern world society may take has not led to such a significant achievement as the United Nations, but it has resulted in the formulation of some interesting views. If one were to ask the secretary-general of the Communist Party of the Soviet Union how he envisages the organization of the future world society, he would in all likelihood not be able to give a very detailed answer. He would nevertheless acknowledge that the creation of a world communist society was the avowed aim of his party, and he would be able to say a good deal about what needs to be done before this goal can be attained. During the 1930's and 1940's not much was said about this long-term prospect, as the immediate problems of industrialization and national defense were foremost in the minds of the Soviet leaders, but the formation of a world society was an explicit goal in the formative years of communism, and after the Second World War it again became a major subject of discussion in the Soviet Union.

This conception of a world communist society is, of course, based on the theories of Marx and Engels, but the original doctrine was particularly vague and general in regard to this question and much has been done by Lenin and his successors to elaborate with more precision the ultimate goal and the means by which it might be achieved. In its simplest theoretical form, the Soviet conception of the development toward a world society is an extension of the class struggle within individual societies. When the proletariat comes to power in all societies, according to this theory, it will be possible to fuse these societies into a single worldwide society. The theories of Marx and Engels were based primarily on a study of Britain, France, and Germany, which they considered to be the most advanced countries. They recognized the diversity of societies around the world, however, and did not have a very clear idea as to the process by which world communism would be achieved. The Soviet leaders shared this uncertainty at first, and only as the revolutionary situation came to a head in Russia did they begin to reinterpret the doctrine to meet the new circumstances and to serve their own needs. Since the communists had seized power there in 1917, the leaders now came to regard Russia as the most advanced society, hence in the forefront of what they considered to be the inevitable worldwide development toward communism.

Throughout the early years of Soviet rule, a world communist society was held up as the ultimate theoretical goal, although circumstances were not yet propitious for its creation, and it was recognized that the concrete implementation of communist doctrine must begin at home. During these early years the view that the Union of Soviet Socialist Republics was the prototype of a future World Soviet Socialist Republic, and a first step toward its realization, was stated explicitly in official documents and repeated frequently on public occasions. Not until after the Second World War, however, did circumstances begin to favor a further elaboration of this scheme. By the 1950's, with the Soviet occupation of Eastern Europe and the victory of communist leaders in China and in neighboring territories, approximately one-third of the world's population was under communist rule, although the leaders of these societies embraced a considerable variety of opinions and policies. These gains, in addition to the achievement of a rough parity between the Soviet Union and the United States in the development of nuclear weapons and the means for their delivery, brought the theoretical goal closer to realization.

Soviet leaders have in recent years discussed alternative plans of implementing their doctrines by both international and domestic means. In the international arena, despite a considerable rigidity of doctrine, they recognize in practice the diversity of the traditions and problems of the various societies. They propose to weld into as close a unity as possible those societies where the communists have already gained power, and elsewhere to assist communists in the seizure of power either directly or as partners of noncommunist leaders. It is assumed that opportunities will arise primarily in the less developed societies, and it is recognized that the advanced countries are not susceptible to communist seizure. The objective is therefore to encircle them with communist-controlled societies and thereby gradually come to dominate them.

At one time it was thought that a major war would be required to achieve this final victory, but since the advent of nuclear weapons, the emphasis has been placed instead on economic and political methods. The Soviet leaders maintain that by extending their control over world markets, they will be able to create economic chaos in the advanced societies. In the course of time this havoc is expected to result in political unrest of a character that would give the communists appropriate opportunities to seize control within these societies by subversive means. Threats of nuclear war would be alternated with propaganda favoring peace and disarmament, as a means of first cowing and then lulling the opponent. Chinese communist leaders have advanced a different conception, under which the countries of Asia, Africa, and Latin America would join forces in a worldwide revolutionary movement against the more advanced countries—by analogy with the encirclement of China's cities by Mao's rural revolutionaries. This alternative Chinese conception is limited to means, however, and does not add anything to the Marxist-Leninist view of an ultimate worldwide communist society.

At the same time, communist leaders have envisaged their essential domestic task as the industrialization of each country under communist rule along the lines pioneered by the Soviet Union. An eventual economy of abundance is foreseen, in which there would be a short working week and a full satisfaction of human needs. It is acknowledged that this goal is still a long way off, especially in Asia and Africa, and the principal effort of communist leaders is directed toward increasing production. No specific timetable for the completion of the process has been announced, but the time it would take to raise the level of production markedly in the less developed countries suggests that the goal is still distant.

The modern world society envisaged by communist theory as the ultimate goal is described only in vague, general, and often contradictory terms. On the one hand, it is recognized that a worldwide economy at a high level of production would require a great deal in the way of centralized administrative controls. On the other hand, the Marxist doctrine of the ultimate withering away of the state calls for a decentralized system. To a certain extent this contradiction can be argued away by maintaining, with Marx, that human nature changes with the system of production and that under communism man will not need to be directed. Some communists have also made the distinction between "state" and "administration," identifying the former with the organs of coercion and the latter with the various economic and social bodies that administer enterprises and institutions. One could certainly imagine a communist party, or even an association of business enterprises, trade unions, and other corporate bodies, administering a society without formal state institutions, but this would simply mean giving the state another name, since a bureaucracy with coercive powers and legal processes for adjudicating conflicts would still be necessary. The question of a world language has also given the communists a great deal of trouble, and they have argued as to whether all languages, or at least the major ones, might not eventually fuse to form a new one, or more recently whether Russian itself might not become the world language. Indeed, the more the future world society has been discussed by Russian communists in recent years, the more it has come to resemble a projection of contemporary Soviet society, with the party, working through the trade unions and other public organizations, gradually supplanting the state. The communists have in any event always recognized the importance of leadership in this future society, whether or not it takes the form of a "state," and they are intent on gaining this leadership.

The essential strength of the Soviet conception of a modern world society lies in its recognition that "modernization," as it is called here, is the central task of mankind and that one can foresee the time when technology will make possible an era of material abundance for all. Its inherent weakness is that apart from vague generalities about an ultimate utopia, it offers little more than a projection, over the entire world, of a modernized version of contemporary Soviet society, with all of its idiosyncrasies. The Soviet leaders have increased industrial production in Russia substantially, and they have modernized it in other respects as well, but they have achieved this at the highest relative human cost previously experienced by a modernizing society. They have evolved a number of institutions, such as the collectivization of agriculture and central planning, that have attracted wide interest. But when these innovations were introduced, the traditions and problems of agriculture in Russia, as well as the practices of the Russian state, were very different from those of other societies before and since.

By failing to give adequate consideration to the many diverse traditions and practices of the various societies, Soviet theory ignores reality. Even within the communist orbit, deep-seated differences have arisen between Soviet, Polish, Hungarian, and Chinese policies, and on the borders of the orbit, Yugoslavia has been evolving yet another variant of operating principles. A significant source of the influence of the Soviet system lies in its demonstration that a small group of vigorous and well-organized leaders can take a society in hand and mobilize its resources and skills for the purpose of thoroughgoing modernization. This demonstration is no doubt exciting to leaders in less developed societies who are concerned with economic and social transformation.

The strength of the conception of a modern world held in the West European and English-speaking societies lies in the high standards that they have achieved, which have in fact served as an inspiration for communist as well as for other programs of modernization. Its principal weakness lies in the fact that it has not been adequately formulated as a world view by responsible political leaders. The societies that modernized relatively early were able to adopt a pragmatic approach to their problems and did not bother to think in general terms about what they were doing. When it comes to presenting a succinct statement of their experience and its relevance to other societies, they are at something of a disadvantage as compared with a communist leadership that has gone to great trouble to conceptualize and rationalize its program. In many instances where rapid modernization is taking place with the methods and assistance of the advanced societies, the indigenous political and intellectual leaders are lacking in ideological goals and incentives.

These contrasting conceptions of the modern world are but two among numerous approaches that have been advocated. From Plato in the fourth century B.C. to K'ang Yu-wei in the nineteenth A.D., many utopian solutions to the problems of mankind have been elaborated. In the twentieth century the prospects of a future modern world are a favorite theme in fiction, philosophy, and political science. These speculations all make interesting reading, but they have not been sufficiently pragmatic to win the support necessary to the formulation of political programs.

The "Western" and "Eastern" conceptions of a modern world that have predominated in the strategy of international relations since the First World War have suffered from the ethnocentric outlook of their proponents, who have oversimplified the historical development of their own societies and have sought to apply their historical theories to the rest of the world in a doctrinaire spirit. The atmosphere of ideological controversy in which the international debate on modernization has been conducted has had the effect of giving both conceptions a greater degree of concreteness than was originally intended, and the ideological protagonists of both views have tended to portray their opponents as leaders of plots of world conquest designed for more or less immediate implementation.

Patterns of International Integration

The components of a more cosmopolitan world view are readily available, and the preliminary work has been done in many fields of scholarship, but leaders in the advanced societies have been too concerned with problems of domestic growth and with maintaining international order—and perhaps also too complacent as a result of their own levels of achievement—to devote adequate attention to the conceptualization of the worldwide task that lies ahead. Certainly much of the economic and social development in societies formerly or still under tutelage has been made possible by the technical knowledge and skilled personnel of the more advanced societies, and in many cases the scope of this assistance has increased after these societies gained independence. But this activity has not been accompanied by a conception of worldwide modernization of such a character as to make its significance generally intelligible.

It is not difficult to foresee that worldwide integration in some form is the logical ultimate consequence of the degree of interdependence already achieved by the dozen or more advanced countries. Integration at the societal level is in a sense the end of the road for modernization insofar as our present perspective permits us to envisage it. When everyone in a given society is well fed, well educated, and well provided with consumer goods, medical care, and social security, there will be nothing more to be done until some new and as yet unforeseen stimulus is available for further change of a different type. The end of this particular road is not yet in sight even for the countries that are presently the most advanced, however, for all are still at an early stage of social integration and are far from mastering its problems.

One must nevertheless consider what lies beyond this hypothetical end of the road for individual societies, for the next set of crises is in sight. Societies do not live alone, but in a world populated by 133 independent societies and about 40 that are still dependent, and it seems clear that the next crises of political modernization will be those arising from problems of international integration. This is something quite different from the national-unification movements that occurred in the United States in the eighteenth century and in Germany and Italy in the nineteenth, and that are now in progress in the Arab world, in Southeast Asia, and perhaps in sub-Saharan

Africa as well. National unification, part of the process of nation-building, normally constitutes a phase of the transfer of power from traditional to modernizing leaders. Similarly the many confederations and alliance systems known to history, including the League of Nations and the United Nations, are of a different order in that they have not involved a genuine fusion of sovereignties. The concern here is not with these, but with movements for international integration in countries already well along toward social integration at the national level. An internationally integrated union of this new type would have the attributes of a state. It would be able to tax, to enforce legislation, and to command the loyalty of its citizens. It would have something of the same relationship to its member states that the United Kingdom, the United States, the Soviet Union, Germany, Italy, and India had to their component subsocieties when they were united.

The motivation of such unions would be much the same as that which originally led to nation-building, and represents a logical continuation of the process of political modernization that is already taking place at the societal level. Chief among the motives would be the desire to promote a better environment for the welfare of their citizens in terms of economic growth—larger markets, greater availability and mobility of resources and skills—as well as more effective protection against economic and political instabilities of the existing international system.

The only union that approaches this model at present is the European Economic Community formed by France, the German Federal Republic, Italy, the Netherlands, Belgium, and Luxembourg under a treaty that went into effect on January 1, 1958. This agreement commits the signatories to a significant degree of integration over a period of twelve to fifteen years, including the elimination of all tariff barriers and a standardization of social-security systems and wage benefits. The EEC, together with the related European Atomic Energy Community and the more loosely organized Council of Europe, has established a pattern that may well define the problems that will be confronted by other integrated societies as they look for ways of extending further the benefits of modern knowledge.

In considering the problems of worldwide integration, it should be recognized that it will be well into the twenty-first century before a majority of the world's societies will have completed the main tasks of economic and social transformation and will have entered the phase of social integration. At the same time, man's knowledge of his environment, as reflected in science and its technological applications, is growing at a more rapid pace today than ever before. The potentialities of the mind are bound only by man's emotional ability to adapt knowledge to human affairs. By the twenty-first century, and perhaps long before, new changes in man's knowledge of and control over his environment of an order of magnitude comparable to the discovery of nuclear energy may well take place. In discussing the foreseeable, then, it is well to keep in mind that the unforeseeable is equally possible.

One may think of the world today, in terms of the foregoing discussion, as comprising fourteen countries with a population of some 445 million that are occupied with the problems of social integration; fifty-five or more with a population of 2,300 million that are in the phase of economic and social transformation; fifty-eight, with a population of 365 million, where modernizing leaders are still in the process of consolidating political power; and about forty territories of varying size and importance that confront the challenge of modernity under foreign tutelage, and the developmental prospects of which lie either with independence under modernizing leaders or in some form of shared sovereignty with more advanced societies.

Such a world is fraught with problems and dangers that extend into and beyond the foreseeable future. One has only to think of the violence that has accompanied the modernization of the fourteen countries that are now in the phase of social integration to imagine what lies ahead for the remaining more than 150 that still have to cope with the earlier phases. Theorists in the advanced countries often appear to assume that all should be well with the world now that their own societies appear to have regained a degree of domestic stability after the long agony of modernization. They hold the rest of the world up to standards that their own countries could never have met at a similar stage of development. Yet there is no reason to believe that the other peoples of the world should or will be able to cope with their problems with any greater skill or moderation than did those that modernized earlier. What reason is there to believe that the peoples of Asia, Latin America, and Africa will be that much more skillful than those of Europe in solving their problems or that they will be able to benefit so much from the European experience as to learn from their errors? The opportunity of the United States and Germany to observe the experience of England and France did not enable them to avoid destructive civil wars, nor did Russia profit sufficiently from the experience of more advanced societies to prevent some of the most violent domestic convulsions that modern history has known. The Christian peoples have certainly been among the most ruthless in their treatment of one another and of peoples of other faiths, and the greatest wars of modern times have been generated within the orbit of their influence, but it remains to be seen whether the peoples of other faiths will be more humane when they face the hard choices posed by modernization. The burden of demonstrating that the world will be less violent in the second half of the twentieth century than in the first half lies with those who believe that 2.8 billion people can modernize in relative comfort because 445 million have reached the relatively and perhaps only temporarily safe haven of social integration.

The functions of modernity are of universal validity, and all societies may be expected to achieve political consolidation, economic growth, social mobilization, and psychological adjustment, but each society has a separate problem either of adapting its own institutions to these functions or of adopting institutions developed by societies that modernized earlier. The institutions of the West European and English-speaking·societies have evolved from a feudalism that encouraged individualism and local initiative and enterprise, and they drew on vast resources. Their institutions cannot be transferred except in a restricted sense to societies that do not share these traditions and resources. Even in India and Pakistan, where the ruling groups have absorbed British culture to a significant degree, it remains to be seen how much of this influence will remain after 50 to 100 million, and ultimately 300 to 400 million, peasants with diverse and very un-British local traditions have become urban workers and salaried officials a few generations from now.

Similarly the Soviet system, despite the concern of Marxist-Leninist doctrine with the universal characteristics of economic and social change, is based on traditions and resources of a special type. The Soviet leaders inherited from tsarist times a tradition of centralized political controls matched by few countries in the world. They also enjoyed agricultural wealth, bounteous by the standards of all but the West European and English-speaking countries, which enabled them to finance with little foreign aid, but with a high human cost, a program of rapid economic growth and social change. No other communist country, however, has been successful in following the Soviet pattern of modernization in detail. Communist governments share some important features—the monopoly of political power by the Communist party, the control of property used for production directly by ownership rather than indirectly by legislation, and a mobilizational style of development that is inclined to run roughshod over human obstacles. Yet the substance of policy—the manner in which capital is accumulated and allocated, the means of controlling agriculture, the organization of management and labor, and the pace and emphases of development—varies considerably from one communist country to another.

Societies can learn much from one another, and there are many instances where it may be easier to adopt the institutions of more modern countries than to adapt native institutions to modern functions. The less institutions are concerned with values and beliefs, and conversely the more they are concerned with technology, the more easily they can be transferred. The process of adaptation itself, however, involves the very type of difficult choice and the challenge to traditional values and interests that in the more advanced societies have been the major sources of violence. Consequently in each of the eighty-five societies that are still facing the challenge of modernity in a traditional setting or are involved in the transfer of political power from traditional to modernizing leaders, one may expect political revolutions and other forms of domestic unrest in the foreseeable future. Even in the more than fifty societies that are now in the phase of economic and social transformation, one must anticipate the same range of domestic disturbances that in the latter half of the nineteenth century and the first half of the twentieth afflicted the societies that are now the most advanced.

Modernization entails the extension from the minority of more advanced peoples of the world to the majority of less advanced not only the opportunity to achieve a higher level of development but also all of the problems the former have encountered in attaining this level. The extension of this agony into the foreseeable future and beyond is further prolonged by the fact that the less advanced societies today are developing at a less rapid pace per capita than the more developed. Population is growing more rapidly than production in many of the less developed societies, and in the first half of the twentieth century the gap between the more advanced and the less advanced grew wider. There is some evidence that this trend changed in the 1950's with respect to such indexes of development as literacy and urbanization, but this is still a matter of dispute among specialists. Not until population growth is brought under control are the less advanced societies likely to start on the long road of per capita growth that may enable them to keep pace with the more advanced.

The pattern of the future development of mankind that is suggested by the available evidence is one that may be envisaged in terms of three distinct but interrelated and to some extent contradictory processes. The first is the transition of the more than 170 independent and dependent societies of the world from a traditional to a modern way of life, culminating so far as one can now foresee in a high degree of social integration. The analysis of this process has been the principal concern of this study, and in worldwide terms it is still at a relatively early stage of development. Each society as it modernizes tends to become more dependent on the others by virtue of the universality of modern knowledge, the growth of international trade, the migration of peoples and of capital, and the myriad of ways in which modernizing societies become increasingly interdependent. The very process of modernization within societies tends to foster international integration without the assistance of formal outside institutions.

The second process, already under way, is the development of several relatively highly integrated regions that may serve as intermediate focuses for international integration. The United States, the European Economic Community, and the system of states organized by the Soviet Union represent alternative prototypes for such regional groupings, and the Commonwealth under British leadership and Japan in Asia may possibly play similar roles. These major regions are investing large sums in other parts of the world and are drawing the ablest individuals from less developed societies to their universities. For individuals desiring education and careers, the bonds of nationalism have not proved to be very strong. The type of integration fostered by these regional centers is not primarily one of political federalism but more one of the integration of resources and skills.

The precedent that suggests this pattern is the way in which the individual more advanced societies have integrated. The component regions of the United Kingdom as they existed a century or more ago have not advanced at an equal pace; nor have the ninety departments of France; or the fifty component states of the United States; or the fifteen republics, comprising twenty autonomous republics, eight autonomous regions, and ten national areas of the Soviet Union. These various component regions and polities have retained some of their local characteristics and in some instances a degree of sovereignty, but substantive integration in these countries has centered around the major metropolitan areas—the megalopolises in which many millions of inhabitants are concentrated in clusters of great cities and constellations of suburbs.

Seen in terms of modernization, these regional nuclei are not merely or even primarily centers of political power, but rather centers of economic and social development that tend to attract to themselves the resources and skills of others. These need not be contiguous blocs of development, but may form a checkerboard pattern or may overlap and interpenetrate one another in a variety of ways—as do the influences of London, Birmingham, and Glasgow; Paris, Brussels, and the cities of the Rhine valley; New York, Chicago, and Philadelphia; and Moscow, Leningrad, and Kiev.

The third concurrent process is integration through the agency of international institutions, which the societies of the world create and to the decisions of which they are prepared to submit. Many international organizations already exist that perform functions assigned to them by member states, and in specialized fields that do not threaten national sovereignties they have achieved substantial results. The United Nations coordinates the most important of these international agencies, and it also serves as the principal instrumentality for the negotiation of matters affecting international security on a worldwide basis. The limited degree of international consensus so far achieved by the United Nations may be explained by the diversity in traditional cultures and in resources and skills of its members. It is significant that the United Nations has achieved as much as it has under the circumstances and that its leading officers have been able to master the inherent difficulties of their task at least to this limited extent.

These three concurrent processes of development—national, regional, and international—are all tending toward an interdependence among politically organized societies and toward an ultimate integration of societies. Although the eventual outcome of each process is the same, they are in significant respects contradictory. The national states, even though they will all eventually reach a degree of domestic integration that will call for closer interrelationships with other societies, will resist both regional and international pressures as long as they are primarily concerned with the consolidation of modernizing leadership and with economic and social transformation. The extent to which individual societies have the capability of undertaking a thoroughgoing transformation within the confines of their own national sovereignties varies a great deal. Nevertheless national states are the only agencies available to undertake many essential features of this process, and to this extent they will tend to oppose initiative by regional and international agencies.

There is likewise a fundamental antagonism between regional and international sources of leadership. The regional have the advantage of a common or dominant institutional heritage and also of a degree of integration not possible in an organization that includes all societies as members. International organizations that are genuinely worldwide in scope must embrace such a variety of institutional heritages and levels of development that the common denominator of agreed policies is likely to be low. For this reason organizational activities based on a worldwide membership are limited primarily to the functions of communication and commerce. The management of more sophisticated problems of worldwide import, such as the control of nuclear testing and the policing of outer space, is in fact the responsibility of the few societies that are capable of participating in these activities.

It is too early to say whether the national, the regional, or the international process will predominate in the eventual formation of an integrated world society. The available evidence would lead one to expect that the regional initiatives that have already gained significant headway are likely to be the principal agencies of international integration until such time as the societies with a majority of the world's inhabitants achieve a level of development that will permit them to participate in international agencies as effectively as those that are now advanced. It is in fact by no means certain that the less advanced will ever catch up with the more advanced, and international agencies may eventually predominate only with the support of one or more regional groupings. The available evidence would also seem to indicate that the conflict between national, regional, and international sources of leadership, as well as among the individual societies, will pose profound and frequently unprecedented problems of policy. It will take skillful leadership to negotiate these problems of policy in the generations ahead, and the decisions will have to be made under circumstances in which the cost of failure may well be widespread destruction by nuclear weapons.

6. Modernization and Policy

History and Policy

Man is not a captive of history, despite the undeniable persistence of historically evolved traditions, and at many critical stages individual or group leadership has been dramatic. It is not so much a question of the accelerating or delaying effect that leaders may exert on the adoption of modern ideas and standards, but rather of the strong imprint that they stamp on the manner in which change takes place. Ideologies are the products of individual minds, and the character of the policies of modernization adopted and the way that they are implemented depend to a considerable degree on leadership. Leaders are limited by their own origins and by the skills and resources at their command, but within these limits differences of vital significance depend on the particular policies adopted.

The same principles of leadership that apply within societies are applicable to leadership among societies. The influence of one society on another—whether by persuasion or by coercion—may counteract decisively both the traditional ideas and institutions of that society and the influence of its own leaders, however wide their following. The knowledge and functions characteristic of the modern era are diffused through the impact of one society on another as well as through the independent development of domestic processes, and a vigorous modernizing society with imaginative leaders may be able, by its successful example alone, to exert a dominant influence on the course of modernization in other societies and generally throughout the world. In thinking about the process of modernization, one must take into consideration not only its universal characteristics, and the fundamental differences in the traditional ideas and institutions of the diverse politically organized societies, but also the vital importance of leadership, both within and among societies, in determining the policies under which traditional institutions are adapted to modern functions.

It is possible to describe processes of change without a deep commitment to values other than those of an objectivity that seeks to examine a subject from all points of view, and with a balance and perspective that correspond as closely as possible to the reality that is perceived by means of a consideration of the available evidence. Indeed, a personal involvement beyond this rather neutral stance would tend to distort the perspective and place a correspondingly greater burden on the reader to take into account the principles of selection used in consulting the evidence and evaluating alternative options.

In writing about policy, on the other hand, one is concerned not with what has happened or what is likely to happen, but with what should happen and what one should do about it within a given framework of perceived reality. To do this one must take sides. The outlook that informs the following remarks maintains that one should distinguish between those institutional changes that are essential to the process of modernization and those that are not; that problems of institutional change must in the last analysis be resolved in terms of the inherited culture of each society, but that the experience of other societies should be drawn upon to the greatest extent possible; and that a reduction of the human costs imposed by violence and disruption should be given the highest consideration in determining policies of modernization.

The role of historical analysis as a guide to the future is essentially one of determining the dimensions of the problems that are likely to engage policy. The pitfalls of the historical perspective as a guide to policy are many. Past trends can be projected without adequate provision for continuing change. Projections may be made on too narrow a basis of past experience, and the range of possible alternatives may be constricted by an often unconscious ethnocentric screening. Predictions based on historical experience are frequently too specific to be valid, for a particular constellation of problems and personalities can never be foreseen.

At the same time, it should be recognized that the entire framework of ideas and institutions is a product of historical development. By far the largest number of factors in any given situation can be accounted for by earlier history rather than by the more recent. Things do not change overnight, and the current circumstances, however different from those of the past, are capable of only a gradual effect on the accumulated experience of mankind. Assuming only a modest understanding of this accumulated experience, one can foresee developments within useful limits. At the very least, an understanding of history should help one to ascertain those changes that are likely to take place regardless of policy, those that are likely to be achieved—if at all—only at enormous human cost, and the range of choices within which policy can operate on the basis of acceptable costs.

The Dimensions of Diversity

The headlong race in which mankind is engaged toward a modernity that is still only dimly perceived has inspired many leaders with a sense of momentum that grossly oversimplifies the inherent problems of adaptation and hence exaggerates the rate at which the process can be expected to develop. This misconception underlies the ruthless and sweeping character of many modernizing policies that appear to seek the transformation of societies within a single lifetime.

Instant modernization is not within the realm of possibility. England faces serious problems after two centuries of modernizing leadership. The United States rates 15 to 20 percent of its citizens as poor—by relatively high standards, to be sure—after many generations of intensive effort at economic growth on the part of a people rich beyond compare in resources and skills. The substantial achievements of the Soviet Union since 1928 are the product of a society with a record of industrial achievement dating from the eighteenth century, and one that enjoyed one of the highest industrial growth rates in the world by the 1890's. Japan's noteworthy attainments in literacy, education, and technology have developed from a base of extensive literacy, a secular literature and philosophy, and a sizable book-publishing business that can be traced back to the seventeenth century. The later-modernizing societies may do better, with the examples and assistance of those that are more advanced. Yet many of them are today less generously endowed in resources and skills than were the earlier-modernizing societies in the seventeenth and eighteenth centuries. It is by no means certain that the knowledge available today is adequate to overcome this gap within the foreseeable future.

The levels of achievement of which diverse societies are capable vary depending on the particular aspect in question. Industrial production can grow by leaps and bounds, the resources of skilled personnel can be increased rapidly, and illiteracy can be substantially reduced in a generation or two. Other aspects of a society, however, change more slowly. The transfer of the economically active population from agricultural to industrial pursuits rarely proceeds at a pace as rapid as 1 percent per year over long periods. Standards of living often undergo a decline before they begin to benefit from the mechanization of labor. The adaptation of popular beliefs, values, and behavior patterns to the insights of modern knowledge is even slower, and the means of mass communication are as efficient in sustaining the traditional as in disseminating the modern. Even if one wished to take a relatively optimistic view, which would not be easy to justify on the basis of the available evidence, one would have to recognize that it will be a great many decades before even China and India, let alone the less developed societies, achieve the level of development per capita of the more advanced societies today.

In considering the prospects for an ultimate modern world society, it must be recognized that historical experience has not yet provided any very satisfactory evidence as to the form that such a society may eventually take. Only a minority of the world's population lives in societies that have achieved even a modest level of well-being, and the experience of this minority is sufficiently varied to warrant the greatest caution in making predictions. Modernization is a continuing process of the utmost complexity, and the assumption that the specific institutions developed so far by the societies that were the first to modernize will in due course be adopted by all other societies —a belief widely held in advanced societies a generation ago—has not been borne out by experience.

What should be of concern to policy is not the unforeseeable future, but rather the more immediate future, the problems of which will be a foreseeable extension of those of today. Even in thinking about this more immediate future, one cannot very well predict the specific issues that will arise or the form that they will take. The only certainty is that the problems raised by modernization are ineluctable. They will take different forms in each society. They will involve, especially for the more advanced societies, difficult choices as to the relativity of values. The institutional pattern of any one society cannot serve as a model for others except in a general sense. Each society must to a considerable extent work out its own solutions.

In comparing modernizing societies, one is struck by the fact that the great diversities in their achievements are due more to their traditional heritage of institutions than to policies of modernizing leadership. There are no doubt dramatic cases of failure to mobilize substantial skills and resources—Salazar in Portugal, Sukarno in Indonesia, and Castro in Cuba are a few instances among many; and of success in making much of meager resources—Switzerland, Norway, Japan, Finland, Turkey; but these are exceptions. One may regret the former cases and commend the latter, but the allocation of censure and praise should be made with due recognition of the complexity of the processes involved and of the humility demanded by our relative ignorance in these matters. Most of the societies that are vigorous and prosperous under modern conditions enjoyed a substantial degree of vigor and prosperity before they took advantage of the opportunities offered by modern knowledge.

Policies of modernization should recognize, at the very least, the profound importance that historically evolved institutions have had in the societies with a substantial modernizing experience. It would be difficult to imagine the British parliamentary system out of the context of the long evolution of the relations between king, lords, and commoners. The constitution of the United States has deep roots in the seventeenth and eighteenth centuries; indeed, some would maintain that it has not kept up with the times. The Soviet political system owes much to a tradition of autocracy that can be traced to the centralizing efforts of the grand dukes of Muscovy. The pattern of elite leadership in Japan has arisen from a long history of relationships within the traditional hierarchy of roles.

Societies that are today at an earlier stage of development have traditional institutions that are likewise firmly embedded, and they will have a profound effect on the form that these societies' modern institutions eventually take. It is often assumed that the later a society undertakes the process of modernization, the greater will be the impact on its institutions of the models represented by the societies that modernized earlier. It is by no means certain that this will be the case in those areas of activity involving the values and loyalties of the great bulk of the population. Frequently the first generation of leaders in new states, more often than not educated in a more modern society, comes to office under the powerful influence of foreign models. Within a generation, however, a much larger group of domestically educated leaders emerges from the peasant population and dilutes this earlier trend with an upsurge of nativist values and attitudes. Even if the influence of foreign models in these areas should prove to be extensive, a significant continuing role remains for the adaptation of native traditional institutions to modern functions. It is often as difficult for policy-makers to accept the possibility that diverse programs of modernization may be equally viable in their respective environments as for religious leaders to accept the validity of other faiths, and it is as necessary.

Societies should be judged by the substance of their modernizing policies and by their success in bringing the benefits of modern knowledge to bear on their political, economic, and social problems at a reasonable human cost, rather than by their labels. There are political leaders that call themselves conservative, or nationalist, or democratic, or liberal, or socialist, or communist who have been relatively successful in these respects. Others bearing the same labels have committed excesses in the belief that they are advancing human welfare. When military regimes come to power in new states, they do so more often than not because the army officers are among the best-trained bureaucrats available, and they should be judged by their performance. The distinction between civilian and military spheres of authority, a vital principle of sound administration in the more advanced countries, is not relevant in new states where a well-trained civil servant is a rarity and where the primary role of armies is administrative rather than military.

In the vocabulary of political scientists China and India are worlds apart, but in the context of comparative modernization they are close in level of achievement and rate of development. There are many dramatic contrasts in the institutional structures of Russia and Japan and in their political development during the past century, but in terms of per capita levels of achievement they have covered much the same range and today occupy about the same rank in the hierarchy of modernizing societies. The universals of the modern era are the common and growing store of knowledge and the functional achievements that it makes possible; but, as noted earlier, the institutional means by which these achievements are implemented are likely to be as diverse as the historical experience of the societies concerned.

The functional requirements of many aspects of human activity are doubtless much the same all over the world, and it is useful to study and record these uniformities. The same can also be said of individuals. It is nevertheless the diversities that extend beyond these uniformities that should command the attention of scholars and enlist the sympathy of policy-makers. Those who seek to correlate democratic government (or any other institution involving societywide participation) with gross national product per capita, literacy, or urbanization, for example, tend to neglect the most vital factors in the viability of institutions. A central problem of later-modernizing societies is the adaptation of foreign models to their own needs, customs, and capabilities. Policy-makers, in turn, must distinguish between the functional goals these societies are seeking to achieve, in regard to which policy must be firm, and the institutional means for achieving them, which must be flexible within an acceptable range of human costs. There is doubtless an interdependence of ends and means in the realm of values, but this interdependence can be sustained under a wide variety of institutional arrangements.

The Dimensions of Instability

The situations faced by modernizing societies are universal, even though the solutions will more often than not be unique for each society. No problem is more general than that of the transfer of political power from traditional to modernizing leaders, and the instability and not infrequently the violence that accompany this process confront policy-makers with some of their most difficult choices. The advanced societies have all passed through periods of profound instability, but once they have achieved a relative degree of law and order, they tend to regard revolution elsewhere as an unjustified disturbance of the peace. Political modernization need not be associated with extensive violence. There are striking instances of societies making this transition without general outbreaks of internal war. Canada, Australia, and New Zealand have developed in a relatively stable fashion. Japan's domestic development, in contrast to its relations with its neighbors, has been more stable than most. Yet in the great majority of cases political, economic, and social development has been accompanied by civil wars, wars of liberation and unification, and domestic violence in many forms. Not only have major revolutions and civil wars marked the decisive stages of political development—those of England, the United States, France, Russia, and China are only the best publicized among many—but there have also been innumerable minor wars, revolts, and disturbances before, during, and after the basic transition from traditional to modernizing leadership. Even today few governments are so stable that they can claim with assurance to be immune to domestic violence of one type or another for the foreseeable future.

Less dramatic than the revolutions and civil wars have been the various forms of breakdown, stagnation, or atavism that have overtaken societies that seemed to be developing in a manner generally believed to be "normal" by the standards of those that modernized earlier. Doubtless the most dramatic case is that of Nazi Germany, where a society that prided itself on its rationalization of economic and social institutions came under the domination of leaders inspired by antimodern conceptions. In Portugal political leaders have held the country back to a point where one has to search among the less developed countries of Latin America to find an equivalent economic and social level. Other countries have developed fitfully, alternating between periods of purposeful activity and of frustrating confusion. These various forms of dysfunction may be attributed to many circumstances. In Germany a combination of defeat, economic depression, and poor judgment undermined the authority of modern-minded leaders. In Portugal, and in other countries as well, men and interest groups of limited vision have gained a stranglehold on political power. In many Latin American countries a European-oriented elite has sought to preserve its monopoly of power from the influence of the Indians and mestizos by restricting economic and social development. The road to modernity is strewn with wrecks and skeletons.

One must anticipate that in the normal course of development there will be prolonged instability in many parts of the world in the generations ahead. Whether it is the struggle between forces of tradition and modernity or between rival programs of development, violence in many forms will be difficult to avoid. It is possible that some societies will receive such skillful guidance from a tutelary society or from the specialized agencies of the United Nations that they will be able to make a transition as great as that from tribalism to a modern bureaucratic state without a serious upheaval. It is more likely that there will be ten to fifteen revolutions a year for the foreseeable future in the less developed societies, in addition to the many forms of domestic strife in the societies that are more developed. If this is not optimistic, it is at least "normal" by the standards established by the evidence available. The task of policy-makers in the more advanced countries is not to prevent revolutions. This is no more possible than it is desirable. Their task is to guide these revolutions in a manner conducive both to successful development at a relatively modest human cost and to the maintenance of international order.

In contemplating the alternatives open to them in the light of this rather dismal prospect, policy-makers in the more advanced and successful countries must recognize that their power to effect change in other countries is not unlimited. It should be acknowledged that these forms of instability are more likely than not to occur, and that they depend on interrelationships of leaders and interest groups within these societies that one would have great difficulty in influencing even with a full-fledged army of occupation. The central concern of policy is not to score a success in imposing institutions on new societies. It is rather to establish reasonable functional standards and maintain workable forms of encouragement and restraint that will serve to influence leadership in the direction of political, economic, and social development at an acceptable human cost. Restraint should never be carried so far as the severance of relations or, at the other extreme, the establishment of an exclusive or satellite relationship. Both policies tend to reduce the possibility of exerting influence, the former by withdrawing too far from the scene of action and the latter by becoming too involved with the interests of the client.

The dilemma that policy-makers face in deciding whether or not to participate in or at least to condone political violence raises a vital question of the relativity of values. It would certainly be unreasonable to judge all societies in terms of the values of those that are the most advanced, but to what extent can their principles be compromised? One must make a distinction here between the relative and the absolute. What is relative is the pattern of traditional ideas and institutions that diverse societies have evolved through the ages, and the different stages of development at which they find themselves. What is absolute is the level of functional achievement that the more advanced societies have attained. One cannot expect societies with diverse traditions and at different levels of development to adopt modern ideas and institutions in the same form as they have been evolved by the advanced societies. It is nevertheless the responsibility of the more advanced societies to make certain that, insofar as their influence can prevail, the policies adopted by the less developed societies will be as humane as possible in any given set of circumstances. There is no formula that will permit one to decide in advance what policy is most conducive to human dignity in any specific situation, for there is no substitute for judgment in these matters. What can safely be predicted, however, is that if the leaders of the advanced societies do not exert their influence to the maximum of their ability, the initiative will pass to the advocates of less humane policies, and that these policies will eventually threaten to engulf not only the newly modernizing societies but the advanced societies as well.

The Bases of International Action

The transcendant problem confronting statesmanship in the modern era is that of guiding the societies of the world in their slow but ineluctable struggle toward worldwide integration. This process is slow because of the adjustments necessitated by the diversity of institutions and policies of modernization among the societies of the world and by the profound domestic instability that will characterize a majority of the world's societies for the foreseeable future. It is nevertheless inevitable because the growth of knowledge is creating functional capabilities that can be realized only by the worldwide organization of mankind.

No doubt the most obvious problem confronting policy-makers concerned with international integration is the question of where to start. Although political integration in some form will ultimately have to be worked out if mankind is to survive, it is clearly the end product and not the starting point of this process. At the present stage of political development only the most advanced societies can contemplate a significant degree of integration with one another, and the experience of the European efforts at integration will serve as a useful primer of the tribulations that confront this enterprise. Societies still coping with the problems of political consolidation under modernizing leaders and of economic and social transformation are much too insecure in their domestic relationships to undertake the sharing of their problems that even a limited degree of integration would involve. It will be many decades before societies embracing a majority of the world's peoples will be prepared to engage in a significant degree of political integration.

The United Nations provides a framework for discussion of and experimentation with elementary problems of international cooperation, but it does not in itself represent an effort at integration. Indeed, it is expressly denied by its own charter the right to intervene in the domestic affairs of member states except in situations judged by the Security Council to endanger international peace and security. This restraint on the United Nations is entirely proper at this stage in the world's development, for the investment of any greater authority in the international organization would not be acceptable to its members.

World trade is expanding rapidly in the second half of the twentieth century, perhaps as rapidly as domestic trade, but the economic relations among states have not yet reached a point where an integrated worldwide economic system is required. The existing national economic systems are flexible enough to maintain the type of international relations necessary for their survival and growth, and a world economy based on discrete national systems still offers vast resources for expansion without resort to institutional change. In the economic sphere as in the political, it is only the few relatively advanced countries, and especially the medium-sized and small ones, that have found some degree of economic integration necessary to sustained growth.

The pressure of political and economic forces in the latter part of the twentieth century will continue to work for division rather than for community at the international level, if only because the great majority of societies do not yet have either the systemic need or the capability to enter into integrative relationships with other societies. The necessity for a consideration of the worldwide organization of mankind comes not from the immediate political or economic needs of the member states but from their security needs. If it were not for the existence of nuclear weapons, the peoples of the world would be able to survive further international wars on their road to integration. It is ironic that the pressing need for some kind of worldwide organization should come at a time when the great majority of the world's population lives in societies that are still in the early throes of modernization and are unprepared for any significant degree of integration, but the threat of worldwide annihilation is sufficiently clear to require decisive action.

The spheres where such action is called for by policy-makers in the more advanced societies are those concerned with the regulation of nuclear weapons, the neutralization of states and strategic areas that might become sources of conflict, and the management of modernizing revolutions in cases where they threaten to upset the existing relations among major powers.

A significant first step in the regulation of nuclear weapons was the partial test-ban treaty agreed to in 1963 by Great Britain, the Soviet Union, and the United States, and signed by more than ninety other states. In the same year further Soviet-American agreements not to place nuclear weapons in space, and to establish a direct line of communication between the Kremlin and the White House, served to nourish the hope that more substantial achievements were possible. These agreements nevertheless represent only a small beginning, and the fate of the world still depends essentially on the self-restraint of American and Soviet leadership. This is not a solid, long-term basis for the survival of mankind. Closely related to international security is the regulation of man's activities in outer space and the restriction of these activities to peaceful uses. It cannot be said that much progress has yet been made in this direction.

The neutralization of states and strategic areas likewise has precedents in recent history that could serve as a guide to action. The neutralization under international guarantees of Switzerland (since 1815) and Belgium (1815–1914) are the leading historical examples of this approach, and Germany's violation of Belgian neutrality in 1914 served to emphasize not the fragility of such arrangements but the consequences of their violation. In the more recent period, the self-neutralization of Austria in 1955 and the neutralization of Laos in 1962 under the guarantee of thirteen states—including China, France, the Soviet Union, the United Kingdom, and the United States—have permitted a relaxation of international tensions in regard to these two countries. This method has also been useful in the case of strategic areas under dispute, such as the Åland Islands (since 1856), Tangiers (1923–1957), and Trieste (1947–1954). In 1959 twelve states with interests in the Antarctic agreed to the neutralization and demilitarization of that region.

Neutralization has worked best in regard to nations and areas that lack substantial power in themselves, but that are considered to be a source of conflict for geographical and strategic reasons. It has proved difficult to extend this principle to larger and more complex regions. Almost two hundred plans were advanced in the first fifteen years after the Second World War for the neutralization of various parts of Europe, but none met with general acceptance. In every case one or more of the interested states came to the conclusion that its security would be less well served by such plans than under the status quo. Such proposals nevertheless deserve continuing study, for political forces are fluid and adjustments that seem impossible at one stage may be feasible at another. Analogous proposals may also find successful application in other parts of the world. The international problems that center on Kashmir, Cuba, Taiwan, and the countries of Southeast Asia might be more amenable to solution under some form of neutralization.

The management of modernizing revolutions is a much more difficult task, for it concerns the very distribution of power in the world that the major nuclear states regard as an essential factor in their security. In every case of revolution the domestic forces involved are likely to have close ties with one or another of the major powers. A victory for one is regarded as a defeat for the other, and many victories for one might lead to a vital shift in the international balance of power that would be perceived as affecting the security of the loser. In the past, nations have resorted to violence to prevent such losses; both world wars arose out of just such situations. In recent years revolutions in Egypt, Hungary, Cuba, the Congo, Laos, and Cyprus have led to crises that have threatened world peace, and in Korea and Vietnam wars of ominous proportions have developed.

Such revolutions confront policy-makers in the more advanced countries with difficult dilemmas. If the revolutions are moderate in their methods and do not become a source of international conflict, they should be allowed to run their course. If they threaten the security of other states, however, and seem likely to become a major international issue, then it is incumbent upon other states to seek to bring them under control. Extensive violence and international conflict are not essential to modernization, even though they have more often than not accompanied it, and in an age of nuclear weapons it is the better part of wisdom to circumscribe the violence before it gets out of control. This can best be done by means of international intervention, and in Palestine, the Congo, and Cyprus such intervention has brought dangerous situations under control without stifling the forces working for vigorous change. Even where international intervention has been undertaken under conditions of great violence, as in the case of Korea, there is good reason to believe that the violence would ultimately have been much greater had there been no intervention. Multilateral intervention to control revolutions is preferable to unilateral, but unilateral intervention is better than no intervention at all if the alternative is a widening of the area of conflict. The decision to intervene must often be taken on short notice, and a reliable estimate of a revolutionary situation may not be available until the time for action has passed. The ultimate criterion for evaluating a decision to intervene is whether intervention will tend to widen or confine the area of conflict. Nevertheless one state intervenes militarily in the affairs of another only at great risk, and a unilateral intervention should be internationalized as soon as possible.

The Formation of an International Consensus

The immediate concrete steps that can be taken on a worldwide scale to safeguard mankind are not many, and they are chiefly in the realm of international security, but meanwhile much can be done toward the creation of an international consensus regarding the common interests of mankind at this stage. The solution of specific problems will require generations of patient work, but the elaboration of a mature understanding of the nature and interrelationship of these problems can be evolved much more rapidly. Political leaders around the world cannot be expected to initiate dramatic changes in the course of human development, but if they are to avoid the type of conflict that can become catastrophic in the nuclear age, they must achieve a consensus regarding the fundamental bases of international order in a changing world.

The United Nations, despite its many shortcomings, is making a fundamental contribution to the establishment of such a consensus. Through the General Assembly in particular, a sense of the common interests of mankind has been created and worldwide standards of action have been elaborated. The Declaration of Human Rights and other statements of principle have served to establish the authority of worldwide values and attitudes in a manner and to a degree that would not otherwise have been possible. The General Assembly has also served as a mediator between larger and smaller states, between early modernizers and late modernizers, and thereby helped to bridge differences that might otherwise present much greater obstacles to understanding. Although the authority of the General Assembly is backed only in exceptional cases by instruments of coercion, it has achieved a significant degree of reality on the basis of a widely recognized need for values and norms that are universal in their application.

The beginnings of an international consensus are also being established on a functional basis, where specific needs and interests often provide deeper roots for an international outlook than do the more general concerns of world politics. The ecumenical movement in the Christian churches has lowered many barriers to understanding. Important branches of manufacturing and commerce have found it necessary to adopt a cosmopolitan outlook. The implementation of large enterprises in the realm of technology, such as the modification of climate and the exploration of outer space, has served as the basis for proposals of international cooperation. The continued search for truth through exploration of man's environment, in the many fields of learning in which it is now being carried on, is likewise conducive to the formation of cosmopolitan standards in many realms of value.

Leadership in the establishment of an international consensus consists not only of issuing declarations and formulating proposals, although these are important, but also in mobilizing domestic sources of support for measures deemed to be essential for the welfare of mankind. In international affairs as in national, the preoccupation with local concerns, interests, and values is the most resistant, as well as the most natural, barrier to be overcome. It is here that leadership is most difficult, for it must challenge the very sources of support on which the authority of leadership is based. Values and norms at the local level can be changed only slowly, through education, both in the abstractions conveyed through teaching, textbooks, and other means of communication and in the concrete form of practical demonstrations of the relationship between international and local welfare.

The problems of worldwide concern that will confront leaders in the years ahead may be seen in terms of adapting diverse traditional institutions to modern functions, managing the continuing instability that will accompany development, establishing the bases of international action, and forming an international consensus. Underlying these main concerns is a dimension of change unprecedented in human experience, which threatens all accepted values and undermines the delicate balance between the patterns of accepted behavior that make for stability and the demands and opportunities provided by an ever-growing knowledge.

The fundamental challenge for the foreseeable future is to the ingenuity of leaders everywhere. They must find the means of adapting the universal imperatives of modern ideas and institutions to the diverse traditions of the various societies, within the framework of an international system that will provide at least a safeguard against widespread destruction. If a stage should eventually be reached at which the various societies are so homogeneous as to be capable of forming a single world state, it will be easy enough to work out the necessary institutional arrangements. In the many generations that lie ahead before this will be possible, mankind faces innumerable problems that will test its ingenuity to the utmost. Leadership in determining the form that a modern world may take will go to that society or group of societies which proves to be most successful in analyzing and resolving these problems.

The Study of Modernization:
A Bibliographical Essay

Varieties of World History

Historians and other scholars concerned with man and his development have not been very successful in treating the problems of mankind as a whole, even though we live in an age in which technology has brought an unprecedented physical unity to mankind on a planet that can now be encircled in a few hours by men and women in outer-space vehicles. This is due in part to the magnitude of the task, in part to the lack of adequate sources and secondary works on many vital subjects, and in part to the education and outlook of the scholars themselves. History has customarily been local, dynastic, and national in outlook, and its practitioners have only recently come to think in broader terms. It is only in the past generation or two that the attempt has been made to write histories of modern Europe, as distinct from compilations of the histories of individual countries, and these attempts have been made primarily by non-Europeans.

It is easier to define what a history of mankind in its totality should not be than what it should be, for there are many examples of what one should avoid. It should certainly not be the histories of all the countries of the world laid end to end, after being divided up into appropriate periods. This approach is characteristic of the long line of world histories that have been written since the eighteenth century. They are useful insofar as they provide a panorama of separate peoples and epochs that serves to dramatize the variety of human experience, but they contribute little to an

175

understanding of this experience. Even the major world histories written by professional historians under the impact of the First World War—such as the *Peoples et civilisations* series (20 vols., 1926–46), edited by Louis Halphen and Philippe Sagnac; the *Propyläen Weltgeschichte* (10 vols., 1929–33), edited by Walter Goetz; and the briefer *Weltgeschichte: Völker, Männer, Ideen* (2 vols., 1939), by Veit Valentin—limited their generalizations to individual geographical regions and chronological periods.

The authors and editors of the principal academic histories of the world published after the Second World War—such as *Les grands courants de l'histoire universelle* (7 vols., 1945–56), by Jacques Pirenne; the *Historia Mundi* (10 vols., 1952–61), edited by Fritz Kern and Fritz Valjavec; the *Histoire général des civilisations* (7 vols., 1952–57), edited by Maurice Crouzet; the *Weltgeschichte der neuesten Zeit* (3 vols., 1951–60), by J. R. von Salis; the *New Cambridge Modern History* (12 vols., 1957–), edited by an advisory committee headed by G. N. Clark; the *Destins du Monde* collection (13 vols., 1957–), edited by Lucien Febvre and Fernand Braudel; the new version of the *Propyläen Weltgeschichte* (10 vols., 1961), edited by Golo Mann and Alfred Heuss; and the multivolume *History of Human Society* (1965–), edited by J. H. Plumb—have likewise not seen it as their task to generalize about mankind as a whole but only about its major component peoples treated separately. The concern of the more recent of these collective works has been more with problems and less with chronology, but the problems selected have been of relatively limited scope. At a more popular level, most textbooks and one-volume narratives share these attributes, although lack of space has frequently forced the authors into some rather unwilling and unenlightening generalizations.

An alternative approach that has had a wide appeal, and that to some extent also characterizes the world histories already mentioned, is the treatment of world history as an extension of Europe. There is some value for teaching purposes in proceeding from the known to the unknown and in introducing non-European peoples as they come within the European ken. When it is assumed that generalizations elaborated on the basis of the European experience are valid for the rest of the world, however, a useful teaching device becomes a source of serious distortion. This attitude is reflected, for example, in the very title of James Harvey Robinson's *The Ordeal of Civilization: A Sketch of the Development and World-Wide Diffusion of Our Present-Day Institutions and Ideas* (1926), although it is in most respects a scholarly and well-balanced account. A widespread reflection of this attitude is the extension to the rest of the world of a periodization that reflects European events alone. The division of history into ancient, medieval, early modern, and modern periods may well make sense for Europe, but is it valid for India or China?

One of the most dramatic methods of discussing the problems of mankind as a whole is to conceive of them in terms of an idea or a conceptual framework that has a predetermined end in view. This end is usually conceived in terms of a solution to problems confronting the author's own society, and by an imaginative leap he tries to rally the forces of world history to the support of the particular solution that he has in mind. This conception of world history found its clearest initial expression in the philosophy of Hegel and its most popular promoters in the writings of Marx and Engels. Although such an approach is not empirical, it at least has the advantage of seeing history in terms of problems and development, and of stimulating a lively debate on matters of concern to mankind as a whole. This stimulus has not, however, borne rich fruits in historiography. Only two general world histories have been immediately Marxist in their inspiration—N. A. Rozhkov's *Russkaia istoriia v sravnitelno-istoricheskom osveshchenii: osnovy sotsialnoi dinamiki* [Russian history from a comparative-historical viewpoint: fundamentals of social dynamics] (12 vols., 1919–26), and the *Vsemirnaia istoriia* [universal history] (10 vols., 1956–65), edited by E. M. Zhukov for the Academy of Sciences of the U.S.S.R. The former sought to fit the societies of all continents and all periods into a series of stages suggested by Marx and Engels, with Russia occupying a central position because of its alleged priority in reaching the stage of "socialism" in 1917. The latter is more traditional in its organization, but in general interpretative sections interspersed through the volumes as well as in the interpretation of individual societies the idea is conveyed that all peoples are moving toward socialism-communism along the path pioneered by the Soviet Union.

Equally productive of debate, but a good deal less conducive to understanding, have been the efforts to discern a pattern in history by means of the comparative study of civilizations. This line of speculation can be traced to Heinrich Rückert's *Lehrbuch der Weltgeschichte in organischer Darstellung* (2 vols., 1857), which posited the existence of a number of separate cultures and anticipated the eventual emergence of a worldwide European culture. The Russian biologist Nikolai Ia. Danilevsky developed a similar scheme in his *Rossiia i Evropa* [Russia and Europe] (1869), but conceived of the future in terms not of a worldwide European-oriented culture but of a predominant Slavic "cultural-historical type." This approach to history was later to be developed more fully in Oswald

Spengler's *Der Untergang des Abendlandes* (2 vols., 1918–22) and Arnold J. Toynbee's *A Study of History* (12 vols., 1934–61), although there is no conclusive evidence that Spengler knew of Danilevsky's work or indeed Danilevsky of Rückert's.

The chain of influence from Rückert to Toynbee has not been established, but the line of reasoning of these works is strikingly similar. They are not only inspired by an immediate concern for the survival of their own society, which is not in itself unreasonable, but they have permitted this concern to dominate their speculations to the point that history serves as illustration rather than as inspiration. Rückert was concerned with the realization of the universal idea, which for him was embodied in the European-Christian cultural world; Danilevsky, with what he assumed to be a growing antithesis between Russia and Europe; Spengler, with the decline of the traditional Europe in the generation before the First World War; and Toynbee, with the dramatic impact of two world wars on the society that he had known as a young man. One has the impression that they knew the answers before they started and permitted themselves to be influenced by these answers in their interpretation of history. By taking the whole world as their laboratory, they have contributed significantly to a reconsideration of the traditional emphasis on national histories and to the acceptance of mankind as a valid subject of historical study. By ignoring empiricism and logic, however, they have stimulated many fruitless debates.

Other world histories have been inspired by advocacy of a predetermined goal, even though the main body of the text may be conventional in structure and the logic of the narrative only indirectly related to the conclusion. H. G. Wells's *Outline of History* (1920), probably the most widely read one-volume history of mankind, concluded a competent if opinionated narrative with a plea for world government. In a similar spirit, Hendrick Van Loon's popular *Story of Mankind* (1922) saw the modern era as only an early stage in man's never-ending struggle for a new and better world. Most of the other more or less popular world histories, and there are many, have had a less lofty goal. They have generally sought to identify, and not infrequently to justify, the positions of individual nations, ethnic or religious groups, or cultures in the larger scheme of things. It is worth noting that the great majority of these have been written by inhabitants of Central and West Europe, the United States, and Russia. There have also been interesting contributions by writers in other parts of the world, from Ibn-Khaldun in the fourteenth century to Nehru in the twentieth, but these have been few and far between.

All of these approaches reflect a concern for world history, but they have generally failed to take into account the experience of mankind as a whole. When they have, the conclusions have been based more on hopes and good intentions than on a considered estimate of what is particular and what is universal. They are concerned typically with nations, civilizations, and cultures, which they combine in a variety of patterns. World history should be concerned not with the accumulation of cultures or with the histories of nations or civilizations, but with the totality of the human experience. World history should be to more local histories what European history is to the history of the individual European countries or what national histories are to the histories of their various component subdivisions. One can write with confidence about a Renaissance, a Reformation, an Industrial Revolution, or a Nationalism in Europe. What generalizations of a similar scope can be made about mankind as a whole?

The Concern for Mankind

The desire to understand mankind in its totality has not yet resulted in widely accepted conclusions, but it has for several generations been a matter of concern on the part of scholars in a number of fields of study other than history. Their goal has been to test accepted generalizations based primarily on the experience of Europe; to study the interactions between European and other cultures and societies; to overcome parochialism, both national and disciplinary, in the relevant disciplines; and to work toward a synthesis of the entire range of disciplines that are concerned with human behavior. "The Church in the Modern World," the statement issued by Pope Paul VI in December 1965 at the end of the Twenty-first Ecumenical Council, is an expression of the concern for mankind characteristic of our era.

A pioneering contribution in scholarship has been made by the anthropologists, whose interest in primitive life has brought them into direct contact with peoples in all parts of the world. Anthropology was the first social discipline to conceive of mankind as a whole, and to be concerned with the universal rather than the particular in human affairs. The generalizing anthropological concepts of culture and acculturation have proved stimulating to scholars in other disciplines, and the totality of the human experience emerges with particular vividness in anthropological studies. Although much anthropological work is essentially local and regional in its concern, its universal scope is well reflected in a number of generalizing works that have as their subject the whole of mankind. Anthropology has also in recent years absorbed and developed further the work in religion and linguistics concerned with the study of uniformities and variations on a worldwide basis. Although much of the earlier work in these fields emphasized historical differences rather than generalizations about mankind as a whole, it resulted in the accumulation of much basic research that continues to be used by scholars who now have a more sympathetic attitude toward alien faiths and cultures.

The experience of Europeans in governing the peoples of Asia, the Americas, and Africa also aroused an interest in the comparison of differing cultures that has had important consequences for scholarship. Although initially most Europeans regarded these peoples more as objects of influence than as subjects of study, experience eventually showed that their cultures had to be understood in their own terms if the process of adaptation and acculturation was to be adequately comprehended. Study of the languages and the political, economic, and social institutions of the peoples of Asia, Latin America, and Africa has now become a major concern of the more advanced nations. Higher education, and to some extent even secondary education, has been affected by this concern; and numerous research organizations have been established to study the traditional institutions of these peoples and the problems that they face in the process of adjustment to modern conditions.

The scope of this research, which is of vital importance to the formulation of generalizations about mankind, may be followed in several scholarly journals that are particularly concerned with the multidisciplinary study of this subject: *L'Afrique et l'Asie* (1948–), published by the Centre des hautes études administratives sur l'Afrique et l'Asie modernes, in Paris; *World Politics* (1948–), published by the Center of International Studies, at Princeton University; *Explorations in Entrepreneurial History*, 1st series (1949–58) published at Harvard University, 2nd series (1963–) published at Earlham College; *Civilisations* (1951–), published by the International Institute of Differing Civilizations, in Brussels; *Economic Development and Cultural Change* (1952–), published at the University of Chicago; *Narody Azii i Afriki* [the peoples of Asia and Africa] (1959), published by the Academy of Sciences of the U.S.S.R., in Moscow; *Tiers Monde* (1960–), published by the Institut d'étude du développement économique et social, in Paris; and the *Journal of Development Studies* (1964–), published in London. Much work along these lines is also being done by the commissions and specialized agencies of the United Nations that are concerned with economic and social problems.

Sociology, psychology, economics, and political science also embrace in principle the totality of human experience, although in practice they have only in recent years extended their vision beyond the limits of Europe and the English-speaking world. Comparative treatments of social institutions, personality types, economic systems, and governments are still exceptional when they undertake a comparison of institutions other than those of the advanced countries, and more exceptional yet when they seek to probe the more general behavioral processes that underlie these institutions. An interest in the underlying processes has nevertheless now come to play a much larger role in the research of social scientists, and many assumptions based on the experience of Europe and the English-speaking countries are being revised in the light of this work. Indeed, the more sophisticated of the social scientists have always extended their interest beyond a single discipline or region. Max Weber, the most important single figure among the founding fathers of contemporary social science, was led by his interest in the relationship between values and behavior from sociology to politics, economics, religion, and psychology—and from the European experience to that of the Indians, the Chinese, the Hebrews, the Russians, and the Americans. This world-encircling pursuit of special topics and themes, reflected in the articles published in the *Archiv für Sozialwissenschaft und Sozialpolitik* (1888–1933), of which Weber was one of the principal editors, is no longer uncommon. Scholars are now frequently encouraged, both during and after their professional training, to think in terms of more than one discipline and region.

Social scientists have also made some interesting and sophisticated contributions to the study of social change, although these have not been adequately tested by historians. Vilfredo Pareto's conception of social change as a cyclical alternation between practical short-range goals and idealistic long-term objectives, for example, is difficult to document. Alfred L. Kroeber and Pitirim A. Sorokin, on the other hand, went to considerable effort to document their own interpretations of the evolution of cultures as reflected in cycles of esthetic expression. Kroeber, to his credit, concluded his lengthy study, *Configurations of Culture Growth* (1944), with a confession that his search for universal patterns had fallen short of success. Sorokin, however, did not lose his faith. Rushton Coulborn, inspired in particular by Kroeber and Sorokin, has suggested that all civilized societies may be seen as passing through stages of faith, reason, and fulfillment before their cycles end in political decline and disintegration. A somewhat different approach was adopted by Ralph E. Turner, a historian strongly influenced by anthropology, who proposed a form of technological determinism that envisaged a cyclical development of societies resulting from periodic stagnations of technological innovation and culminating in a worldwide acceptance of the scientific method.

It seems clear enough that, with reference to the main problems that they face, societies or civilizations develop a level of understanding—an ideology, style, religion, or value system—that tends to permeate all modes of expression. This level of understanding is constantly being challenged, however, by new experiences, threats from without, and the growth of knowledge. Societies or civilizations may be regarded as systems of conflict management, which must cope with the tensions arising from the never-ending struggle between forces of stability and forces of adaptation. This struggle is essentially one that takes place among intellectual and political leaders who, for a wide variety of reasons and in myriads of patterns—and no two of them share quite the same point of view—seek to maintain some sort of a balance between the accepted way of doing things and the innovations that appear to be unavoidable. This attempt at conflict management has always been ultimately unsuccessful, and it is self-evident that all societies and civilizations except those now in existence have failed to survive. This experience underlies the many cyclical theories that have become one of the principal themes of world histories, and it is not difficult to understand how historians excavating the great graveyard of societies and civilizations should have hit upon the human life-cycle as a dominant analogy. These cyclical theories are credible enough as a general organizing principle, for it is obvious that all major forms of human organization have undergone periods of success and failure, but they are presented in such subjective and abstract terms that even the cyclists themselves have great difficulty in describing what they mean and how the materials of history can be fitted into their schemes. The explanatory value of these theories has therefore not been substantial.

A much more refined approach to this subject has been developed by Talcott Parsons, whose work has benefited much from the experiments of his predecessors and from the research and criticism of an unusually productive generation of empirical and theoretical sociologists. His theory of action—which may be described, at the risk of gross oversimplification, as one that sees social change in terms of the alternating emphasis of human actors on adaptation, goal-attainment, pattern-maintenance, and integration—may seem excessively abstract to historians accustomed to the simple dichotomies of stability and change or reform and reaction. Yet it is the first such theory that seeks to take full account of the interrelationships of personalities, cultures, societies, and social organisms —as well as the pattern variables that affect human attitudes—in a manner that reflects in some measure the infinitely complex reality that is so familiar and so baffling to historians. Theoretical history has suffered more from oversimplification than from overcomplexification, and any theory that seeks to give complexity its due is deserving of sympathetic consideration.

The holistic approach to the complexities of social structure and change characteristic of anthropological and more recently of sociological method has stimulated an interest in problems of multidisciplinary synthesis. The creation from many related facts of a pattern—whether narrative or analytical, local or general—has always been the central problem of historical writing. It has become infinitely more complex, however, as the accumulated knowledge in history and the related social sciences has increased in volume and sophistication. The interest of professional historians has broadened from one that was primarily political to one that concerns itself extensively with economic and social institutions, and has even become in some degree antagonistic to political history. The awakening of interest in economic and social history was greeted with bitter criticism in the nineteenth century by political historians inspired by the rise of the national state, and a certain amount of antagonism and controversy between the two approaches have survived to the present day. At the same time, since the turn of the century there have been numerous efforts to promote a synthesis of the various branches of history, and of history and related disciplines.

The most systematic efforts in this direction have been those of the Centre international de synthèse, established in Paris by Henri Berr in 1900. Its journal, the *Revue de synthèse* (1931–), succeeding the *Revue de synthèse historique* (1900–30); its *semaines,* which have sought through discussion by scholars from a variety of disciplines to clarify such concepts as civilization, society, individuality, and statistics; and its continuing series of volumes on universal history, *L'Evolution de l'humanité* (1920–), of which over sixty of a projected one hundred have now been published—these and other activities have served to focus attention, in a judicious and scholarly fashion, on the problems of multidisciplinary synthesis.

As interest in synthesis has developed, it has come to embrace the natural as well as the behavioral sciences. The unprecedented pace of the growth of knowledge in the twentieth century has nourished this interest, and the possibilities of a more general synthesis are being explored not only in the *Revue de synthèse* but also in such new journals as *Synthèse* (1936–) in the Netherlands, *Studium Generale* (1947–) in Germany, *General Systems* (1956–) in the United States, and *Minerva* (1962–) and *Systematics* (1963–), both in the United Kingdom. This concern is reflected likewise in the preparation of the *International Encyclopedia of Unified Science* (1938–). Conferences, research, and publications in a variety of fields have also been supported since 1952 by the Council for the Study of Mankind, in Chicago.

In this effort of scholars to understand their environment in all of its complexity, the biologists have found themselves in a strategic position, since their rapidly changing discipline not only involves man and nature but also has a uniquely historical interest that goes back to the beginnings of geological time. The noted Russian biologist V. I. Vernadsky was interested in generalizations about living matter that sought the common elements in human, animal, and plant life; and Pierre Teilhard de Chardin went beyond this to formulate a conception of evolution extending from the formation of the earth from gases to the future development of man and nature. Teilhard found it useful in his speculations to adopt the term "nöosphere" to describe the universality of knowledge in modern times as a terrestrial sphere of thinking substance that is developing an organic life of its own apart from the biological existence of mankind—a form of world brain.

Generalizations at this cosmic level can hardly be said to be of immediate concern to the problems of synthesis faced by working historians, but they should inspire them to raise their sights beyond the source materials on which their monographs are based and to appreciate the scope of knowledge that it is ultimately their task to understand. While awaiting the time when it will be possible to generalize usefully about the common experience of man and nature, a beginning has been made in writing the history of the world in such a way as to take into account not only those experiences that are local, national, regional, continental, or civilizational in scope but also those that are common to mankind as a whole. This view of world history has had many theorists, from Jean Bodin in the sixteenth century to N. I. Kareev in the twentieth, but it did not have effective practitioners until after the First World War. One of the first of these was the Swiss scholar Eduard Fueter, who in his *Weltgeschichte der Letzten hundert Jahre, 1815–1920* (1921) sought to write history from a universal point of view and took as his main theme what he called "the Europeanization of the World." The difficulties of this task are reflected in the tentative character of the effort to generalize about mankind as a whole in recent world histories. An interesting attempt is made in the *Handbuch der Weltgeschichte* (3rd ed., 4 vols., 1962), edited by Alexander Randa, in most respects a routine compendium of events and dates, to conclude with a brief *Totalbild der Menschheit*. These brief topical syntheses by well-known scholars provide a suggestive example of what might be done on a larger scale. Another approach is adopted by the *Weltgeschichte der Gegenwart* (2 vols., 1962–63), planned by the late

Fritz Valjavec and edited by Felix von Schroeder, of which the first volume is devoted to national histories and the second to worldwide developments and forces. The shortcoming of this experiment is that the topical chapters by individual authors are not coherently organized and that the initial chapter on foundations and basic forces in the modern world is more of an introduction than a synthesis.

On a much more comprehensive and sophisticated level, William H. McNeill's *The Rise of the West: A History of the Human Community* (1963) offers a scheme of organization and explanation in terms of the innovating centers, or civilizations, that have exerted a predominant influence in their periods of greatest accomplishment. The approach is diffusionist rather than comparative in its treatment of civilizations, which are organized in terms of three periods: Middle Eastern dominance (to 500 B.C.), Eurasian cultural balance (500 B.C. to A.D. 1500), and Western dominance (since 1500). The title suggests a reply to Spengler and implies a confidence in modern industrial society, which he regarded as a period of decline. McNeill's explanation is not in terms of cycles, like that of the civilizational historians, but of competition among metropolitan centers and of the predominance of the few that prove best able to offer solutions to the characteristic problems of their era. This is a distinctive approach, original in its execution, that offers valuable perspectives for further study.

Somewhat similar in conception, but much more narrowly focused on the innovating process, is the *History of Mankind* (6 vols., 1963–), in preparation by the International Commission for a History of the Scientific and Cultural Development of Mankind, under the auspices of UNESCO. The sponsors seek to improve on previous histories of mankind not only by stressing cultural and scientific aspects at the expense of political, economic, and military but also by inviting the participation of specialists from many nationalities and submitting for comment drafts of the texts to the many national commissions of UNESCO. The resulting product, if one may judge from the first two volumes, reflects the absence of a dominant interpretation and the interference of too many critics. Collaboration is indeed necessary in such magisterial projects, but the number and formal authority of critics and experts should be kept within reason and subordinated as far as possible to the discipline of a single mind. Perhaps later volumes will benefit from the experience of the earlier ones. In the meantime, the range of ideas and materials that form a part of this work may be followed in the *Journal of World History* (1953–), a unique international venture published under the same auspices.

Underlying this new interest on the part of historians in the experience of mankind as a whole in modern times is the problem of gaining control over the enormous and diverse materials that form the basis of historical work. General histories cannot be written except on the basis of special histories, and if these are to be useful for the formulation of generalizations about mankind as a whole they also must have a worldwide perspective. The most fruitful results along these lines so far have come from the study of specific problems or institutions common to a number of societies in one or more historical periods. Occasionally individual scholars can gain sufficient command of sources and secondary works to undertake broad comparative studies of such subjects as war, imperialism, revolutions, river-valley civilizations, despotisms, social strata, and urban cultures. An outstanding study of this type is Robert R. Palmer's *The Age of Democratic Revolution* (2 vols., 1959–64).

More often such comparisons require the cooperative skills of scholars representing a variety of fields of specialization. Valuable collaborative studies have been made, for example, of irrigation civilizations, feudalism, and political modernization. The important series of collaborative volumes issued since 1936 by the *Société Jean Bodin pour l'histoire comparative des institutions,* in Brussels, on feudal obligations and immunities, serfdom, land tenure, the domain, fairs, cities, foreigners, women, and peace, is among the most imaginative of works of this type. Other forms of interdisciplinary and comparative history have been stimulated by such scholarly journals as *Annales: Economies-Sociétés-Civilisations,* founded in Paris in 1929 by Lucien Febvre and Marc Bloch; and more recently by *Saeculum* (1950–), published in Munich; *Past and Present* (1952–), published at Corpus Christi College, Oxford; the *International Review of Social History* (1956–), published in Amsterdam; *Vestnik Istorii Mirovoi Kultury* [journal of the history of world culture] (1957–) and *Novaia i Noveishaia Istoriia* [modern and contemporary history] (1958–), both published in Moscow by the Academy of Sciences of the U.S.S.R.; *Comparative Studies in Society and History* (1958–), published at the University of Michigan; and the *Journal of Contemporary History* (1966–), published by the Wiener Library, in London.

Conceptions of Modernization

The contemporary literature on modernization draws on this rich and diverse heritage of research and thought, and is still in the process of defining its subject and of making the fundamental distinctions between the universal characteristics of modernity and the distinctive institutions of individual societies and cultures. The purpose of this relatively new approach is the multidisciplinary study of mankind, with a view to describing and explaining in all their complexity the processes of change that are now recognized to be of worldwide significance. This work has been greatly stimulated by the experience of the countries that have gained independence since the Second World War. The study of the peoples of Asia, Latin America, and Africa has a long tradition, but not until many peoples suddenly emerged to independent nationhood have the conceptions of political development, economic growth, and social change that were based primarily on the experience of the earlier-modernizing societies been challenged.

A useful brief introduction to the study of modernization is S. N. Eisenstadt's *Modernization: Growth and Diversity,* published in 1963 as a pamphlet by the Department of Government, Indiana University, and later as an article in *India Quarterly,* XX (January–March 1964), 17–42. It is both a bibliographical review and an essay on the nature and variety of research problems confronting this field of study. He stresses the need to be concerned both with quantitative indexes of development and with the institutional changes accompanying this process, but calls attention to the fact that the institutional patterns present the most perplexing problems. It was the initial impulse of students in this field to assume a more or less direct relationship between quantitative growth and institutional change, on the basis of the experience of the earlier-modernizing societies, and there are still those who seek to correlate literacy, gross national product per capita, and similar indexes with representative government and civil liberties. Eisenstadt's review of research in this field points to the conclusion, however, that different societies vary greatly in the means by which they seek to institutionalize the capacity for continuous change.

The study of modernization at this early stage in its development should start with a series of questions about the institutional structure of traditional societies; the nature and commitments of leadership groups; the relationship between the political, economic, social, and cultural spheres and their differing sequences of modernization; characteristic critical problems that confront all modernizing societies; and the not infrequent breakdowns and stagnations that have accompanied modernization. Eisenstadt also stresses the importance of comparative studies of modernizing societies as a means of distinguishing between the universal and the particular. Eisenstadt himself is the author of a series of papers, some collected in *Essays on Sociological Aspects of Political and Economic Development* (1961) and *Essays on Comparative Institutions* (1965), that discusses a number of the key problems in this field. He is also the author of *The Political Systems of Empires* (1963), a fundamental study of the structure of traditional societies, to which further reference is made below.

Readers seeking a general introduction to this subject will be interested in the views of twenty-five American scholars presented in *Modernization: The Dynamics of Growth* (1966), edited by Myron Weiner. These short essays, originally presented as a series of radio programs sponsored by the Voice of America and broadcast throughout the world, represent a comprehensive and authoritative statement of the major questions to which answers are being sought.

The most systematic theoretical approach to the study of modernization is provided by *Modernization and the Structure of Society: A Setting for International Affairs* (2 vols., 1966), by Marion J. Levy, Jr. Levy defines modernization as "the uses of inanimate sources of power and the use of tools to multiply the effect of effort," and within the framework of this broad definition he is primarily concerned with the basic distinction between relatively modernized and relatively nonmodernized societies. This fundamental distinction is the principal point of reference in the three main sections of the book, which are concerned with (1) aspects of social systems (role definition, solidarity, economic allocation, political allocation, and integration and expression); (2) the organizational contexts of societies (kinship and family organization, governments and associated units, economic organizations, armed forces organizations, and organizations devoted to religion, education, and recreation); and (3) common elements, variations, and problem focuses, in which he differentiates between universal and particular elements of societies, and discusses the central problem of the impact of modernization on stability.

Readers of Levy's earlier *Structure of Society* (1952) will find much of the logical framework and terminology of the more recent study familiar, and the essential difference between these two studies is that in the latter the structure is set in motion by constant reference to the distinction between relatively modernized and relatively nonmodernized societies. Although the description in the preceding paragraph is no more than a summary of the table of contents, it should at least convey a sense of the scope of Levy's analysis. He takes pains to point out that he is presenting hypotheses about the facts, and is not primarily concerned with empirical demonstrations. He cites numerous examples, taken primarily from the United States, China, and Japan, but his main emphasis is on the logical exposition of the uniformities and variations in the various categories of structure and function that he uses for analyzing societies.

The value of Levy's work lies in its holistic approach to human action as reflected in organized societies, which enhances the sensitivity of the understanding that he conveys of the phenomenon of modernization. Its quality as an exercise in sociological theory will make it seem unduly abstract to many historians and political scientists accustomed to simpler forms of narrative and analysis, but the force of its logic will not fail to sensitize careful readers to the scope and variety of the structures in terms of which human beings act. They will also be impressed by the theoretical demonstration of the reasons that modernization as a universal solvent is so subversive of traditional societies and that it has such a profoundly destabilizing effect on developing societies.

David E. Apter's *Politics of Modernization* (1965) is dedicated to Levy, and it employs some of his categories of analysis, but it is much more limited in scope and purpose. Apter treats modernization not in terms of the entire process of transformation from tradition to modernity but more particularly in terms of the transitional phase between traditionalism and industrialization. Apter is more concerned with process than with the distinction between relatively modernized and relatively nonmodernized societies, and he focuses his attention on ideology, motivation, and mobility as reflected in the changing roles of the members of modernizing societies. He presents his analysis in terms of rather simple categories— consummatory and instrumental values; hierarchical, pyramidal, and segmental authority types; traditionalist, accommodationist, and innovative role types; secular-libertarian and sacred-collectivity models of policy —but he draws extensively on recent research in the United States and conveys a vivid impression of the range of choices faced by modernizing societies.

I. Robert Sinai, in his volume *The Challenge of Modernisation: The West's Impact on the Non-Western World* (1964), is also concerned with changing roles in modernizing societies, and he centers his attention on the need for determined leadership to mobilize their resources. He is impressed by the marked absence of vigorous and self-disciplined leadership in the new states, and contrasts in dramatic terms their declarations of intent with their modest achievements. His approach draws attention to the setting of traditional cultures in which modernization is undertaken and raises the question whether societies that do not have a record of purposeful organization in their traditional heritage can be expected to develop the capacity to adapt their institutions to modern functions. In a forthcoming work Sinai will pursue this theme in more detail with reference to five societies at various stages of development—China, Japan, Mexico, Russia, and Turkey—that have demonstrated an unusual aptitude for directed social change.

In studying the diverse ways in which different societies have sought to adapt their institutions to the revolution in functions represented by modernization, particular emphasis has naturally been placed on political development. Edward Shils, a pioneer in this field, in his *Political Development in the New States*—originally published in *Comparative Studies in Society and History,* II (1959–60)—is explicit in emphasizing the variety of traditional systems, hence the different political forms that change is likely to take. The alternative forms of political developments that he envisages include not only political democracy but also tutelary democracy, modernizing oligarchies, totalitarian oligarchy, and traditional oligarchy. He sees these as diverse paths toward democracy, however, rather than as ends in themselves. He agrees with Sinai that the critical variable is the quality of the modernizing elite, but he is more optimistic that the new states will find adequate leadership.

Similarly influential among political scientists has been the work of Gabriel A. Almond, who with James S. Coleman edited *The Politics of Developing Areas* (1960). Almond's introductory chapter places particular emphasis on structural-functional analysis as a means of understanding the ways in which a variety of political systems may be mobilized to perform the tasks required by political, economic, and social change. This approach has had a beneficial influence on political scientists who were wedded to the view that contemporary Western institutions were inherently and exclusively "modern," but the other chapters on selected countries in this symposium did not make systematic use of his model. Almond and his colleagues have also planned the important series "Studies in Political Development," sponsored by the Committee on Comparative Politics of the Social Science Research Council, in New York. The collaborative volumes in this series on bureaucracy, education, communications, and political culture have brought together the ablest scholars in these fields. This series also includes a comparative study of Japan and Turkey, which is discussed below. Further volumes on political parties and on crises in political development are in preparation.

Fred W. Riggs, in his *Administration in Developing Countries: The Theory of Prismatic Society* (1964), seeks to conceptualize the problems of institutional change in transitional societies. The term "prismatic" is intended to describe the intermediate stage between "fused" traditional agrarian societies and "diffused" modern industrial societies, and Riggs examines their problems as they pass through this transitional "prism." Insofar as he is concerned with the problems of increasing functional specificity at the administration level, on the basis of his research in the Philippines, Riggs makes a useful contribution. He does not draw on the much more voluminous evidence, however, of the European societies that were passing through the "prism" in the seventeenth, eighteenth, and nineteenth centuries.

The economists, like the sociologists, are inclined toward a rather parochial determinism. W. W. Rostow, in his *Stages of Economic Growth* (1960), does not seriously take into account the differences represented by traditional institutions. He appears to be a liberal economic determinist, who believes that the achievement of "high mass consumption" will tend to dissolve institutional differences among societies and orient them toward the model represented by the earlier-modernizing societies. His ideas have nevertheless provoked fruitful debates, and at an international conference at which his views were discussed—the papers are collected in *The Economics of Take-off into Sustained Growth* (1963), which he edited—many interesting issues were presented. A. F. K. Organski's *Stages of Political Development* (1965) likewise presents a periodization—primitive unification, industrialization, national welfare, abundance—that is essentially economic in its determinism.

The forthcoming study of Dankwart A. Rustow, *A World of Nations: The Dynamics of Modern Politics,* is more properly political and is concerned with the various ways within the democratic-totalitarian continuum by which modernizing societies institutionalize change. Similarly, *New Nations: The Problem of Political Development,* a symposium edited by Karl von Vorys—published as Volume 358 of the *Annals of American Academy of Political and Social Science*—treats problems of development, patterns of leadership, and policies in selected countries. The essays of Lucian W. Pye, one of the leading students of this subject, are collected in *Aspects of Political Development* (1966).

Much interesting work is also being done on the problem of modernization as seen from the perspective of human behavior. Karl W. Deutsch's *Nerves of Government: Models of Political Communication and Control* (1963) draws on cybernetic theory as a means of understanding how governments achieve the tension-management necessary to attain a viable stability in times of rapid change. Similarly Everett E. Hagen, in *On the Theory of Social Change: How Economic Growth Begins* (1962), focuses primarily on the changes in attitude that social psychologists have found to underlie the ability of leaders in traditional societies to comprehend the potentialities of economic opportunity. Particularly stimulating is Lucian W. Pye's *Politics, Personality, and Nation-Building: Burma's Search for Identity* (1964), which describes in graphic detail the problems of identity of leaders after they leave the relative stability of the traditional way of life, and the means by which they seek to create a new identity while retaining an organic link with their followers.

This discussion of the leading conceptions of modernization may seem excessively parochial insofar as it is limited primarily to books published in the United States, but it is a fact that most of the generalizing work at this early stage in the study of modernization has been done by Americans. Much of it has been done by scholars who have conducted research in other parts of the world and in a variety of foreign languages, and one of its strengths is that it reflects the fresh view of the New World looking at the Old. At the same time it has some of the weaknesses of events described at too great a distance from the scene of action, and of an excessive abstraction that tends to focus on organizing concepts and methodology at the expense of substance—to the extent that the latter is sometimes completely dissolved without leaving a visible trace.

An investigation of the more specialized topics on which these generalizations are based, in the various relevant disciplines, would soon lead one to works of scholarship in many languages. A great deal of the research in recent generations in the humanities and social sciences is relevant in one way or another to the study of modernization, if one defines this subject broadly enough, and to consult this accumulated scholarship requires the resources of a major library. Its current flow may be followed in the annual international bibliographies published by UNESCO on anthropology, economics, history, political science, and sociology. Suffice it here to examine a few of the more specialized works concerned with the comparison of modernizing societies.

Problems of Comparison

Central to the problem of modernization as a process is the interrelationship of the historically evolved institutions of individual societies and the universally valid standards of value and performance that have resulted from the rapid growth of knowledge in recent centuries. This problem involves most of the points at issue among the various students of modernization, and it is particularly susceptible to study by the comparative method.

Quantification is one of the points at issue, and only in recent years have satisfactory comparative statistics become generally available. A pioneer work in this field is the *World Handbook of Political and Social Indicators* (1964), edited by Bruce M. Russett and others for the Political Data Program, at Yale University. This handbook brings together virtually all essential quantitative data on measurable characteristics that are available for a large number of countries and arranges them for comparative purposes in both gross and per capita tables. It also correlates the political and social indexes into patterns and proposes a ranking of countries into five stages of development on the basis of nine indexes. The highest stage, comprising fourteen countries, has been used in Chapter 3 above, pages 82–83, in defining those societies that can be considered to be in the phase of integration. The editors are reasonably modest in regard to the accuracy and comparability of their figures, although they do not go so far as Oskar Morgenstern, in *On the Accuracy of Economic Statistics* (2nd ed., 1963), in questioning the validity of these estimates.

This *World Handbook* is less ambitious in scope than the compilations *World Population and Production* (1953) and *World Commerce and Governments* (1955), edited by W. S. and E. S. Woytinsky, but it is much more sophisticated in the presentation of its materials. Other attempts to compile comparative statistics, including the fundamental series issued by the United Nations, are referred to in the footnotes of the *World Handbook*.

Of particular interest as an experiment in the comparison of political, economic, and social variables is *A Cross-Polity Survey* (1963), by Arthur S. Banks and Robert Textor, which rates 115 societies in terms of fifty-seven political and social variables. These variables are then dichotomized, and cross-referenced by computer methods for all countries. This permits one, for example, not only to find out which countries have a high (over 66 percent) or medium (34–66 percent), medium or low (16–33 percent), or low or very low (under 16 percent) agricultural population but also which of the other fifty-six variables correlate with each of these four levels. It should be added that two of the variables selected for this exercise are the periodization and typology set forth in chapters 3 and 4 above, in an earlier formulation. By consulting pages 77–80 of the text of Banks and Textor, and paragraphs 81–86 of the appended computer printout, the reader can test the degree of correlation among the societies thus grouped.

A limitation of the *Cross-Polity Survey* is that only one-third of the variables is based on objectively testable criteria, primarily statistical. Another dozen are based on subjective criteria, but are sufficiently clearly defined to be susceptible to reasonable discussion. These include, for example, the aforementioned periodization and typology, as well as "electoral systems," "freedom of group opposition," "character of bureaucracy," and similar characteristics. These may well be universal attributes of societies, but the extent to which they are shared is a matter of subjective judgment and to this extent controversial. The variables of a third group, almost half of the fifty-seven, are not only based on subjective criteria but also are either inadequately defined or are primarily

Western rather than universal in their orientation. Such variables include "Westernization," "governmental stability," "leadership charisma," "interest articulation by associational groups," among others.

It must be recognized that this situation reflects the state of the behavioral sciences rather than the judgment of Banks and Textor. The authors selected the best criteria available to them, but the state of our knowledge is such that not many political and social characteristics have been sufficiently studied to be accepted as universally applicable. Granted these limitations, the uses to which the *Survey* can be put are well illustrated by Philip M. Gregg and Arthur S. Banks in their "Dimensions of Political Systems: Factor Analysis of *A Cross-Polity Survey*," *American Political Science Review*, LIX (September 1965), 602–614.

Among the many other efforts at quantification, particular attention should be drawn to the value for students of comparative modernization of "Quantitative Aspects of the Economic Growth of Nations," a series of articles published by Simon Kuznets in *Economic Development and Cultural Change* (1956–64); Norton Ginsburg, *Atlas of Economic Development* (1961); Karl W. Deutsch, "Social Mobilization and Political Development," *American Political Science Review*, LV (September 1961), 493–514; and the comparative index of levels of human resource development elaborated in Frederick Harbison and Charles A. Myers, *Education, Manpower, and Economic Growth: Strategies of Human Resource Development* (1964), Chapter 3.

Attention should also be drawn to the sources of the quantitative measures cited in the earlier chapters of this book. The estimates on page 12 of the proportion of resources devoted to the production and the distribution of knowledge are from Fritz Machlup, *The Production and Distribution of Knowledge in the United States* (1962), Chapter 9; the figures on the growth of scientific publications and personnel on pages 12–13 are from Derek J. de Solla Price, *Science Since Babylon* (1961), pages 94–111; the estimates on page 33 of the growth of violence in the nineteenth and twentieth centuries are from Lewis F. Richardson, *Statistics of Deadly Quarrels* (1960); the analogy between structure and function in animals and in human affairs on page 44 is borrowed from John T. Bonner, *Cells and Societies* (1955); and the various references to levels of political, economic, and social development in chapters 1, 3, and 4 draw on the resources of the *Cross-Polity Survey* of Banks and Textor and the *World Handbook* edited by Russett and his colleagues.

It would take another full volume to do justice to the problems of comparative modernization raised by recent research. Suffice it to say that the strong bias toward the view that modernization will dissolve tradition, based on the theoretical assumption that form follows function, an essentially Westernizing view in this context, held by most sociologists and economists, and by many political scientists, has not been supported by the empirical research done so far. Anthropologists and historians are by training and experience more impressed by the staying power of tradition, and political scientists are divided on this issue depending on their education and the direction of their research. It is their view that form follows function only in the limited sense of adaptation to changing functions. Forms are so diverse to start with, and so varied in their ability to adapt to changing functions, that theoretical assumptions should rest on diversity, and research should be directed toward the study of these diverse forms and their adaptability.

A good statement of this case, although in a different setting and for a different purpose, is available in *A Theory of Stable Democracy*, "Research Monograph No. 10, Center of International Studies, Princeton University" (1961), by Harry Eckstein. Eckstein develops the theme that political systems, to be stable, must have an authority pattern that is congruent with the prevailing familial, economic, and associational authority patterns within the society. A similar line of analysis is developed in several works on political culture, especially Gabriel A. Almond and Sidney Verba, *The Civic Culture* (1963), which compares political attitudes in the United States, England, Germany, Italy, and Mexico; Clifford Geertz, ed., *Old Societies and New States: The Quest for Modernity in Asia and Africa* (1963); J. J. Spengler and R. Braibanti, eds., *Tradition, Values, and Socioeconomic Development* (1961); and Lucian W. Pye and Sidney Verba, eds., *Political Culture and Political Development* (1965). In a somewhat different vein, *The Transfer of Institutions* (1964), edited by William B. Hamilton, despite its title, stresses transformation of indigenous institutions, rather than transfer of institutions from more advanced societies, as the course that is more likely to succeed.

Comparisons embracing a wide spectrum of countries raise problems that are still in an early stage of investigation. The best introduction to these problems is *Comparing Nations: The Use of Quantitative Data in Cross-National Research* (1966), edited by Richard L. Merritt and Stein Rokkan, like the *World Handbook* a product of the Yale Political Data Program. Only a few examples of the many special studies in this field can be cited here: Julian H. Steward, "Cross-Cultural Regularities of Contemporary Change," *Kyoto American Studies Seminar Publications*, No. 2 (1956), 9–17; *The Comparative Study of Economic Growth and Structure: Suggestions on Research Objectives and Organization* (1959), published by the National Bureau of Economic Research; Stanley H.

Udy, Jr., *Organization of Work: A Comparative Analysis of Production Among Non-industrial Peoples* (1959); and Amitai Etzioni, *A Comparative Analysis of Complex Organizations* (1961).

East Asia is one of the principal testing grounds of the controversy over adoption versus adaptation, and John K. Fairbank, Edwin O. Reischauer, and Albert M. Craig, in the second volume of their *History of East Asian Civilization,* entitled *East Asia: The Modern Transformation* (1965), take pains to point out that modernization in China, Japan, and neighboring countries is taking place within the traditional context. They reach the conclusion that there is "no reason to suppose that a thoroughly modernized East Asia will be merely a reflection of the modernized West either in its superficial cultural patterns or in its more fundamental ideals and values" (page 9). In his essays entitled "A New Look at Modern History" (1962) and "Toward a Definition of 'Modernization'" (1965), published in Japanese periodicals and reprinted in English as pamphlets by the U.S. Information Service, Edwin O. Reischauer develops more fully the theme of common functions performed by a variety of institutions. A similar point is made by Hideo Kishimoto in "Modernization versus Westernization in the East," *Journal of World History,* VII (1963), 871–874.

The theme of cultural diversity is being explored in detail in the five symposia planned by the Conference on Modern Japan of the Association for Asian Studies, of which two—Marius B. Jansen, ed., *Changing Japanese Attitudes Toward Modernization* (1965), and William W. Lockwood, ed., *The State and Economic Enterprise in Japan* (1965)— have already appeared. This series draws on the extensive Japanese research on modernization and promises to be a most important investigation of the relationship between the unique and the universal in the Japanese experience.

There is no work on China of similar scope and penetration, but a beginning has been made by John K. Fairbank, Ssu-yü Teng, and others, in *China's Response to the West, a Documentary Survey 1839–1923* (1954), with an accompanying volume of notes and bibliography. In his article "China's Response to the West: Problems and Suggestions," *Journal of World History,* III (1956), 381–406, Fairbank suggests a framework of periodization for the study of this problem. Another relevant East Asian study, with an anthropological approach, is Manning Nash, *The Golden Road to Modernity: Village Life in Contemporary Burma* (1965).

Considerable attention has also been given to comparisons of the divergent experiences of Japan and China. This work is summarized in

Allan B. Cole, "Contrasting Modernization in China and Japan," *Chung Chi Journal* (Hong Kong), IV (May 1965), 99–138. A broader comparative view, embracing Japan, China, and Russia, is suggested in Cyril E. Black, "Ajiya kindaika no dotei" [Asia's path to modernization], *Jiyu*, VII (October 1965), 92–99. The results of a conference at Hokkaido University on this subject are reported in " 'Kindaika' o meguru hokoku to toron" [reports and discussion on "modernization"], *Slavic Studies* (Hokkaido University), X (1966), 71–84, by Shigeto Toriyama and Tsuguo Togawa.

Bridging East and West Asia, Robert E. Ward and Dankwart A. Rustow's *Political Modernization in Japan and Turkey* (1964) is a unique international venture that draws on scholars from England, Japan, Turkey, and the United States. Although both countries had a heritage of effective government, and neither came under direct foreign rule, there are many contrasts in traditional institutional structure that help to explain the differences in their levels of development today.

Valuable general interpretations of modernization in the Middle East are Daniel Lerner, *The Passing of Traditional Society: Modernizing the Middle East* (1958), a pioneering study, and Manfred Halpern, *The Politics of Social Change in the Middle East and North Africa* (1963). Important studies of individual countries are Douglas E. Ashford, *Political Change in Morocco* (1961); Bernard Lewis, *The Emergence of Modern Turkey* (1961); Roderic H. Davison, *Reform in the Ottoman Empire, 1856–1876* (1963); William R. Polk, *The Opening of South Lebanon, 1788–1840: A Study of the Impact of the West on the Middle East* (1963); Charles A. Micaud, Clement Moore, and L. Carl Brown, *Tunisia: The Politics of Modernization* (1964); Robert L. Tignor, *Modernization and British Colonial Rule in Egypt, 1882–1914* (1966); and the forthcoming *Oman in the Late Nineteenth Century and After,* by Robert G. Landen.

To this brief introductory list of books in English one would wish to add, if space permitted, the extensive fundamental research on social change in Islamic societies by such French scholars as Georges Balandier, Jacques Bercque, Roger Le Tourneau, Robert Montagne, and Jean-Louis Miège. Significant work has also been done in Arabic and Turkish, and by scholars of these countries writing in Western languages.

Russia—so much a part of Europe yet so different in institutional heritage from the societies of Western Europe that have established the frame of reference for modernizing theory—has of course been a major subject of study. Yet the Bolshevik revolution so heightened ideological tensions that it was not until after the Second World War that the Soviet

Union began to be studied as an example of modernization. In *The Transformation of Russian Society: Aspects of Social Change Since 1861* (1960), edited by Cyril E. Black, thirty-eight contributors sought to distinguish elements of continuity and change, and in effect the unique and the universal, in the entire period since the emancipation of the serfs. For the Soviet period alone, similar questions are discussed in Barrington Moore, Jr., *Terror and Progress USSR: Some Sources of Change and Stability in the Soviet Dictatorship* (1954); Raymond A. Bauer, Alex Inkeles, and Clyde Kluckhohn, *How the Soviet System Works: Cultural, Psychological, and Social Themes* (1956); and a forthcoming symposium, *The Prospects for Soviet Society*, edited by Allen Kassof.

In a comparative vein, Zbigniew Brzezinski and Samuel P. Huntington, in *Political Power: USA/USSR* (1961), examine the main categories of power and policy in the two countries and reach the conclusion that they are likely to modernize along separate paths congruent with their distinctive traditional heritages.

Soviet theorists naturally approach these questions from a different point of view, and the official textbook on the subject, *Fundamentals of Marxism-Leninism* (2nd ed., 1963), develops a theory of history centered on the assumption that the Soviet pattern of development is the true exemplar of Marxism and the model that all other countries are destined to follow. A more scholarly and pragmatic Soviet interpretation is presented in *Sotsiologiia v SSSR* [sociology in the USSR] (2 vols., 1965), edited by G. V. Osipov, which provides extensive documentation of selected economic and social problems as well as some international comparisons. Representative Soviet views on the development of the new states are presented in *The Third World in Soviet Perspective* (1965), edited by Thomas P. Thornton. Soviet scholars also write extensively on the peoples and problems of Africa, Asia, and Latin America, and research is conducted under the auspices of the Academy of Sciences.

An alternative Marxist view is developed by Henri Lefebvre in *Introduction à la modernité* (1962). A leading Communist intellectual, expelled from the party in 1958, Lefebvre seeks to reinterpret Marxism in terms of contemporary sociological theory as a means of defining the essential elements of the modernizing process.

The emphasis placed by anthropologists, historians, and some political scientists on the continuing influence of political institutions inherited from the past has led to a renewed interest in earlier history as seen from a modern perspective. The most broadly based of these works is *The Political Systems of Empires* (1963), by S. N. Eisenstadt, a leading student of modernization; this volume describes and compares traditional political systems on the basis of a detailed scheme of analysis. Similar studies of more limited groups of societies are available in Julian H. Steward, ed., *Irrigation Civilizations: A Comparative Study* (1955), and Karl A. Wittfogel, *Oriental Despotisms: A Comparative Study of Total Power* (1957).

The important symposium *Feudalism in History* (1956), edited by Rushton Coulborn, studies the uniformities in the development of feudalism not only in Western Europe but also in Japan, China, ancient Mesopotamia, Iran, Egypt, India, the Byzantine Empire, and Russia. The relevance of the traditional institutions of Europe to the modern era is explored in *Twelfth-Century Europe and the Foundations of Modern Society* (1961), edited by Marshall Clagett, Gaines Post, and Robert Reynolds. Joseph R. Strayer, a leading contributor to these two volumes, has compared the English and French cases in "The Historical Experience of Nation-Building in Europe," in *Nation Building* (1963), edited by Karl W. Deutsch and W. J. Foltz, pages 17–27. Samuel P. Huntington also draws on earlier history in his interesting article "Political Modernization: America vs. Europe," *World Politics*, XVIII (April 1966), 378–414. Seymour M. Lipset's *The First New Nation: The United States in Historical and Comparative Perspective* (1963) reinterprets American history in a comparative framework.

These are but a few of the more pertinent titles among many that one could cite that compare modernizing change in societies at different stages of development. The work that has been done thus far is only a beginning, but it is adequate to permit an appreciation of the dimensions of the two interdependent problems that require further study before our generalizations can be more adequately tested: the development of theory with a view to elaborating categories of assumptions and questions applicable to all societies, and the thoughtful study and comparison of the individual experiences—both traditional and modernizing—of the societies that constitute mankind.

Let us continue to ask questions and seek answers.

Index

70 71 72 73   12 11 10 9 8 7 6 5

ḣarper ⚡ ϲorcḣbooks

† The New American Nation Series, edited by Henry Steele Commager and Richard B. Morris.
‡ American Perspectives series, edited by Bernard Wishy and William E. Leuchtenburg.
α History of Europe series, edited by J. H. Plumb.
§ The Library of Religion and Culture, edited by Benjamin Nelson.
ǁ Researches in the Social, Cultural, and Behavioral Sciences, edited by Benjamin Nelson.
Σ Harper Modern Science Series, edited by James A. Newman.
○ Not for sale in Canada.
+ Documentary History of the United States series, edited by Richard B. Morris.
# Documentary History of Western Civilization series, edited by Eugene C. Black and Leonard W. Levy.
Λ The Economic History of the United States series, edited by Henry David et al.
¶ European Perspectives series, edited by Eugene C. Black.
** Contemporary Essays series, edited by Leonard W. Levy.
* The Stratum Series, edited by John Hale.

EDMUND S. MORGAN: The Puritan Family: *Religion and Domestic Relations in Seventeenth Century New England* TB/1227

RICHARD B. MORRIS: Government and Labor in Early America TB/1244

WALLACE NOTESTEIN: The English People on the Eve of Colonization: 1603-1630. † *Illus.* TB/3006

FRANCIS PARKMAN: The Seven Years War: *A Narrative Taken from Montcalm and Wolfe, The Conspiracy of Pontiac, and A Half-Century of Conflict. Edited by John H. McCallum* TB/3083

LOUIS B. WRIGHT: The Cultural Life of the American Colonies: 1607-1763. † *Illus.* TB/3005

YVES F. ZOLTVANY, Ed.: The French Tradition in America + HR/1425

American Studies: The Revolution to 1860

JOHN R. ALDEN: The American Revolution: 1775-1783. † *Illus.* TB/3011

MAX BELOFF, Ed.: The Debate on the American Revolution, 1761-1783: *A Sourcebook* TB/1225

RAY A. BILLINGTON: The Far Western Frontier: 1830-1860. † *Illus.* TB/3012

STUART BRUCHEY: The Roots of American Economic Growth, 1607-1861: *An Essay in Social Causation. New Introduction by the Author.* TB/1350

WHITNEY R. CROSS: The Burned-Over District: *The Social and Intellectual History of Enthusiastic Religion in Western New York, 1800-1850* TB/1242

NOBLE E. CUNNINGHAM, JR., Ed.: The Early Republic, 1789-1828 + HR/1394

GEORGE DANGERFIELD: The Awakening of American Nationalism, 1815-1828. † *Illus.* TB/3061

CLEMENT EATON: The Freedom-of-Thought Struggle in the Old South. *Revised and Enlarged. Illus.* TB/1150

CLEMENT EATON: The Growth of Southern Civilization, 1790-1860. † *Illus.* TB/3040

ROBERT H. FERRELL, Ed.: Foundations of American Diplomacy, 1775-1872 HR/1393

LOUIS FILLER: The Crusade against Slavery: 1830-1860. † *Illus.* TB/3029

DAVID H. FISCHER: The Revolution of American Conservatism: *The Federalist Party in the Era of Jeffersonian Democracy* TB/1449

WILLIAM W. FREEHLING, Ed.: The Nullification Era: *A Documentary Record* ‡ TB/3079

WILLIM W. FREEHLING: Prelude to Civil War: *The Nullification Controversy in South Carolina, 1816-1836* TB/1359

PAUL W. GATES: The Farmer's Age: *Agriculture, 1815-1860* △ TB/1398

FELIX GILBERT: The Beginnings of American Foreign Policy: *To the Farewell Address* TB/1200

ALEXANDER HAMILTON: The Reports of Alexander Hamilton. ‡ *Edited by Jacob E. Cooke* TB/3060

THOMAS JEFFERSON: Notes on the State of Virginia. ‡ *Edited by Thomas P. Abernethy* TB/3052

FORREST MCDONALD, Ed.: Confederation and Constitution, 1781-1789 + HR/1396

BERNARD MAYO: Myths and Men: *Patrick Henry, George Washington, Thomas Jefferson* TB/1108

JOHN C. MILLER: Alexander Hamilton and the Growth of the New Nation TB/3057

JOHN C. MILLER: The Federalist Era: 1789-1801. † *Illus.* TB/3027

RICHARD B. MORRIS, Ed.: Alexander Hamilton and the Founding of the Nation. *New Introduction by the Editor* TB/1448

RICHARD B. MORRIS: The American Revolution Reconsidered TB/1363

CURTIS P. NETTELS: The Emergence of a National Economy, 1775-1815 △ TB/1438

DOUGLASS C. NORTH & ROBERT PAUL THOMAS, Eds.: *The Growth of the American Economy to 1860* + HR/1352

R. B. NYE: The Cultural Life of the New Nation: 1776-1830. † *Illus.* TB/3026

GILBERT OSOFSKY, Ed.: Puttin' On Ole Massa: *The Slave Narratives of Henry Bibb, William Wells Brown, and Solomon Northup* ‡ TB/1432

JAMES PARTON: The Presidency of Andrew Jackson. *From Volume III of the Life of Andrew Jackson. Ed. with Intro. by Robert V. Remini* TB/3080

FRANCIS S. PHILBRICK: The Rise of the West, 1754-1830. † *Illus.* TB/3067

MARSHALL SMELSER: The Democratic Republic, 1801-1815 † TB/1406

TIMOTHY L. SMITH: Revivalism and Social Reform: *American Protestantism on the Eve of the Civil War* TB/1229

JACK M. SOSIN, Ed.: The Opening of the West + HR/1424

GEORGE ROGERS TAYLOR: The Transportation Revolution, 1815-1860 △ TB/1347

A. F. TYLER: Freedom's Ferment: *Phases of American Social History from the Revolution to the Outbreak of the Civil War. Illus.* TB/1074

GLYNDON G. VAN DEUSEN: The Jacksonian Era: 1828-1848. † *Illus.* TB/3028

LOUIS B. WRIGHT: Culture on the Moving Frontier TB/1053

American Studies: The Civil War to 1900

W. R. BROCK: An American Crisis: *Congress and Reconstruction, 1865-67* ° TB/1283

T. C. COCHRAN & WILLIAM MILLER: The Age of Enterprise: *A Social History of Industrial America* TB/1054

W. A. DUNNING: Reconstruction, Political and Economic: 1865-1877 TB/1073

HAROLD U. FAULKNER: Politics, Reform and Expansion: 1890-1900. † *Illus.* TB/3020

GEORGE M. FREDRICKSON: The Inner Civil War: *Northern Intellectuals and the Crisis of the Union* TB/1358

JOHN A. GARRATY: The New Commonwealth, 1877-1890 ° TB/1410

JOHN A. GARRATY, Ed.: The Transformation of American Society, 1870-1890 + HR/1395

HELEN HUNT JACKSON: A Century of Dishonor: *The Early Crusade for Indian Reform.* ‡ *Edited by Andrew F. Rolle* TB/3063

ALBERT D. KIRWAN: Revolt of the Rednecks: *Mississippi Politics, 1876-1925* TB/1199

ARTHUR MANN: Yankee Reforms in the Urban Age: *Social Reform in Boston, 1800-1900* TB/1247

ARNOLD M. PAUL: Conservative Crisis and the Rule of Law: *Attitudes of Bar and Bench, 1887-1895. New Introduction by Author* TB/1415

JAMES S. PIKE: The Prostrate State: *South Carolina under Negro Government.* ‡ *Intro. by Robert F. Durden* TB/3085

WHITELAW REID: After the War: *A Tour of the Southern States, 1865-1866.* ‡ *Edited by C. Vann Woodward* TB/3066

FRED A. SHANNON: The Farmer's Last Frontier: *Agriculture, 1860-1897* TB/1348

2

VERNON LANE WHARTON: The Negro in Mississippi, 1865-1890 TB/1178

American Studies: The Twentieth Century

RICHARD M. ABRAMS, Ed.: The Issues of the Populist and Progressive Eras, 1892-1912 + HR/1428
RAY STANNARD BAKER: Following the Color Line: *American Negro Citizenship in Progressive Era.* ‡ *Edited by Dewey W. Grantham, Jr. Illus.* TB/3053
RANDOLPH S. BOURNE: War and the Intellectuals: *Collected Essays, 1915-1919.* ‡ *Edited by Carl Resek* TB/3043
A. RUSSELL BUCHANAN: The United States and World War II. † *Illus.*
Vol. I TB/3044; Vol. II TB/3045
THOMAS C. COCHRAN: The American Business System: *A Historical Perspective, 1900-1955* TB/1080
FOSTER RHEA DULLES: America's Rise to World Power: 1898-1954. † *Illus.* TB/3021
JEAN-BAPTISTE DUROSELLE: From Wilson to Roosevelt: *Foreign Policy of the United States, 1913-1945. Trans. by Nancy Lyman Roelker* TB/1370
HAROLD U. FAULKNER: The Decline of Laissez Faire, 1897-1917 TB/1397
JOHN D. HICKS: Republican Ascendancy: 1921-1933. † *Illus.* TB/3041
ROBERT HUNTER: Poverty: *Social Conscience in the Progressive Era.* ‡ *Edited by Peter d'A. Jones* TB/3065
WILLIAM E. LEUCHTENBURG: Franklin D. Roosevelt and the New Deal: 1932-1940. † *Illus.* TB/3025
WILLIAM E. LEUCHTENBURG, Ed.: The New Deal: *A Documentary History* + HR/1354
ARTHUR S. LINK: Woodrow Wilson and the Progressive Era 1910-1917. † *Illus.* TB/3023
BROADUS MITCHELL: Depression Decade: *From New Era through New Deal, 1929-1941* ʌ TB/1439
GEORGE E. MOWRY: The Era of Theodore Roosevelt and the Birth of Modern America: 1900-1912. † *Illus.* TB/3022
WILLIAM PRESTON, JR.: Aliens and Dissenters: *Federal Suppression of Radicals, 1903-1933* TB/1287
WALTER RAUSCHENBUSCH: Christianity and the Social Crisis. ‡ *Edited by Robert D. Cross* TB/3059
GEORGE SOULE: Prosperity Decade: *From War to Depression, 1917-1929* ʌ TB/1349
GEORGE B. TINDALL, Ed.: A Populist Reader: *Selections from the Works of American Populist Leaders* TB/3069
TWELVE SOUTHERNERS: I'll Take My Stand: *The South and the Agrarian Tradition. Intro. by Louis D. Rubin, Jr.; Biographical Essays by Virginia Rock* TB/1072

Art, Art History, Aesthetics

CREIGHTON GILBERT, Ed.: Renaissance Art ** *Illus.* TB/1465
EMILE MALE: The Gothic Image: *Religious Art in France of the Thirteenth Century.* § *190 illus.* TB/344
MILLARD MEISS: Painting in Florence and Siena After the Black Death: *The Arts, Religion and Society in the Mid-Fourteenth Century. 169 illus.* TB/1148
ERWIN PANOFSKY: Renaissance and Renascences in Western Art. *Illus.* TB/1447
ERWIN PANOFSKY: Studies in Iconology: *Humanistic Themes in the Art of the Renaissance. 180 illus.* ‒ TB/1077

JEAN SEZNEC: The Survival of the Pagan Gods: *The Mythological Tradition and Its Place in Renaissance Humanism and Art. 108 illus.* TB/2004
OTTO VON SIMSON: The Gothic Cathedral: *Origins of Gothic Architecture and the Medieval Concept of Order. 58 illus.* TB/2018
HEINRICH ZIMMER: Myths and Symbols in Indian Art and Civilization. *70 illus.* TB/2005

Asian Studies

WOLFGANG FRANKE: China and the West: *The Cultural Encounter, 13th to 20th Centuries. Trans. by R. A. Wilson* TB/1326
L. CARRINGTON GOODRICH: A Short History of the Chinese People. *Illus.* TB/3015
DAN N. JACOBS, Ed.: The New Communist Manifesto and Related Documents. *3rd revised edn.* TB/1078
DAN N. JACOBS & HANS H. BAERWALD, Eds.: Chinese Communism: *Selected Documents* TB/3031
BENJAMIN I. SCHWARTZ: Chinese Communism and the Rise of Mao TB/1308
BENJAMIN I. SCHWARTZ: In Search of Wealth and Power: *Yen Fu and the West* TB/1422

Economics & Economic History

C. E. BLACK: The Dynamics of Modernization: *A Study in Comparative History* TB/1321
STUART BRUCHEY: The Roots of American Economic Growth, 1607-1861: *An Essay in Social Causation. New Introduction by the Author.* TB/1350
GILBERT BURCK & EDITORS OF *Fortune:* The Computer Age: *And its Potential for Management* TB/1179
JOHN ELLIOTT CAIRNES: The Slave Power. ‡ *Edited with Introduction by Harold D. Woodman* TB/1433
SHEPARD B. CLOUGH, THOMAS MOODIE & CAROL MOODIE, Eds.: Economic History of Europe: *Twentieth Century* # HR/1388
THOMAS C. COCHRAN: The American Business System: *A Historical Perspective, 1900-1955* TB/1180
ROBERT A. DAHL & CHARLES E. LINDBLOM: Politics, Economics, and Welfare: *Planning and Politico-Economic Systems Resolved into Basic Social Processes* TB/3037
PETER F. DRUCKER: The New Society: *The Anatomy of Industrial Order* TB/1082
HAROLD U. FAULKNER: The Decline of Laissez Faire, 1897-1917 ʌ TB/1397
PAUL W. GATES: The Farmer's Age: *Agriculture, 1815-1860* ʌ TB/1398
WILLIAM GREENLEAF, Ed.: American Economic Development Since 1860 + HR/1353
J. L. & BARBARA HAMMOND: The Rise of Modern Industry. ‖ *Introduction by R. M. Hartwell* TB/1417
ROBERT L. HEILBRONER: The Future as History: *The Historic Currents of Our Time and the Direction in Which They Are Taking America* TB/1386
ROBERT L. HEILBRONER: The Great Ascent: *The Struggle for Economic Development in Our Time* TB/3030
FRANK H. KNIGHT: The Economic Organization TB/1214
DAVID S. LANDES: Bankers and Pashas: *International Finance and Economic Imperialism in Egypt. New Preface by the Author* TB/1412
ROBERT LATOUCHE: The Birth of Western Economy: *Economic Aspects of the Dark Ages* TB/1290

3

History: Renaissance & Reformation

JACOB BURCKHARDT: The Civilization of the Renaissance in Italy. *Introduction by Benjamin Nelson and Charles Trinkaus. Illus.* Vol. I TB/40; Vol. II TB/41

JOHN CALVIN & JACOPO SADOLETO: A Reformation Debate. *Edited by John C. Olin* TB/1239

FEDERICO CHABOD: Machiavelli and the Renaissance TB/1193

THOMAS CROMWELL: Thomas Cromwell. *Selected Letters on Church and Commonwealth, 1523-1540.* ¶ *Ed. with an Intro. by Arthur J. Slavin* TB/1462

R. TREVOR DAVIES: The Golden Century of Spain, 1501-1621 ° TB/1194

J. H. ELLIOTT: Europe Divided, 1559-1598 α ° TB/1414

G. R. ELTON: Reformation Europe, 1517-1559 ° α TB/1270

DESIDERIUS ERASMUS: Christian Humanism and the Reformation: *Selected Writings. Edited and Translated by John C. Olin* TB/1166

DESIDERIUS ERASMUS: Erasmus and His Age: *Selected Letters. Edited with an Introduction by Hans J. Hillerbrand. Translated by Marcus A. Haworth* TB/1461

WALLACE K. FERGUSON et al.: Facets of the Renaissance TB/1098

WALLACE K. FERGUSON et al.: The Renaissance: *Six Essays. Illus.* TB/1084

FRANCESCO GUICCIARDINI: History of Florence. *Translated with an Introduction and Notes by Mario Domandi* TB/1470

WERNER L. GUNDERSHEIMER, Ed.: French Humanism, 1470-1600. * *Illus.* TB/1473

MARIE BOAS HALL, Ed.: Nature and Nature's Laws: *Documents of the Scientific Revolution* # HR/1420

HANS J. HILLERBRAND, Ed., The Protestant Reformation HR/1342

JOHAN HUIZINGA: Erasmus and the Age of Reformation. *Illus.* TB/19

JOEL HURSTFIELD: The Elizabethan Nation TB/1312

JOEL HURSTFIELD, Ed.: The Reformation Crisis TB/1267

PAUL OSKAR KRISTELLER: Renaissance Thought: *The Classic, Scholastic, and Humanist Strains* TB/1048

PAUL OSKAR KRISTELLER: Renaissance Thought II: *Papers on Humanism and the Arts* TB/1163

PAUL O. KRISTELLER & PHILIP P. WIENER, Eds.: Renaissance Essays TB/1392

DAVID LITTLE: Religion, Order and Law: *A Study in Pre-Revolutionary England.* § *Preface by R. Bellah* TB/1418

NICCOLO MACHIAVELLI: History of Florence and of the Affairs of Italy: *From the Earliest Times to the Death of Lorenzo the Magnificent. Introduction by Felix Gilbert* TB/1027

ALFRED VON MARTIN: Sociology of the Renaissance. ° *Introduction by W. K. Ferguson* TB/1099

GARRETT MATTINGLY et al.: Renaissance Profiles. *Edited by J. H. Plumb* TB/1162

J. E. NEALE: The Age of Catherine de Medici ° TB/1085

J. H. PARRY: The Establishment of the European Hegemony: 1415-1715: *Trade and Exploration in the Age of the Renaissance* TB/1045

J. H. PARRY, Ed.: The European Reconnaissance: *Selected Documents* # HR/1345

BUONACCORSO PITTI & GREGORIO DATI: Two Memoirs of Renaissance Florence: *The Diaries of Buonaccorso Pitti and Gregorio Dati. Edited with Intro. by Gene Brucker. Trans. by Julia Martines* TB/1333

J. H. PLUMB: The Italian Renaissance: *A Concise Survey of Its History and Culture* TB/1161

A. F. POLLARD: Henry VIII. *Introduction by A. G. Dickens.* ° TB/1249

RICHARD H. POPKIN: The History of Scepticism from Erasmus to Descartes TB/1391

PAOLO ROSSI: Philosophy, Technology, and the Arts, in the Early Modern Era 1400-1700. || *Edited by Benjamin Nelson. Translated by Salvator Attanasio* TB/1458

FERDINAND SCHEVILL: The Medici. *Illus.* TB/1010

FERDINAND SCHEVILL: Medieval and Renaissance Florence. *Illus.* Vol. I: *Medieval Florence* TB/1090

Vol. II: *The Coming of Humanism and the Age of the Medici* TB/1091

R. H. TAWNEY: The Agrarian Problem in the Sixteenth Century. *Intro. by Lawrence Stone* TB/1315

H. R. TREVOR-ROPER: The European Witch-craze of the Sixteenth and Seventeenth Centuries and Other Essays ° TB/1416

VESPASIANO: Rennaissance Princes, Popes, and XVth Century: *The Vespasiano Memoirs. Introduction by Myron P. Gilmore. Illus.* TB/1111

History: Modern European

RENE ALBRECHT-CARRIE, Ed.: The Concert of Europe # HR/1341

MAX BELOFF: The Age of Absolutism, 1660-1815 TB/1062

OTTO VON BISMARCK: Reflections and Reminiscences. *Ed. with Intro. by Theodore S. Hamerow* ¶ TB/1357

EUGENE C. BLACK, Ed.: British Politics in the Nineteenth Century # HR/1427

EUGENE C. BLACK, Ed.: European Political History, 1815-1870: *Aspects of Liberalism* ¶ TB/1331

ASA BRIGGS: The Making of Modern England, 1783-1867: *The Age of Improvement* ° TB/1203

ALAN BULLOCK: Hitler, A Study in Tyranny. ° *Revised Edition. Illus.* TB/1123

EDMUND BURKE: On Revolution. *Ed. by Robert A. Smith* TB/1401

E. R. CARR: International Relations Between the Two World Wars. 1919-1939 ° TB/1279

E. H. CARR: The Twenty Years' Crisis, 1919-1939: *An Introduction to the Study of International Relations* ° TB/1122

GORDON A. CRAIG: From Bismarck to Adenauer: *Aspects of German Statecraft. Revised Edition* TB/1171

LESTER G. CROCKER, Ed.: The Age of Enlightenment # HR/1423

DENIS DIDEROT: The Encyclopedia: *Selections. Edited and Translated with Introduction by Stephen Gendzier* TB/1299

JACQUES DROZ: Europe between Revolutions, 1815-1848. ° *a Trans. by Robert Baldick* TB/1346

JOHANN GOTTLIEB FICHTE: Addresses to the German Nation. *Ed. with Intro. by George A. Kelly* ¶ TB/1366

ROBERT & ELBORG FORSTER, Eds.: European Society in the Eighteenth Century # HR/1404

C. C. GILLISPIE: Genesis and Geology: *The Decades before Darwin* § TB/51

5

Literature & Literary Criticism

Philosophy

7

MIRCEA ELIADE: Myths, Dreams and Mysteries: *The Encounter Between Contemporary Faiths and Archaic Realities* § TB/1320
MIRCEA ELIADE: Rites and Symbols of Initiation: *The Mysteries of Birth and Rebirth* § TB/1236
HERBERT FINGARETTE: The Self in Transformation: *Psychoanalysis, Philosophy and the Life of the Spirit* || TB/1177
SIGMUND FREUD: On Creativity and the Unconscious: *Papers on the Psychology of Art, Literature, Love, Religion. § Intro. by Benjamin Nelson* TB/45
J. GLENN GRAY: The Warriors: *Reflections on Men in Battle. Introduction by Hannah Arendt* TB/1294
WILLIAM JAMES: Psychology: *The Briefer Course. Edited with an Intro. by Gordon Allport* TB/1034
C. G. JUNG: Psychological Reflections. *Ed. by J. Jacobi* TB/2001
KARL MENNINGER, M.D.: Theory of Psychoanalytic Technique TB/1144
JOHN H. SCHAAR: Escape from Authority: *The Perspectives of Erich Fromm* TB/1155
MUZAFER SHERIF: The Psychology of Social Norms. *Introduction by Gardner Murphy* TB/3072
HELLMUT WILHELM: Change: *Eight Lectures on the I Ching* TB/2019

Religion: Ancient and Classical, Biblical and Judaic Traditions

W. F. ALBRIGHT: The Biblical Period from Abraham to Ezra TB/102
SALO W. BARON: Modern Nationalism and Religion TB/818
C. K. BARRETT, Ed.: The New Testament Background: *Selected Documents* TB/86
MARTIN BUBER: Eclipse of God: *Studies in the Relation Between Religion and Philosophy* TB/12
MARTIN BUBER: Hasidism and Modern Man. *Edited and Translated by Maurice Friedman* TB/839
MARTIN BUBER: The Knowledge of Man. *Edited with an Introduction by Maurice Friedman. Translated by Maurice Friedman and Ronald Gregor Smith* TB/135
MARTIN BUBER: Moses. *The Revelation and the Covenant* TB/837
MARTIN BUBER: The Origin and Meaning of Hasidism. *Edited and Translated by Maurice Friedman* TB/835
MARTIN BUBER: The Prophetic Faith TB/73
MARTIN BUBER: Two Types of Faith: *Interpenetration of Judaism and Christianity* ° TB/75
MALCOLM L. DIAMOND: Martin Buber: *Jewish Existentialist* TB/840
M. S. ENSLIN: Christian Beginnings TB/5
M. S. ENSLIN: The Literature of the Christian Movement TB/6
ERNST LUDWIG EHRLICH: A Concise History of Israel: *From the Earliest Times to the Destruction of the Temple in A.D. 70* ° TB/128
HENRI FRANKFORT: Ancient Egyptian Religion: *An Interpretation* TB/77
ABRAHAM HESCHEL: The Earth Is the Lord's & The Sabbath. *Two Essays* TB/828
ABRAHAM HESCHEL: God in Search of Man: *A Philosophy of Judaism* TB/807
ABRAHAM HESCHEL: Man Is not Alone: *A Philosophy of Religion* TB/838
ABRAHAM HESCHEL: The Prophets: *An Introduction* TB/1421

T. J. MEEK: Hebrew Origins TB/69
JAMES MUILENBURG: The Way of Israel: *Biblical Faith and Ethics* TB/133
H. J. ROSE: Religion in Greece and Rome TB/55
H. H. ROWLEY: The Growth of the Old Testament TB/107
D. WINTON THOMAS, Ed.: Documents from Old Testament Times TB/85

Religion: General Christianity

ROLAND H. BAINTON: Christendom: *A Short History of Christianity and Its Impact on Western Civilization. Illus.* Vol. I TB/131; Vol. II TB/132
JOHN T. MCNEILL: Modern Christian Movements. *Revised Edition* TB/1402
ERNST TROELTSCH: The Social Teaching of the Christian Churches. *Intro. by H. Richard Niebuhr* Vol. I TB/71; Vol. II TB/72

Religion: Early Christianity Through Reformation

ANSELM OF CANTERBURY: Truth, Freedom, and Evil: *Three Philosophical Dialogues. Edited and Translated by Jasper Hopkins and Herbert Richardson* TB/317
MARSHALL W. BALDWIN, Ed.: Christianity through the 13th Century # HR/1468
W. D. DAVIES: Paul and Rabbinic Judaism: *Some Rabbinic Elements in Pauline Theology. Revised Edition* ° TB/146
ADOLF DEISSMAN: Paul: *A Study in Social and Religious History* TB/15
JOHANNES ECKHART: Meister Eckhart: *A Modern Translation by R. Blakney* TB/8
EDGAR J. GOODSPEED: A Life of Jesus TB/1
ROBERT M. GRANT: Gnosticism and Early Christianity TB/136
WILLIAM HALLER: The Rise of Puritanism TB/22
GERHART B. LADNER: The Idea of Reform: *Its Impact on the Christian Thought and Action in the Age of the Fathers* TB/149
ARTHUR DARBY NOCK: Early Gentile Christianity and Its Hellenistic Background TB/111
ARTHUR DARBY NOCK: St. Paul ° TR/104
GORDON RUPP: Luther's Progress to the Diet of Worms ° TB/120

Religion: The Protestant Tradition

KARL BARTH: Church Dogmatics: *A Selection. Intro. by H. Gollwitzer. Ed. by G. W. Bromiley* TB/95
KARL BARTH: Dogmatics in Outline - TB/56
KARL BARTH: The Word of God and the Word of Man TB/13
HERBERT BRAUN, et al.: God and Christ: *Existence and Province. Volume 5 of Journal for Theology and the Church, edited by Robert W. Funk and Gerhard Ebeling* TB/255
WHITNEY R. CROSS: The Burned-Over District: *The Social and Intellectual History of Enthusiastic Religion in Western New York, 1800-1850* TB/1242
NELS F. S. FERRE: Swedish Contributions to Modern Theology. *New Chapter by William A. Johnson* TB/147
WILLIAM R. HUTCHISON, Ed.: American Protestant Thought: *The Liberal Era* ‡ TB/1385
ERNST KASEMANN, et al.: Distinctive Protestant and Catholic Themes Reconsidered. *Volume 3 of Journal for Theology and the Church,*

edited by Robert W. Funk and Gerhard Ebeling TB/253

SOREN KIERKEGAARD: On Authority and Revelation: *The Book on Adler, or a Cycle of Ethico-Religious Essays. Introduction by F. Sontag* TB/139

SOREN KIERKEGAARD: Crisis in the Life of an Actress, *and Other Essays on Drama. Translated with an Introduction by Stephen Crites* TB/145

SOREN KIERKEGAARD: Edifying Discourses. *Edited with an Intro. by Paul Holmer* TB/32

SOREN KIERKEGAARD: The Journals of Kierkegaard. ° *Edited with an Intro. by Alexander Dru* TB/52

SOREN KIERKEGAARD: The Point of View for My Work as an Author: *A Report to History.* § *Preface by Benjamin Nelson* TB/88

SOREN KIERKEGAARD: The Present Age. § *Translated and edited by Alexander Dru. Introduction by Walter Kaufmann* TB/94

SOREN KIERKEGAARD: Purity of Heart. *Trans. by Douglas Steere* TB/4

SOREN KIERKEGAARD: Repetition: *An Essay in Experimental Psychology* § TB/117

SOREN KIERKEGAARD: Works of Love: *Some Christian Reflections in the Form of Discourses* TB/122

WILLIAM G. MCLOUGHLIN, Ed.: The American Evangelicals: 1800-1900: *An Anthology* TB/1382

WOLFHART PANNENBERG, et al.: History and Hermeneutic. *Volume 4 of Journal for Theology and the Church, edited by Robert W. Funk and Gerhard Ebeling* TB/254

JAMES M. ROBINSON, et al.: The Bultmann School of Biblical Interpretation: New Directions? *Volume 1 of Journal for Theology and the Church, edited by Robert W. Funk and Gerhard Ebeling* TB/251

F. SCHLEIERMACHER: The Christian Faith. *Introduction by Richard R. Niebuhr.*
Vol. I TB/108; Vol. II TB/109

F. SCHLEIERMACHER: On Religion: *Speeches to Its Cultured Despisers. Intro. by Rudolf Otto* TB/36

TIMOTHY L. SMITH: Revivalism and Social Reform: *American Protestantism on the Eve of the Civil War* TB/1229

PAUL TILLICH: Dynamics of Faith TB/42

PAUL TILLICH: Morality and Beyond TB/142

EVELYN UNDERHILL: Worship TB/10

Religion: The Roman & Eastern Christian Traditions

A. ROBERT CAPONIGRI, Ed.: Modern Catholic Thinkers II: *The Church and the Political Order* TB/307

G. P. FEDOTOV: The Russian Religious Mind: *Kievan Christianity, the tenth to the thirteenth Centuries* TB/370

GABRIEL MARCEL: Being and Having: *An Existential Diary. Introduction by James Collins* TB/310

GABRIEL MARCEL: Homo Viator: *Introduction to a Metaphysic of Hope* TB/397

Religion: Oriental Religions

TOR ANDRAE: Mohammed: *The Man and His Faith* § TB/62

EDWARD CONZE: Buddhism: *Its Essence and Development.* ° *Foreword by Arthur Waley* TB/58

EDWARD CONZE: Buddhist Meditation TB/1442

EDWARD CONZE et al, Editors: Buddhist Texts through the Ages TB/113

ANANDA COOMARASWAMY: Buddha and the Gospel of Buddhism TB/119

H. G. CREEL: Confucius and the Chinese Way TB/63

FRANKLIN EDGERTON, Trans. & Ed.: The Bhagavad Gita TB/115

SWAMI NIKHILANANDA, Trans. & Ed.: The Upanishads TB/114

D. T. SUZUKI: On Indian Mahayana Buddhism. ° *Ed. with Intro. by Edward Conze.* TB/1403

Religion: Philosophy, Culture, and Society

NICOLAS BERDYAEV: The Destiny of Man TB/61

RUDOLF BULTMANN: History and Eschatology: *The Presence of Eternity* ° TB/91

RUDOLF BULTMANN AND FIVE CRITICS: Kerygma and Myth: *A Theological Debate* TB/80

RUDOLF BULTMANN AND KARL KUNDSIN: Form Criticism: *Two Essays on New Testament Research. Trans. by F. C. Grant* TB/96

WILLIAM A. CLEBSCH & CHARLES R. JAEKLE: Pastoral Care in Historical Perspective: *An Essay with Exhibits* TB/148

FREDERICK FERRE: Language, Logic and God. *New Preface by the Author* TB/1407

LUDWIG FEUERBACH: The Essence of Christianity. § *Introduction by Karl Barth. Foreword by H. Richard Niebuhr* TB/11

ADOLF HARNACK: What Is Christianity? § *Introduction by Rudolf Bultmann* TB/17

KYLE HASELDEN: The Racial Problem in Christian Perspective TB/116

MARTIN HEIDEGGER: Discourse on Thinking. *Translated with a Preface by John M. Anderson and E. Hans Freund. Introduction by John M. Anderson* TB/1459

IMMANUEL KANT: Religion Within the Limits of Reason Alone. § *Introduction by Theodore M. Greene and John Silber* TB/FG

WALTER KAUFMANN, Ed.: Religion from Tolstoy to Camus: *Basic Writings on Religious Truth and Morals. Enlarged Edition* TB/123

H. RICHARD NIEBUHR: Christ and Culture TB/3

H. RICHARD NIEBUHR: The Kingdom of God in America TB/49

ANDERS NYGREN: Agape and Eros. *Translated by Philip S. Watson* ° TB/1430

JOHN H. RANDALL, JR.: The Meaning of Religion for Man. *Revised with New Intro. by the Author* TB/1379

WALTER RAUSCHENBUSCHS Christianity and the Social Crisis. ‡ *Edited by Robert D. Cross* TB/3059

Science and Mathematics

JOHN TYLER BONNER: The Ideas of Biology. Σ *Illus.* TB/570

W. E. LE GROS CLARK: The Antecedents of Man: *An Introduction to the Evolution of the Primates.* ° *Illus.* TB/559

ROBERT E. COKER: Streams, Lakes, Ponds. *Illus.* TB/586

ROBERT E. COKER: This Great and Wide Sea: *An Introduction to Oceanography and Marine Biology. Illus.* TB/551

W. H. DOWDESWELL: Animal Ecology. *61 illus.* TB/543

9

C. V. DURELL: Readable Relativity. *Foreword by Freeman J. Dyson* TB/530
GEORGE GAMOW: Biography of Physics. Σ *Illus.* TB/567
F. K. HARE: The Restless Atmosphere TB/560
J. R. PIERCE: Symbols, Signals and Noise: *The Nature and Process of Communication* Σ TB/574
WILLARD VAN ORMAN QUINE: Mathematical Logic TB/558

Science: History

MARIE BOAS: The Scientific Renaissance, 1450-1630 ° TB/583
STEPHEN TOULMIN & JUNE GOODFIELD: The Architecture of Matter: *The Physics, Chemistry and Physiology of Matter, Both Animate and Inanimate, as it has Evolved since the Beginnings of Science* TB/584
STEPHEN TOULMIN & JUNE GOODFIELD: The Discovery TB/576
STEPHEN TOULMIN & JUNE GOODFIELD: The Fabric of the Heavens: *The Development of Astronomy and Dynamics* TB/579

Science: Philosophy

J. M. BOCHENSKI: The· Methods of Contemporary Thought. *Tr. by Peter Caws* TB/1377
J. BRONOWSKI: Science and Human Values. *Revised and Enlarged. Illus.* TB/505
WERNER HEISENBERG: Physics and Philosophy: *The Revolution in Modern Science. Introduction by F. S. C. Northrop* TB/549
KARL R. POPPER: Conjectures and Refutations: *The Growth of Scientific Knowledge* TB/1376
KARL R. POPPER: The Logic of Scientific Discovery TB/1376
STEPHEN TOULMIN: Foresight and Understanding: *An Enquiry into the Aims of Science. Foreword by Jacques Barzun* TB/564
STEPHEN TOULMIN: The Philosophy of Science: *An Introduction* TB/513

Sociology and Anthropology

REINHARD BENDIX: Work and Authority in Industry: *Ideologies of Management in the Course of Industrialization* TB/3035
BERNARD BERELSON, Ed.: The Behavioral Sciences Today TB/1127
JOSEPH B. CASAGRANDE, Ed.: In the Company of Man: *Twenty Portraits of Anthropological Informants. Illus.* TB/3047
KENNETH B. CLARK: Dark Ghetto: *Dilemmas of Social Power. Foreword by Gunnar Myrdal* TB/1317
KENNETH CLARK & JEANNETTE HOPKINS: A Relevant War Against Poverty: *A Study of Community Action Programs and Observable Social Change* TB/1480
LEWIS COSER, Ed.: Political Sociology TB/1293
ROSE L. COSER, Ed.: Life Cycle and Achievement in America ** TB/1434
ALLISON DAVIS & JOHN DOLLARD: Children of Bondage: *The Personality Development of Negro Youth in the Urban South* || TB/3049
PETER F. DRUCKER: The New Society: *The Anatomy of Industrial Order* TB/1082
CORA DU BOIS: The People of Alor. *With a Preface by the Author*
Vol. I *Illus.* TB/1042; Vol. II TB/1043
EMILE DURKHEIM et al.: Essays on Sociology and Philosophy: *with Appraisals of Durkheim's Life and Thought. || Edited by Kurt H. Wolff* TB/1151

LEON FESTINGER, HENRY W. RIECKEN, STANLEY SCHACHTER: When Prophecy Fails: *A Social and Psychological Study of a Modern Group that Predicted the Destruction of the World* || TB/1132
CHARLES Y. GLOCK & RODNEY STARK: Christian Beliefs and Anti-Semitism. *Introduction by the Authors* TB/1454
ALVIN W. GOULDNER: The Hellenic World TB/1479
ALVIN W. GOULDNER: Wildcat Strike: *A Study in Worker-Management Relationships* || TB/1176
CESAR GRANA: Modernity and Its Discontents: *French Society and the French Man of Letters in the Nineteenth Century* TB/1318
L. S. B. LEAKEY: Adam's Ancestors: *The Evolution of Man and His Culture. Illus.* TB/1019
KURT LEWIN: Field Theory in Social Science: *Selected Theoretical Papers. || Edited by Dorwin Cartwright* TB/1135
RITCHIE P. LOWRY: Who's Running This Town? *Community Leadership and Social Change* TB/1383
R. M. MACIVER: Social Causation TB/1153
GARY T. MARX: Protest and Prejudice: *A Study of Belief in the Black Community* TB/1435
ROBERT K. MERTON, LEONARD BROOM, LEONARD S. COTTRELL, JR., Editors: Sociology Today: *Problems and Prospects* ||
Vol. I TB/1173; Vol. II TB/1174
GILBERT OSOFSKY, Ed.: The Burden of Race: *A Documentary History of Negro-White Relations in America* TB/1405
GILBERT OSOFSKY: Harlem: The Making of a Ghetto: *Negro New York 1890-1930* TB/1381
TALCOTT PARSONS & EDWARD A. SHILS, Editors: Toward a General Theory of Action: *Theoretical Foundations for the Social Sciences* TB/1083
PHILIP RIEFF: The Triumph of the Therapeutic: *Uses of Faith After Freud* TB/1360
JOHN H. ROHRER & MUNRO S. EDMONSON, Eds.: The Eighth Generation Grows Up: *Cultures and Personalities of New Orleans Negroes* || TB/3050
ARNOLD ROSE: The Negro in America: *The Condensed Version of Gunnar Myrdal's An American Dilemma. Second Edition* TB/3048
GEORGE ROSEN: Madness in Society: *Chapters in the Historical Sociology of Mental Illness. || Preface by Benjamin Nelson* TB/1337
PHILIP SELZNICK: TVA and the Grass Roots: *A Study in the Sociology of Formal Organization* TB/1230
PITIRIM A. SOROKIN: Contemporary Sociological Theories: *Through the First Quarter of the Twentieth Century* TB/3046
MAURICE R. STEIN: The Eclipse of Community: *An Interpretation of American Studies* TB/1128
EDWARD A. TIRYAKIAN, Ed.: Sociological Theory, Values and Sociocultural Change: *Essays in Honor of Pitirim A. Sorokin* ° TB/1316
FERDINAND TONNIES: Community and Society: *Gemeinschaft und Gesellschaft. Translated and Edited by Charles P. Loomis* TB/1116
SAMUEL E. WALLACE: Skid Row as a Way of Life TB/1367
W. LLOYD WARNER: Social Class in America: *The Evaluation of Status* TB/1013
FLORIAN ZNANIECKI: The Social Role of the Man of Knowledge. *Introduction by Lewis A. Coser* TB/1372

10